Dedicated to the men and women of the Merchant Navy
and
In memory of all who fell in the Falklands War

There are those men that go down to the sea in ships and make their living on the oceans of the world.
These men see the works of the Lord and his wonders of the deep.
Psalm 107

THE QE2 IN THE FALKLANDS WAR

TROOPSHIP TO THE SOUTH ATLANTIC

COMMODORE RONALD W. WARWICK OBE
AND DAVID HUMPHREYS

Dedication page anchor image designed by Freepik

First published 2025

The History Press
97 St George's Place, Cheltenham,
Gloucestershire, GL50 3QB
www.thehistorypress.co.uk

© Ronald W. Warwick and David Humphreys, 2025

The right of Ronald W. Warwick and David Humphreys
to be identified as the Authors of this work has been asserted in
accordance with the Copyright, Designs and Patents Act 1988.

All rights reserved. No part of this book may be reprinted
or reproduced or utilised in any form or by any electronic,
mechanical or other means, now known or hereafter invented,
including photocopying and recording, or in any information
storage or retrieval system, without the permission in writing
from the Publishers.

British Library Cataloguing in Publication Data.
A catalogue record for this book is available from the British Library.

ISBN 978 1 80399 738 4

Typesetting and origination by The History Press
Printed and bound in Great Britain by TJ Books Limited, Padstow, Cornwall

Trees for Life

Contents

Foreword by Admiral The Rt Hon. the Lord West of Spithead   7

Introduction   9

1	The Falkland Islands and South Georgia	11
2	The Argentinian Invasion	15
3	Cunard Ships at War	19
4	*QE2* is Requisitioned	23
5	Conversion to a Troopship	31
6	The Volunteers	55
7	5 Infantry Brigade	65
8	The Voyage South to Freetown	73
9	Freetown to South Georgia	123
10	Grytviken, South Georgia Island	185
11	The Survivors and Their Ships	207
12	Homeward Bound to Southampton	213
13	*QE2* Arrives Home	241
14	Military Units Embarked on *QE2*	253
15	*QE2* Logbook Extract	255

16	The Cost of the Requisition	261
17	The Volunteer Crew of *QE2*	267
18	Afterword	287

Notes	299
Bibliography and Sources	307
Acknowledgements	310
The Authors	312
Subject Index	314
Vessel Index	320

Foreword

Commodore Ronald Warwick and Professor David Humphreys' book is a fascinating account of the part *QE2* played in the Falklands War. It was a maritime war and only a nation with significant maritime capability could have prosecuted it and emerged victorious. Although steadily eroded since the Second World War, the Royal Navy remained a force of considerable power with global reach.

The UK merchant marine, although only a shadow of its former self, was still of appreciable size and there remained a large cadre of trained seamen. It was a diverse fleet including some magnificent cruise ships and liners. By far the most significant of these was Cunard's *Queen Elizabeth 2*.

To prosecute the war in the South Atlantic, some 8,000 miles away from the United Kingdom, it was necessary to use many of these merchant ships to assist the Royal Navy. In total, forty-five merchant ships were requisitioned in addition to the twenty-four merchant-crewed Royal Fleet Auxiliary ships. This compares with the thirty-nine Royal Navy warships ships that took part.

Transporting large numbers of troops when there was no friendly air-field of any size within 4,000 miles necessitated the use of troop ships and, as Warwick and Humphreys explain, *QE2* was perfect for the role. Indeed, she was following in the footsteps of her illustrious predecessors, RMS *Queen Elizabeth* and *Queen Mary*, which transported tens of thousands of troops across the Atlantic in the Second World War, with Churchill later saying their contribution had shortened the war.

Requisitioned on 3 May 1982, *QE2* departed on the 12th carrying 2,988 troops of 5 Infantry Brigade that were required for the final assault on Port Stanley.

They arrived safely, having transhipped to the *Canberra*, *Norland* and other ships in South Georgia, in time to ensure the collapse of the Argentinian forces before the full rigours of the Antarctic winter impacted on military operations.

Having disembarked 5 Brigade, *QE2* took on board the survivors of three sunken Royal Navy ships and returned them to the UK. I was one of those survivors and this book describes in detail how life was on board on that passage home. What was amazing was the kindness and care the *QE2* ship's company lavished on us. I will never forget them.

QE2 was crucial to victory and this tale of her part in it is a wonderful tribute to the ship and her crew.

Admiral The Rt Hon. the Lord West of Spithead GCB DSC PC

Introduction

Although Britain and Argentina never formally declared war on each other, most military and maritime historians refer to this moment in time as 'the *Falklands War*'. Until now the full story of *Queen Elizabeth 2* (*QE2*), the most famous ship to take part in the 1982 Falklands War, has not been told. Yet *QE2* made a vital contribution to the outcome, considerably shortening the seventy-four-day conflict despite being at anchor in an area of danger for only forty-six hours.

QE2 was launched by Her Majesty Queen Elizabeth the Second in 1967 and entered into commercial service as the Cunard Line flagship in 1969. Thirteen years later she was one of the last ships to be requisitioned for service in the South Atlantic. Here is the story of her most epic voyage, from the moment this majestic ship was requisitioned, to her conversion to a troopship, to the risks and dangers of the voyage that followed.

We believe we are well qualified to tell the story of *QE2*'s South Atlantic odyssey because we were there. We served as members of her volunteer crew: one as chief officer, the other as a senior petty officer in the accounts department. We had the privilege of sailing with wonderful crew members: hard-working seafarers who are generous, entertaining and humble.

While writing this book we reached out to the crew of *QE2*, the embarked soldiers whom we took to the South Atlantic and the survivors who returned home with us, asking them for their recollections of the voyage and to share their experiences. We thank everyone who so kindly contributed for entrusting their memories to us so that we can share them with you.

This is more than the story of a famous liner engaged unexpectedly in a military operation. It is the story of those on board who lived through and experienced that astonishing voyage. Everyone who worked as crew members on board continues to feel a great sense of pride and loyalty to *QE2*.

This is not just our story. It is a story that belongs to everyone who served on board *QE2* during her finest hour.

Ronald W. Warwick and David Humphreys
January 2025

1

The Falkland Islands and South Georgia

The Falkland Islands (known in Argentina as the Islas Malvinas) is an archipelago in the South Atlantic about 300 miles east of mainland South America. The archipelago comprises two large islands – West Falkland and East Falkland – and approximately 740 smaller islands. West and East Falkland are separated by a stretch of water known by the British as Falkland Sound. The capital of East Falkland is Port Stanley.

It has been claimed that the first sighting of the islands was by the Italian explorer Amerigo Vespucci in 1502.[1] Another claim is that the islands were first discovered in 1519 by the Portuguese.[2] The first known sighting by the British was in 1592, by the crew of the *Desire* commanded by Captain John Davis. The first recorded landing was in January 1690 from HMS *Welfare*. Her master, Captain John Strong, named the islands after Viscount Falkland, the Royal Navy treasurer.[3]

Over ensuing years, ships from France, Spain and Britain visited the islands, laying claims of sovereignty and establishing settlements. It is believed the islands were first occupied by French explorer Louis-Antoine de Bougainville, who established a settlement on East Falkland in 1764. He named the islands the Malouines, which later became Las Malvinas in Spanish.[4] In 1765 Captain John Byron landed on the islands and raised the Union flag. In 1767, France sold its interest in the islands to Spain.[5] In January 1771, Britain and Spain signed a peace treaty over the islands, although both continued to reserve their rights on sovereignty. British settlers departed the islands in 1774 for economic reasons, while continuing to claim sovereignty.[6] Spain maintained a settlement until 1811.[7]

The origins of the present disagreement between Argentina and Britain lie in the early decades of the nineteenth century. In what is now Argentina, a succession of wars were fought from 1810 to 1818 between pro-independence forces and pro-royalist forces loyal to Spain. In July 1816, the foundation of the state of Argentina was declared. The new country laid claim to all territories formerly governed by the Spanish vice-royalty, including Spain's acquisition in 1767 of France's interest in the Falkland Islands. In 1826 the first colonists from Argentina settled on the islands.[8]

In January 1833, HMS *Clio* captained by James Onslow arrived at the Falklands, lowered the Argentinian flag and raised the Union Jack.[9] Britain then set about settling the islands. Since then Argentina has claimed the islands are a legitimate part of its territory. However, the islanders have consistently supported rule by Britain. By the time of the invasion, the population was approximately 2,000. About 80 per cent of these were born on the islands. All of the population, most of whom are of British decent, have known only British rule.

The island of South Georgia is more remotely situated in a more southerly latitude and some 800 nautical miles further to the east. The island is believed to have first been sighted in the late 1600s. Captain James Cook set foot on South Georgia in January 1775, naming the large inlet where he landed Cumberland Bay. In 1908, both South Georgia and the South Sandwich Islands were formally annexed by Britain. Seven whaling stations were established on the island with the largest at Grytviken and Stromness. The Grytviken station remained active until it closed down in 1965.

In 1927 the dispute over the Falklands was widened when Argentina made a claim to South Georgia and the South Sandwich Islands. However, the UK has continued to maintain a presence on the island of South Georgia. This included a group of scientists from the British Antarctic Survey backed up with periodic visits of HMS *Endurance*.

Argentina's claim to sovereignty over the Falklands Islands, South Georgia and the South Sandwich Islands gained momentum in the 1960s. Negotiations between Argentina and the UK took place from 1966 to 1968. It later emerged that in 1968 the two countries drafted a memorandum of understanding that included the provision: 'The government of the United Kingdom will recognise Argentina's sovereignty over the Islands with effect from a date to be agreed.'[10] However, while the text of the memorandum was agreed, for reasons that are unclear it was never formalised as a diplomatic communiqué.

In 1975, Lord Edward Shackleton, the son of the Antarctic explorer Sir Ernest Shackleton, was commissioned by the UK Foreign and Commonwealth Office to prepare a report on the economic future of the Falkland Islands. Argentina was invited to participate in the survey but declined. Shackleton carried out the survey in a ship named after his father, the Royal Research Ship (RRS) *Shackleton*. At the start of the survey in February 1976, the Argentine destroyer *Almirante Storni* fired a shot across the RRS *Shackleton*'s bow.[11] After this incident the British Ambassador to Argentina was withdrawn. At the time, Argentina was under the presidency of Isabel Perón, who was overthrown in a military coup a few weeks later.

Lord Shackleton's 1976 report argued that the UK had neglected the economic development of the islands, both in Port Stanley and in the camp (as the countryside outside the capital is known). He recommended increased financial assistance, lengthening the runway at Stanley airport, the development of offshore fishery resources and an expansion in tourism.[12] Shackleton's report pleased those in the UK seeking to keep the islands under British rule. However, the report was not welcomed by those concerned with the economic cost of the islands to the UK and who were seeking increased cooperation with Argentina. The Labour government of James Callaghan gave no indication that it intended to implement Shackleton's recommendations. Neither did the Conservative government elected in 1979.

In 1980, the Conservative government of Margaret Thatcher drew up a proposal whereby Britain would hand over titular sovereignty of the Falklands to Argentina. Argentina would then lease the islands back to the UK for ninety-nine years. As Lawrence Freedman reveals in *The Official History of the Falklands Campaign*, a secret meeting took place between British and Argentine officials at which the plan was discussed.[13] In November a junior foreign office minister, Nicholas Ridley, visited the Falklands. The islanders he met were strongly opposed to the proposal.[14]

In 1981, a UK Defence Review proposed extensive cuts to the Royal Navy including the withdrawal of HMS *Endurance*,[15] a Royal Navy ice patrol vessel that maintained a presence in Antarctica, the Falkland Islands and South Georgia. The Defence Review estimated that withdrawing *Endurance*, the only British ship to connect the Falklands to the UK, would save about £4 million a year. At the same time, proposals were under consideration to close the British Antarctic Survey station at Grytviken. In Buenos Aires, the military junta interpreted these developments as a signal the British were losing interest in the islands and their protection.

In February 1982, the UK and Argentina held discussions about the Falklands at the British and Argentine diplomatic missions in New York. Enrique Mos, the deputy of Argentina's foreign minister Nicanor Costa Méndez, proposed establishing a permanent British–Argentine commission to consider the question of sovereignty. The commission would hold monthly meetings with chairmanship rotating between the two countries. The British reacted favourably to the idea and a communiqué was issued that affirmed the resolve of the two governments to find a solution. However, the communiqué, which described the talks as 'cordial and positive',[16] was not welcomed by the Argentine government, which had wanted the talks to push the UK into a corner. In Buenos Aires, the Foreign Ministry issued a statement that if Argentina were not given sovereignty over the islands, it would use other means to secure them.[17]

These events provided the contextual background to the South Atlantic crisis of 1982. Argentina had been pressing its claims for several decades. The country's position had become firmer in the early months of 1982. Meanwhile, it could be argued that the UK's willingness to consider a possible transfer of sovereignty, the failure to commit to Lord Shackleton's recommendations and the planned withdrawal of HMS *Endurance* suggested a declining interest in the Falklands – at least, that is how the military junta in Buenos Aires appears to have judged British intentions.

2

The Argentinian Invasion

At the time of the invasion, Argentina had been under military rule since March 1976 when President Isabel Perón was overthrown in a coup. A military junta comprising the heads of the Army, Navy and Air Force took over the government.

The sequence of events that led to Argentina's invasion of the Falklands began in 1979 when Constantino Davidoff, an Argentinian businessman and scrap metal merchant, obtained a contract to buy and remove scrap metal from abandoned whaling stations on South Georgia.[18] Davidoff and seven salvage workers sailed with British permission to South Georgia to inspect the Stromness whaling station in December 1981.

Davidoff returned to Stromness with a workforce, arriving at Leith Harbour on 19 March 1982. However, before landing on South Georgia, Davidoff was required to obtain a landing permit, which he failed to do. A few days later the group was sighted by scientists from the British Antarctic Survey, who also spotted the Argentine flag flying. This was reported to Rex Hunt, the British governor in the Falklands. He in turn instructed the scientists to send a message to the contractors instructing them to lower the flag and requesting one of their party to travel to Grytviken to obtain the landing permit. The flag was lowered but nobody attempted to obtain the requested documentation. In London the government ordered HMS *Endurance*, under the command of Captain Nicholas Barker, to proceed to Stromness and evict the workers.[19]

The situation on South Georgia and the demands of the British government appear to have provided the junta with a convenient pretext and the motivation to proceed with an invasion. At this same time, the Argentine naval fleet was preparing to carry out fleet manoeuvre exercises with Brazil off Montevideo in Uruguay. All it took was a change of orders for the ships to be diverted. Several ships from the Argentine fleet assembled at Puerto Belgrano. They included the aircraft carrier *Veinticinco de Mayo* (ex-Royal Navy, launched in 1943 as HMS *Venerable*) and the submarine *Santa Fe* (ex-US Navy, launched in 1944 as USS *Catfish*).

A further factor concerned the foreign relations between Argentina and the United States. When Ronald Reagan assumed the US presidency in January 1981, he regarded Argentina as a useful ally against Communism and left-wing movements in Latin America. Leopoldo Galtieri received a warm welcome when he visited Washington as commander-in-chief of the Army in November 1981, two months before Reagan became president.[20] The junta appear to have judged that, while an invasion would not be welcomed by Washington, it would probably be accepted. They were wrong.

By 1 April the Argentine naval fleet was off the coast of the Falklands. Rex Hunt ordered all sensitive and classified documents to be shredded and burned.[21] He conferred with Major Mike Norman, the head of the island's detachment of sixty-nine Royal Marines based at the Moody Brook barracks to the west of Stanley. It was recognised that the marines were heavily outnumbered and outgunned. The plan was for the marines, supported by the Falkland Islands Defence Force, a local civilian volunteer force, to resist and delay the Argentine forces as long as possible while avoiding civilian casualties. Hunt made a broadcast advising all citizens to remain indoors.

In the early hours of 2 April 1982, Argentine forces made an amphibious landing on the Falkland Islands. This was known as Operation Rosario. Argentine soldiers heavily outnumbered the Royal Marines detachment. After several exchanges of fire, Hunt asked Major Norman to lay down arms at 0925 hours.[22] Later that day Hunt, his family and the Royal Marines were flown to the UK via Montevideo, Uruguay. The following day, Argentinian forces landed on South Georgia and overwhelmed the detachment of twenty-two Royal Marines at Grytviken. However, before the Royal Marines surrendered they shot down a Puma helicopter which had taken off from the Argentine vessel *Bahía Paraíso*.

The news that British territory had been seized through military force led to a sense of shock and national shame. On Saturday, 3 April, both the House of Commons and the House of Lords met in emergency session. This was only the third time the House of Commons had met on a Saturday since the Second World War, the last occasion being the Suez crisis of 1956. Prime Minister Margaret Thatcher pledged the government's support for the islanders, noting that the people of the Falkland Islands, like those of the UK, were island people:

> I must tell the House that the Falkland Islands and their dependencies remain British territory. No aggression and no invasion can alter that simple fact. It is the Government's objective to see that the islands are freed from occupation and are returned to British administration at the earliest possible moment ... The people of the Falkland Islands ... have the right to live in peace, to choose their own way of life and to determine their own allegiance. Their way of life is British: their allegiance is to the Crown.[23]

The leader of the opposition, Michael Foot, responded:

> ... there is the longer-term interest to ensure that foul and brutal aggression does not succeed in our world. If it does, there will be a danger not merely to the Falkland Islands, but to people all over this dangerous planet.[24]

On the same day as the sittings at Parliament, an emergency session of the United Nations Security Council convened in New York, where it passed Resolution 502. This stated that the Security Council was:

> *Deeply disturbed* at reports of an invasion on 2 April 1982 by armed forces of Argentina.
> *Determining* that there exists a breach of the peace in the region of the Falkland Islands (Islas Malvinas),
> 1. *Demands* an immediate cessation of hostilities.
> 2. *Demands* an immediate withdrawal of all Argentine forces from the Falkland Islands (Islas Malvinas).
> 3. *Calls* on the Governments of Argentina and the United Kingdom of Great Britain and Northern Ireland to seek a diplomatic solution to their differences and to respect fully the purposes and principles of the Charter of the United Nations.[25]

The resolution was adopted by ten votes to one. The countries that voted in favour were three of the five permanent members (UK, USA, France) plus seven temporary members (Guyana, Ireland, Japan, Jordan, Togo, Uganda and Zaire). Panama was the only country to vote against. Four countries abstained: two permanent members (China and the Soviet Union) and two temporary members (Poland and Spain).

The US secretary of state, Alexander Haig, attempted to mediate a settlement through 'shuttle diplomacy', flying between Buenos Aires, Washington and London in an effort to broker a deal. Haig's mission ended when the governments of the two countries adhered to positions that were unacceptable to each other: Argentina would agree to withdraw its forces only if the UK first recognised Argentine sovereignty over the islands, while the UK insisted on immediate withdrawal without preconditions.

The British government decided to take action and a task force was formed with the code name Operation Corporate under the leadership of Admiral Sir John Fieldhouse. Included in the task force were the aircraft carriers HMS *Invincible* (Captain J.J. Black) and HMS *Hermes* (Captain L.E. Middleton). The main task force put to sea on 5 April 1982. For support, several Merchant Navy vessels were requisitioned by the government. They were known as Ships Taken Up From Trade (STUFT). In all, the task force comprised forty-five STUFTs, five trawlers manned by Royal Navy personnel, thirty-nine Royal Navy ships and twenty-four Royal Fleet Auxiliary ships. The P&O cruise liner *Canberra* was converted at Southampton to carry troops and sailed a few days later on 9 April.

Three Cunard ships contributed to the task force. They were the container ships *Atlantic Conveyor* (Captain Ian North) and *Atlantic Causeway* (Captain Michael Twomey RNR) and the refrigerated cargo vessel *Saxonia* (Captain H. Evans). Cunard ships have a long tradition of serving the British Crown by supporting naval campaigns in wartime. However, as the task force sailed south, it appeared that there would be no role in Operation Corporate for QE2.

3

Cunard Ships at War

Several Cunarders were requisitioned to support Britain during the Crimean War (1853–56).[26] A total of fourteen Cunard ships served in the campaign.[27] Of those, *Arabia* transported all the horses used in the Charge of the Light Brigade.

During the American Civil War (1861–65), the Cunard liners *Australasia* and *Persia* transported British troops to reinforce the British and Canadian position of neutrality.[28] Cunard ships also served in the first and second Boer wars.

The company's ships were central to British naval strategy during the First World War. The liner *Mauretania* (launched 1906) started the war by making several voyages transporting British soldiers to fight in the Gallipoli campaign. *Aquitania* (launched 1913) also served as a troop ship, after which she became a hospital ship evacuating casualties from Gallipoli. Both ships finished the war serving on the North Atlantic, carrying American troops to Europe, while transporting fare-paying passengers on their westbound passages.[29]

Cunard's transatlantic liner *Carmania* (launched 1905) was requisitioned in August 1914. She was converted into an armed merchant cruiser and fitted with eight 4.7in guns for defensive purposes. *Carmania* was ordered to the Caribbean, where she made history by participating in the first, and so far only, liner-versus-liner naval battle. This was against the German ship *Cap Trafalgar*, which like *Carmania* had been converted to an armed merchant ship. The two armed liners encountered each other off the coast of Trinidad in September 1914. *Carmania* fired a warning shot across the German ship's bow. *Cap Trafalgar*'s response was to open fire on the Cunarder. *Carmania* responded, aiming fire at the waterline of the German ship, causing severe flooding and leading the *Cap Trafalgar* to roll on her side.[30]

The Cunarder *Lusitania* (launched 1906) held the prestigious Blue Riband in 1908 for the fastest Atlantic crossing. However, while under the command of Captain William T. Turner she was sunk by the German submarine *U-20* (Kapitän Walther Schwieger), south of Ireland in May 1915. Her sinking led to the loss of nearly 1,200 lives, turning public opinion in North America against Germany and contributing to the USA entering the conflict in 1917.[31]

Other Cunard losses during the First World War included *Ivernia*,[32] *Andania, Aurania, Caria, Folia, Feltria, Franconia, Alaunia* and *Lycia*.[33] One of the last Cunard ships sunk by a U-boat in the First World War was *Carpathia*, sunk by *U-55* (Commander Wilhelm Werner). *Carpathia* had become famous in April 1912 as the ship which responded to the SOS telegraphed by White Star Line's *Titanic* after she struck an iceberg and sank in the North Atlantic on her maiden voyage.

In the Second World War, the two Cunard *Queens* of that era – *Queen Mary* (launched 1934) and *Queen Elizabeth* (launched 1938) – were requisitioned. The two *Queens* were much faster than any other troopships during the war. After being launched, *Queen Elizabeth* went straight into service as a troop carrier.[34] In 1940, *Queen Mary* sailed to Sydney, Australia, where she was converted to carry troops. She then carried Australian troops to Scotland via Cape Town. Between them, the two *Queens* delivered some 80,000 Australian soldiers to Suez and the Middle East. A port that the two ships visited en route was Freetown, then part of British Sierra Leone.[35]

Throughout the latter part of the Second World War, *Queen Mary* and *Queen Elizabeth* plied the North Atlantic, bringing thousands of Canadian and American troops to the UK in preparation for the Normandy landings. '*Mary*' and '*Lizzie*', as they were affectionately known, made several transatlantic crossings, carrying as many as 15,000 troops on each eastbound voyage. On westbound crossings they carried wounded military personnel and civilian evacuees from the war in Europe.

German submarines were a constant threat during these crossings. Three Cunard ships were sunk by German U-boats during the Second World War. Two were torpedoed: *Carinthia* (launched 1925) and *Andania* (launched 1921). *Laurentic* (launched 1908) was sunk by a German mine. A fourth vessel, *Lancastria* (launched 1920) under the command of Captain Rudolph Sharp, was destroyed in June 1940 by Luftwaffe dive-bomber aircraft off the coast of St-Nazaire, France, while evacuating British troops and civilians. Estimates of total lives lost vary but number at least 6,000,[36] the greatest loss of life on a single ship in British maritime history.

At war's end, *Queen Elizabeth* and *Queen Mary* remained in service transporting troops, making westbound transatlantic crossings to return home some of the victorious troops to North America, and eastbound crossings to bring home British prisoners of war held captive by Japan as well as transporting fresh Canadian and American troops to garrison Germany.

Franconia (launched 1922) served as a troopship during the Second World War.[37] In January 1945, she sailed to the Black Sea to serve as the base for the British delegation to the Yalta Conference between Winston Churchill, Franklin Roosevelt and Joseph Stalin. They met to discuss the final stages of the war and the post-war division of Europe.[38] Meanwhile, *Aquitania* served on the North Atlantic, transporting troops from New York to the UK in preparation for D-Day.[39] She was the only Cunarder to see service in both world wars.

Cunard suffered the loss of ships due to submarine attacks in the two world wars. In the Second World War, there was the additional risk of losing ships to aerial bombing. However, the two wars highlighted the significant strategic advantages that could be gained from using requisitioned ocean liners to transport troops to a theatre of war. At the end of the war, the Supreme Allied Commander in Europe, General Dwight D. Eisenhower, said:

> The officers and men of the Merchant Marine by their dedication to duty in the face of enemy action as well as the natural dangers of the sea have brought to us the tools to finish the job. This contribution to Final Victory will long be remembered.[40]

Prime Minister Winston Churchill also spoke with great appreciation:

> The Merchant Navy, with its Allied comrades, night and day, in weather fair or foul, faces not only the ordinary perils on the sea, but the sudden assaults of war from beneath the waters or from the sky. We feel confident that the proud tradition of our island will be upheld today, wherever the Ensign of a British Merchantman is flown.[41]

After the Second World War, Churchill made several crossings on *Queen Mary* and *Queen Elizabeth*, which, he said, had helped shorten the war by at least a year.

Thirty-seven years after the end of the Second World War, there was no expectation that *QE2* would become a troopship as so many Cunard ships had done earlier in the century.

4

QE2 is Requisitioned

I never thought I'd go to war again.

Captain Peter Jackson, Master of *QE2*

The year 1982 had started in normal fashion for the great liner. In January, she departed New York on an eastbound world cruise. On 4 March, she put into Hong Kong, then governed by the UK. She docked at the Kowloon Passenger Terminal, occupying the north-side berth. Occupying the south-side berth was SS *Canberra*, which like *QE2* was on her annual world cruise but sailing westbound. Over the years, these two great ships were occasionally together in their home port of Southampton. However, it was rare for them to be in port together outside the UK. Just a few months later, *QE2* and *Canberra* would again be together but in circumstances that could not have been foreseen at the time.

On 20 April, *QE2* left Southampton for a transatlantic crossing to Philadelphia to take part in the tercentennial anniversary of the city's foundation in 1682 by William Penn. On 25 April, the day when *QE2* arrived in Philadelphia, British forces recaptured South Georgia from Argentina. This led to one of the most memorable signals of the war. Captain Brian Young RN, commander of HMS *Antrim*, signalled London 'Be pleased to inform Her Majesty that the White Ensign flies alongside the Union Jack in South Georgia. God save the Queen'.[42]

QE2 departed from Philadelphia on 29 April, putting to sea in anticipation of a normal eastbound transatlantic crossing. With the British task force sailing south, some crew members wondered whether *QE2* might yet take part in the campaign. First Officer Philip Rentell and Second Officer

Paul Jowett were on the Bridge for the 8 to 12 watch when they decided to calculate the fuel, time and distance for a voyage from Southampton to the Falklands. Their calculations were filling a notepad when Captain Alexander J. Hutcheson RD RNR appeared, observed the two officers and joked, 'You two will have us down there!' Within days their calculations would be of interest. The officers had calculated that *QE2* would cover the 8,000-mile route at a speed of 27½ knots over ten and a half days, during which her engines would consume 6,000 tons of oil. That oil would have a retail value of $1,080,000 at $180 per ton for the one-way trip.

QE2 crew traditionally referred to the evening before the ship docked in Southampton as 'channels night'. As the ship approached the English Channel, there would be a growing anticipation among the crew, some of whom would be preparing to sign off on leave. Those not signing off who lived in the Southampton area would be looking forward to spending a few hours with family and friends. Channels night on this crossing was Sunday, 2 May.

The following day, Monday, 3 May, was a memorable one. *QE2* was due to dock near midnight at Southampton, change passengers and take on board stores for a thirteen-day Mediterranean cruise. The cruise never took place. At 1230 hours, as the Cunarder sailed along the southern coast of England just past Land's End, several officers and crew picked up the news from BBC radio that *QE2* had been requisitioned. The news bulletin came as something of a shock as no official notification had been received.

Most crew members can remember where they were on the ship and what they were doing when they heard the news that day. Hotel officer Terry Foskett was preparing immigration documentation. It was normal procedure for a UK immigration officer to board the ship in the USA, then sail with her east across the Atlantic Ocean, processing passengers in order to expedite immigration clearance in Southampton. Terry and the immigration official were working in a passenger cabin when a bedroom steward opened the door and asked if he could provide any beverages or lunch, before adding, 'By the way, have you heard? We've been requisitioned.' Cruise director Tim Castle was in his office on One Deck forward when he heard a cheer from the nearby crew mess. Other crew members who heard the news responded with enthusiasm.

Hairdresser Timothy Williams was working in the Steiners salon on One Deck aft when the news reached him. Crew member Clive Dalley was on his way to the Six Deck working alley, descending the crew-only part of 'A' Stairway, when a crew member told him the news. Hotel officer Rupert Ballantyne was working in the Double Down Room Bar when his bleeper sounded, requesting he telephone a colleague. He made the call and was told the news. Stewardess Elena Littlehales was having a cup of tea with friends in the One Deck aft pantry when the news arrived. She was preparing to clean cabins and remake beds in preparation for the next cruise, now cancelled.

First Officer Rentell had accepted an invitation for a lunchtime drink with friends in one of the penthouse suites to bid farewell to one of the shop staff. Also there was Anthony Dance, the shop manager, who was due to sign off the ship on arrival and join an Italian ship. The group were listening to BBC Radio 2's lunchtime show when the host Jimmy Young announced that QE2 had been requisitioned.

One of the radio officers who heard the BBC broadcast went to the Bridge and reported the news to the 12 to 4 watch. When Captain Hutcheson was telephoned by an enterprising BBC reporter and asked about the requisitioning, he responded that he knew nothing officially. There was some feeling among the officers that the ship should have been forewarned before the media. Following official confirmation, Captain Hutcheson made a Tannoy announcement throughout the ship shortly after 1300 hours, informing everyone that QE2 would be withdrawn from commercial service upon arrival at Southampton. Contacted again by a reporter and asked his thoughts about the news, he replied, 'I think the troops will enjoy Cunard luxury.' By now there was a growing air of excitement around the ship, among crew and passengers. Crew members sought out television sets with good reception to watch the *BBC One O'clock News*.

The officers' Wardroom on Boat Deck was bustling with off-duty officers. In the Columbia Restaurant, waiter Pierre Cornlouer watched the news on an old television secreted in a dumb waiter no longer in use. Meanwhile, the Petty Officers' Club on Two Deck forward, the social space for senior cooks, carpenters, mechanics, office crew and security staff, was packed with standing room only. The news broadcast showed the formal announcement of the requisitioning by Ian McDonald, Ministry of Defence spokesman. McDonald said that the government had requisitioned more Merchant Navy vessels:

Among the ships being requisitioned is the *QE2* … The *QE2*'s speed, size and facilities make her uniquely suited to carry substantial numbers of troops.[43]

In the Petty Officers' Club the news was greeted with a cheer. Later, the message Cunard received from the government was released:

Your vessel *Queen Elizabeth 2* is requisitioned by the Secretary of State for Trade under the Requisitioning of Ships Order 1982 and you are accordingly required to place her at his disposal forthwith. The Master should report for directions on the employment of the vessel to Mr R. Brooks, Department of Trade Sea Transport Officer, Southampton who will act as the principal link between the Master and all other civil and naval/military authorities until sailing.[44]

That afternoon the shop staff received a message from Ocean Trading, the owners of *QE2*'s shops' concession, ordering them to box up stock ready for unloading in Southampton. They started packing items but soon encountered a problem: there was not enough packaging on board. The job of unloading so much stock at short notice had never been anticipated and the staff rapidly ran out of packing cases and boxes. They resorted to packing items in shopping carrier bags. Packing glassware and chinaware was particularly time consuming to avoid breakages. The staff also had to document the stock, manifesting everything for declaration to Her Majesty's Customs. All these tasks were implemented while the shops remained open to serve passengers making last-minute purchases.

The firm Mecca Sportsman held the on-board casino concession. When news of the requisitioning came through, the staff were preparing to open the casino. Casino supervisor and dealer Maggie O'Connell recalls, 'The ship was buzzing at the news when we received instructions to start dismantling everything in the casino. The camaraderie on board between all crew was a special experience.' Maggie did not sail on the voyage to the South Atlantic but remembers:

I was proud to be on board and part of the team that was preparing the ship to be taken over. It was very emotional knowing some of our friends and colleagues would be joining the ship to go to the Falklands. We had many celebrations saying good luck and also worried about our precious *QE2* and whether it would come back safely with all crew on board.

In her memoirs, Margaret Thatcher noted that the requisitioning of *QE2* was not planned at the start of the conflict, with the decision being taken only after the main task force had sailed. She wrote of a meeting of the war cabinet the Sunday before the ship was requisitioned:

> ... we approved reinforcements for the Falklands which would be taken there in the *QE2*. It surprised me a little that the need for reinforcements had not been clear sooner. I asked whether it was really necessary or advisable to use this great ship and to put so many people in it, but as soon as I was told that it was necessary to get them there in time I gave my agreement. I was always concerned that we would not have sufficient men and equipment when the time came for the final battle and I was repeatedly struck by the fact that even such highly qualified professionals as advised us often under-estimated the requirements.[45]

QE2 was due to dock that evening at the Queen Elizabeth II Passenger Terminal. As she steamed up the Channel with lights ablaze, there was considerable anticipation. The 3,203-mile voyage from Philadelphia to Southampton had been accomplished at an average speed of 27.19 knots. The ship was tied up alongside her berth at 0002 hours on 4 May 1982 and was immediately requisitioned for war service.

Two military jeeps were parked on the quayside as the ship docked. The military had clearly wasted no time in sending an advance party to make contact with the ship's officers. *QE2* was no longer a Cunard liner. She was now under the control of the government and became a civilian 'Ship Taken Up From Trade' (STUFT). The legal authority for requisitioning *QE2* and other STUFT ships was the Requisitioning of Ships Order in Council that was issued on 4 April 1982. Cunard announced that all passengers booked on cancelled cruises would receive a full fare refund. Some of those who had booked cruises on *QE2* had done so after their cruise booked on *Canberra* was cancelled.[46]

One of the first military officers to board after *QE2*'s arrival was Captain N.C.H. James RN, the Commanding Officer of Naval Party 1980 (NP1980). Naval parties are formed to perform specific functions in an operational environment. NP1980 became the Royal Navy presence on board *QE2* for the duration the ship was involved in the conflict. Members of the party had duties which included helicopter flight deck operations, radio communications, defensive weapons and assisting on the Bridge. Supporting Captain James within NP1980 were his first lieutenant, Lieutenant Commander D.A.C. Poole RN, supply officer Lieutenant Commander B. Warlow RN, and Lieutenant Commander N.B. Shaw RN, who was responsible for flight operations. Major H. E. Affleck-Graves of the Royal Marines, an operations officer on board to instruct troops on amphibious landings, was also in NP1980. Captain James's primary role would be to liaise with the military ashore and work closely with the master of *QE2*. In effect, he would have strategic control of the liner with the aim of protecting her and those on board from enemy attacks.

On boarding, Captain James was met at the gangway by Captain Hutcheson and escorted to captain's quarters. There he was introduced to Captain Peter Jackson, who had just arrived on board from leave to take over command of the ship; Captain T.D. Ridley, the company's nautical adviser; and Ralph Bahna, the president of Cunard Line, who had flown from the company's head office in New York. Mr Bahna had expressed a deep concern about what was happening to 'his' ship. He said he hoped that the military would not be using the luxury penthouse suites. Captain James replied that the accommodation would be used for senior officers.

Captain Jackson was the most senior master in the fleet and it was assumed he would be in command for the forthcoming voyage. However, a less senior captain in Cunard volunteered to take command for the voyage, suggesting he was better suited as he was in List One of the Royal Naval Reserve (RNR) and trained in naval customs and strategy. List One of the RNR is a volunteer reserve force of serving Merchant Navy officers who are qualified to serve with the Royal Navy and can be called upon when requested by the Ministry of Defence. While not himself a member of the RNR, Captain Jackson had the support of his staff captain, Alexander J. Hutcheson, an RNR captain who had tasted action as a cadet during the Second World War.[47] Captain Hutcheson was due to remain on board but as second in command in the position of staff captain. In a supporting role was Chief Officer Ronald W. Warwick, a lieutenant commander in the RNR. The debate about who was the best qualified to captain *QE2* was an important one and an early decision needed to be made. Cunard's fleet personnel management sought the opinion of Captain James RN, who said this was for Cunard to decide. Cunard then confirmed that Peter Jackson would remain in command of *QE2* to the South Atlantic.

Captain Peter Jackson's service in the Second World War made him qualified to serve as master during the forthcoming voyage.[48] He had served in the Second World War as a junior officer with the Blue Funnel Line, helping ferry the British Expeditionary Force to Cherbourg. He later took part in the Norwegian campaign. In June 1940, he made several crossings of the English Channel, repatriating troops from Dunkirk, Brest and St-Jean-de-Luz. Two years later his ship *Mentor* (Captain Alexander Pope) was torpedoed north of Cuba by the German submarine *U-106* (Kapitän Hermann Rasch). Jackson's lifeboat was adrift for five days before being rescued by another Blue Funnel ship, the *Antilochus*. Peter Jackson was helped on board by one of *Antilochus*'s junior officers, Robert Arnott. By remarkable coincidence both these young officers would later captain *QE2*. Robert Arnott relates in his book *Captain of the Queen:*

> Since that first meeting so many years ago, Peter Jackson and I have met many times and after hostilities ended, we both joined the Cunard Line. Much later, I took over command of Peter's ship, *Cunard Adventurer*, so that he could join the *Queen Elizabeth 2*. That first meeting in 1942 was very much in both our thoughts as Peter handed over command to me in such different circumstances.[49]

Only three task force ship's captains had Second World War experience, all of them of Cunard ships. The other two were Captain Michael Twomey of the *Atlantic Causeway* and Captain Ian North of *Atlantic Conveyor*.[50] As well as Captain Peter Jackson and Staff Captain Alex Hutcheson, other *QE2* volunteers for the South Atlantic voyage had served in the Merchant Navy during the Second World War. Long-serving Cunard crew members waiter Phillip Ward and bedroom steward Edward Worsley, both of whom were in their sixties, had served on board the *Queen Mary* and *Queen Elizabeth*. Financial manager, Gerry Nolan, had also served at sea during the war but did not talk about his service. Purser Brian Vickers had seen service in the Pacific theatre. Herbert Thornton, a bedroom steward and long-serving Cunard employee, had served on board MV *Fort Halket* (Captain William Walker) when she was torpedoed on 6 August 1943.

5

Conversion to a Troopship

When *QE2* docked on 4 May, at 0002 hours, there were no cranes available to unload packaged surplus stock items. The only way to unload the high-value shop stock was to walk it through the ship's passageways and down the gangplank. Anthony Dance recalls walking off the ship with a large, sealed cardboard box full of luxury jewellery valued at approximately £3 million. He handed the box to his shoreside area manager, who deposited it in a duty-free, bonded warehouse. Later, despite the arrival of more packaging, it proved impossible to unload all the unrequired shop stock before the ship sailed. Expensive watches and perfumery remained on board when *QE2* sailed.

Shortly after *QE2* berthed, the ship's chief cashier, Stephen Ward, was preparing to go on leave when he saw a group of military officers dressed in khaki in the midships lobby. They were gathered around a deck plan of *QE2* spread out on the grand piano and seemingly oblivious to the curious glances from disembarking passengers heading for the gangway. Other military officers embarked throughout the day, requesting meeting rooms to plan the conversion of *QE2* to a troopship. Hotel officer Terry Foskett escorted the American actor Larry Hagman down a lower-deck service gangway so that he and his family could avoid the press, who by now were gathering at the Two Deck passenger gangway. Passenger disembarkation was complete before noon.

While *QE2* had been steaming along the south coast towards Southampton, news had come through that the Royal Navy submarine HMS *Conqueror* (Commander Christopher Wreford-Brown) had torpedoed the second largest ship in the Argentine Navy, ARA *General Belgrano*

(Captain Hector Bonzo). This ship was previously the USS *Phoenix* and had survived the Japanese attack on Pearl Harbor in 1941. *General Belgrano* sank with 323 sailors in the icy waters of the South Atlantic, with 772 survivors rescued from life rafts. *Conqueror* was the first nuclear submarine to sink a warship in combat. The attack led to Argentine naval forces withdrawing to their coastal waters, from which they rarely ventured after 2 May.

After the initial excitement about the requisitioning, the mood of *QE2* hardened and became more serious. On 10 May the RN Type 42 destroyer, HMS *Sheffield* (Captain James Salt), was badly damaged by an Exocet missile fired from an Argentinian Super-Etendard aircraft and later foundered. *Sheffield* was the first British warship lost to enemy action since the Second World War. The war was heating up and some Cunard officers and crew became concerned with writing wills and setting their personal affairs in order.

QE2 was to depart for the South Atlantic as soon as possible. The eight-day period of conversion from liner to troopship was a busy one. Military advance parties, shoreside contractors, telecommunications experts, Cunard staff from Southampton, and Ministry of Defence officials were up and down the gangway at all hours of the day and night.

Chief Officer Ronald W. Warwick recalls this time as being incredibly busy, with the area outside his office resembling a doctor's waiting room as people patiently waited to ask questions about what could be removed, what needed to stay and where things should be stowed.

Important discussions had to take place and decisions reached on a variety of matters including:

- structural alterations to enable the ship to support helicopter operations at sea
- the removal of equipment and stores not required
- where military equipment and stores could be safely stowed on board
- alterations to enable the ship to be refuelled at sea
- identifying which crew members would be required on the voyage
- safety measures to accommodate the extra number of souls
- protection of the fabric of the ship
- the monitoring of stability as extra weight was added to the ship
- the siting and installation of a secure communications system.

Major structural changes were needed to transform *QE2* from a luxury passenger ship into a troop carrier. Some of the conversion work commenced on 4 May as soon as all passengers had disembarked and continued in earnest the following day. The ship's helicopter landing area astern of the funnel was suitable for small helicopters but was not designed to bear the weight of military helicopters. The broad, open expanses of the ship's decks fore and aft would be perfectly suited for large helicopters once some structural changes were made to the ship's upper decks. Chief Officer Warwick and First Officer Philip Rentell studied the plans of the ship with Lieutenant Commander David Poole RN, whom they then escorted around the open decks. During discussions about the modifications that needed to be made, it was decided it would be preferable if *QE2* was laying starboard side to the quay. At 2200 hours, tugboats arrived and carefully swung around the 963ft liner-troopship in the turning area so that her starboard side lay against the quay.

The scale of the task sunk in as the decision was made to cut away the superstructure of the Upper Deck Lido in line with the Q4 Room as well as all associated superstructure down to Quarter Deck level. This would enable the aft end of Quarter Deck to be extended and converted into a landing pad and service area for two helicopters.

This raised the question of how the added weight of a helicopter deck would be supported. It was calculated that the two outdoor swimming pools on Quarter Deck and One Deck, which were designed to hold tons of seawater, could provide the foundations of the flight deck. The structural work was carried out by Vosper Thornycroft shipyard in Southampton. The company had already modified the *Canberra* and would play an important part in supplying the steel and labour for the modification of *QE2*. Steel plates were laid over the bottoms of the pools to support and distribute evenly the weight through an intricate network of vertical girders. As steel plating was welded in place, the helicopter decks slowly took shape. Able Seaman Thomas Young was one of those tasked to stand by with fire extinguishers in case any welding sparks ignited inflammable material. Fortunately, there were no such incidents. The completed landing area was able to accommodate two Sea King helicopters. The incredible achievements of Vosper Thornycroft's company employees as they rose to the task of converting *QE2* right before our eyes in less than eight days was inspiring for those of us who witnessed their superhuman efforts. Foreman welder Eddie Sholing commented, 'The lads have done a smashing job. I am proud to have been working with them.'

At the forward end, a further helicopter deck was added. Again the question of support for the enormous weight of the steel pads and the added weight of a Sea King helicopter was critical. The bow of the ship is particularly strong and designed to withstand exposure to the elements in stormy weather. On Atlantic crossings it was not unusual to have large waves cascading over the bow onto the deck. However, there was not enough clear room to land a helicopter because space was taken up with the capstan, the machinery used to lower and raise the ship's anchors. The solution was to extend Quarter Deck over the capstan to create enough room for one Sea King helicopter to land. *QE2* would now have helicopter landing pad space for three helicopters and their payloads.

These structural changes, along with the additional stores and equipment to be carried south, had a significant impact on the weight and stability of the liner. Ensuring the modified *QE2* remained stable at sea was of paramount importance. Second Officer Chris Haughton was assigned the important task of monitoring the changes in the distribution of weight around the ship and its impact on the ship's stability. He kept running calculations of weight and stability throughout the conversion process. For a ship to float upright in a stable position, it must be designed and built so that the centre of gravity remains above the centre of buoyancy. The distance between the two centres is known as the metacentric height, which is abbreviated to 'GM' by mariners. Calculating the GM involves determining and listing the weight of every single space on a ship in relation to the ship's centre of gravity. The higher the value of the GM, the more stable a ship will be. A negative GM will, in most cases, cause a ship to capsize.

In order to calculate the GM of *QE2* for her voyage to the South Atlantic, it was necessary to calculate the new weight of the ship after all structural changes had been made. This entailed deducting the weights of the superstructure cut away from the Upper Deck and Quarter Deck. The weights of the new steel beams and plates used to construct the flight decks fore and aft were added. The value of the changed weight then became part of a mathematical formula used to calculate the new GM. In addition, the weight of all items in every storage area had to be included in the formula. These items included ammunition and ordnance, weapons, military equipment and stores. Items stowed on the open decks, including helicopters, drums of fuel and Land Rovers, also had to be added.

Allowance also had to be made for every person sailing with the ship. For cruise passengers the weight was normally calculated at fourteen souls per tonne. This figure included the average weight of a passenger with luggage. For the troops a different figure was required. Given the additional weight of equipment each soldier would carry, the weight was calculated at eight souls per tonne. An allowance had to be added for the weight of fuel and water on board and how the stability would change as fuel and water were consumed. One final calculation was added for the possibility of ice accretion on the ship in the cold South Atlantic winter. Second Officer Haughton's calculations kept *QE2* safe outward and homeward bound.

As *QE2* prepared for sea in Southampton, more weight was added than was cut away with the result that *QE2* sailed below her Plimsoll line for the first and only time. The Plimsoll line is a reference mark located amidships on the outside of the hull that indicates the maximum depth to which a vessel is certified to be immersed in accordance with UK maritime safety regulations. A marine surveyor from the Ministry of Transport was notified that the ship was 'below her marks' and a special dispensation was issued to permit her to sail.

The extensive work required to construct the helicopter pads continued throughout the period the ship was in Southampton prior to her departure. When the ship departed eight days later, the construction work was complete, although the painting of the decks was not yet finished and was completed at sea after the ship had sailed.

QE2 did not have the fuel tank capacity to travel non-stop to the South Atlantic and back. Modifications were required to prepare her for refuelling at sea. Normally, *QE2* put into port every two or three days when cruising, and the longest uninterrupted period she was normally at sea was five days when crossing the Atlantic or Pacific Ocean. For the voyage to the South Atlantic, it was possible the ship could be at sea for several weeks with no opportunity to refuel in port. This is a situation Royal Navy ships regularly experience. They are refuelled at sea by ships from the Royal Fleet Auxiliary (RFA). The RFA is a civilian-crewed fleet that delivers logistical and operational support at sea to Royal Navy ships. The technical expression for transferring fuel or other stores between two ships at sea is replenishment at sea (RAS). This process is known as RASing (pronounced 'razzing').

The foredeck of *QE2* before conversion. (R.W. Warwick)

The forward helicopter deck was constructed over the anchor-lifting machinery. (Stephen Hallam)

Conversion to a Troopship

Viewed from the Bridge: the forward helicopter deck under construction forward of the cargo hold. (Stephen Hallam)

The new helicopter landing platform is temporarily supported by metal props while vertical girders are welded in place. (Stephen Hallam)

A floating crane came alongside to lift the pieces of the new helicopter deck into place. (Patrick Hewetson)

The two swimming pools on Upper Deck and Quarter Deck aft formed part of the foundation for the new aft landing platform. (R.W. Warwick)

Conversion to a Troopship

The tiled pool surround is being removed to make way for the new landing platform. (Patrick Hewetson)

Wood decking across the width of the ship was removed in preparation for cutting away the aft section of Upper Deck. Hardboard sheets were loaded on board for internal protection. (Patrick Hewetson)

The QE2 in the Falklands War

Background centre: floodlights were erected on the deck to enable construction to continue throughout the night. (Stephen Hallam)

The removal of the aft end of Upper Deck provided more space for construction of the landing platform. (Patrick Hewetson)

Conversion to a Troopship

Pieces of *QE2*'s superstructure that have been cut away lie on the dockside. (Stephen Hallam)

The weight of the extra steel used in the construction of the helicopter decks had to be taken into account when calculating and monitoring the stability of the ship. (Stephen Hallam)

Extra support at the end of One Deck enabled the platform to be extended as far aft as possible. (R.W. Warwick)

All the new plating has been welded in place and a safety railing installed where the end of Upper Deck was removed. (R.W. Warwick)

Conversion to a Troopship

Troops lend a hand to apply a coat of paint before departure. (Stephen Hallam)

The underside of the aft landing deck provided storage space for military equipment. (Patrick Hewetson)

QE2's designated helicopter landing area is marked with a white cross. It was not used during the voyage because the deck was not strong enough to bear the weight of Sea Kings. (R.W. Warwick)

Sheets of hardboard were affixed to provide protection to the vast area of the ship's carpeting. (Stephen Hallam)

Conversion to a Troopship

Containers holding equipment for the Ministry of Defence SCOT satellite communications system were loaded on the open deck aft of the Bridge. (Stephen Hallam)

Elevation drawing showing the stowage spaces in the cargo hold down to the lowest level on Eight Deck. The cargo space on Eight Deck extended out to the sides of the ship. (R.W. Warwick)

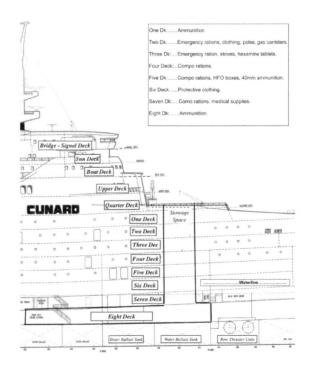

The cargo hold was used for storing military equipment including large quantities of ammunition. This photograph shows stores having been loaded on Eight Deck. The flap for Seven Deck is partially in place. (Stephen Hallam)

Military equipment on deck ready to be lowered into the cargo hold. (Stephen Hallam)

Stores have been craned on board from the dockside and now they have to be lowered into the hold. (R. Smith)

All hands turned to help with the loading and one of them made a record of where everything was stowed. (R. Smith)

Stacks of supplies were secured in place by wood battens, known on ships as 'tomming off'. (R. Smith)

Drums of aviation fuel and vehicles are already in place as extra life rafts are loaded. (Stephen Hallam)

Stowage space for the equipment required by 5 Infantry Brigade was at a premium. Some equipment had to be stowed on the top deck forward of the funnel. (Stephen Hallam)

Normally *QE2* was refuelled through a shell door opening on Five Deck very close to the waterline. Refuelling through Five Deck is problem free when the ship is stable in the calm waters of port with no motion, but a replenishment at sea via Five Deck would have been hazardous in the often treacherous seas of the South Atlantic Ocean. Royal Navy and Cunard officers discussed the matter and a decision was made to install an 8in pipe from the midships baggage entrance on Two Deck starboard side. The pipe was routed a short way along Two Deck at knee height and then into crew stairway number five. The pipe had chequered danger markings to alert personnel there was a hazard to be stepped over. The pipe then followed the stairway down to the fuel tanks at the bottom of the ship. The potential peril involved in refuelling at sea, with heavy oil coursing through piping that ran through passenger accommodation, was considerable. The installation required careful planning and workmanship of the highest quality.

Protecting the ship's luxury carpeting required 2,000 sheets of hardboard purchased from the Vosper Thornycroft shipyard. The hardboard was laid over several miles of carpet in public rooms, passageways and some of the cabins, while stair carpets were covered in thick canvas. The hardboard covering was laid by the ship's carpenters assisted by the hotel crew.

Another important area of preparation concerned equipment and supplies. All the trappings and accoutrements of a cruise ship were offloaded, including deck chairs, fine crockery, cutlery, paintings and ornaments. *QE2*'s silverware, glassware and fine china was collected, securely packaged and offloaded. This was replaced with light, plain crockery and stainless-steel cutlery supplied by the Ministry of Defence. The military also supplied 1,000 stacking chairs, 1,000 camp beds and folding trestle tables. Between 5 May and 9 May, most of the decorative pictures and valuable furniture were removed from the ship. Gambling machines and card tables were removed from the casino. Lorries waited quayside to take the trappings of the twentieth-century cruise liner into storage. Most furnishings and equipment were stored in warehouses owned by the removals and storage company Pickfords. The concessionaire providing all the flowers and potted plants was asked to remove them from the ship. Luckily, the owner was able to rent storage space from Wills of Romsey, a well-known local tomato grower.[51]

Around the ship, departments carried out stock checks. It was necessary to know the value of on-board stock before the liner sailed so that anything consumed during the voyage could be billed to the Ministry of Defence. A check of the stocks of drugs, dressings and consumable medical supplies in the ship's hospital revealed an estimated stock value of £60,000 with a further £2,000 of dental supplies. However, it was anticipated that none of the ship's medical supplies would be used because the Army had placed sufficient supplies on board to meet its needs for about three months. Meanwhile the ship's catering officers liaised with the military on food stores. A computer printout was prepared of all on-board food provisions. Catering crew worked to change the ship's food stores from those expected by passengers travelling on board a world-class ocean liner to food that provided the practical, balanced diet required for an infantry brigade. A few first-class foodstuffs did remain on board with the result that during the voyage military officers were occasionally pleased to discover suckling pigs, lobster tails, caviar and foie gras on the menu.

Secure communications in any war situation are critical. For global ship-to-shore communication, *QE2* was fitted with an Inmarsat terminal. While the equipment was very versatile, it was not suitable for military operations as messages had to be encrypted. If this time-consuming process had not been carried out, messages could have been read or heard by others. To avoid the risk of strategic messages being compromised, an additional satellite communication system was installed to enable secure encrypted two-way communication between the ship and military units in the South Atlantic. The official name of this equipment was UK/SSC 002, although it was referred to as SCOT (Satellite Communications Terminal). The SCOT terminal was installed behind the chart room on the Bridge. When the ship was launched, this large empty space was referred to by deck officers as the 'barn'. The name stuck. While the ship was prepared for war service in Southampton, a secure and enclosed radio room was constructed of wood in the centre of the barn. The SCOT system was installed but unfortunately was not operational before *QE2* departed. Two Marconi technicians sailed with the ship to complete the task. The remainder of the barn was a secure South Atlantic map-plotting area that was off limits to almost all personnel. Ultra-high-frequency aerials were fitted on the Bridge wings, and satellite communication domes were installed on the deck forward of the funnel.

QE2 was required to carry sufficient lifeboat and life raft capacity for everyone on board. On a passenger cruise, the number of passengers and crew would never exceed 2,915 souls. This time, the number would be much higher. The ship had received an official exemption from normal regulations with the requirement that:

> ... the number of persons on board shall not exceed 4,000 provided that sufficient life saving equipment was carried in accordance with the Merchant Shipping (Life Saving Appliances) Regulations of 1980.[52]

On this voyage, *QE2* carried the most souls she ever sailed with, and so the safety equipment loaded in Southampton included extra life rafts and additional life jackets to meet the requirement of one for every person on board. The exemption also required a list naming every person sailing to be maintained ashore. The authors have not been able to locate a list of the names of all military personnel who embarked.

The loading of military stores commenced on Sunday, 9 May. Military stores were loaded on board along with flight deck stores, foul weather clothing, metal drums of aviation fuel and safes for classified documents. Most of the ammunition assigned to the ship was loaded into No. 1 Hold, accessed through a hatch on the forecastle head. In this hold during a normal voyage, imperishable stores were kept, all of which were offloaded. Also loaded into No. 1 Hold were compo rations, medical supplies, protective clothing, field stoves and gas canisters. A sign warning 'Danger – Live Ammo' was erected while the ship was in port. Additional quantities of ammunition were loaded in containers on the Sports Deck, forward of the funnel near what was normally the dog kennels. The ship had received a formal notice from the Department of Trade notifying Cunard that *QE2* was exempt from regulations on dangerous goods 'in so far as they prohibit the carriage of explosives on passenger ships'.[53]

Equipment too large for convenient stowage or which it was felt might be needed quickly for offloading by helicopters was stored on the open decks aft, on the raised Boat Deck and on what remained of the aft end of Upper Deck. This included seven Land Rovers, two trailers loaded with equipment, helicopter parts, fuel and rations. The presence of high-octane aviation fuel stowed on deck was a risk given the possibility of air raids or the ship being hit by an Exocet missile. However, virtually no part of *QE2* was completely secure against attack.

QE2 crew with the responsibility for ordering stores responded to the requisitioning by placing additional orders. The normal procedure for ordering stores in Southampton was for *QE2* stores petty officers to liaise with colleagues working in the Cunard offices at South Western House, just across the road from the dock entrance in Southampton. The ship would be heading into new territory, so nautical charts had to be ordered. Petty officer David Humphreys ordered charts for the Falkland Islands and South Georgia. This was an urgent order for charts of an area of the world not in high demand and it took several days for Cunard staff to procure them from the Hydrographic Office in Taunton. The charts arrived on board just days before departure.

The ship's hospital was busy while the vessel was in Southampton preparing to sail. As well as providing medical cover for crew and shoreside contractors working on board during the conversion, the medical team also had to prepare for the voyage south. Trucks delivered medical stores to the quayside from the Ludgershall military depot on Salisbury Plain. Known as 'frigate packs', these were crates of medical stores kept ready for immediate despatch to any part of the world. The packs were large crates that contained a range of medical supplies that Army personnel might need in different climates from the tropics to the polar regions. Senior nurse Sister Jane Yelland was asked by an Army officer if she considered any medical supplies had not been delivered that might be required. She replied that there were no sea sickness tablets, an item not normally required by the Army but which might be needed in rough seas by even the toughest soldiers. The next day several boxes of Stugeron travel sickness tablets were delivered to the ship. The hospital sailed with one more nurse than the normal complement. Cunard nurse Sister Diane McLean was a member of the Territorial Army (TA). It was agreed that she would perform her TA service on board *QE2* rather than be seconded to a military hospital. Approximately 150 members of the Brigade were qualified medical professionals and they were happy to assist the ship's medical team on the journey south.

6

The Volunteers

All the deck officers volunteered to sail on the voyage. First Officer Philip Rentell had qualified as an RNR lieutenant the year before the ship was requisitioned. He had been due to go on leave at Southampton but volunteered to remain. His offer was accepted and it was decided that he would serve as liaison officer between Captain Jackson and his officers and the Royal Navy personnel embarked with NP1980. He adopted his naval rank and became Lieutenant Rentell RNR for the duration of the voyage. In making this change, he was required to wear the insignia of his RNR rank. This meant that he had to swap the two-and-a-half gold stripes of a first officer for the two stripes of a Royal Navy lieutenant. The 'loss' of half a stripe led to some joking in the officers' Wardroom that he had been demoted!

Cunard announced the arrangements for deciding which crew would sail on the ship. Only those who were signed on the ship's articles at the time of the requisition were asked to sail. The ship's articles are a contractual document between the master (captain) of a ship and her crew. All crew members are required to sign on the articles when joining a ship, then to sign again when leaving.

Officers and ratings had different leave rotations. Officers usually served two months on duty followed by one month off. Different departments would make their own arrangements for officers' leave. The situation was different for ratings, who worked to a 'three on, one off' rotation. Crew changes for ratings would take place about once a month with a third of the ratings signing off and a third returning from leave. After the end of her world cruise, *QE2* would put into Southampton on average twice a month from April through to December, so generally there would be one change of crew ratings in every two visits to the home port. The ship's arrival in Southampton from Philadelphia was not one of those occasions, so there was no scheduled crew change. Almost all crew on leave would not be required to sail. They would remain signed off and receive full pay while the ship was away. Many volunteered their services but few were accepted. One exception was waiter John Davies. He was one of the few ratings to have signed off when the ship returned from Philadelphia. After two days of leave, he called Cunard and volunteered to sail. 'I am very proud that I did,' he recalls.

Most officers who were on leave remained on leave, but there were exceptions. Senior Sister Jane Yelland was at home decorating her kitchen when she heard on local radio that the ship had been requisitioned. She received a call from the office of the Cunard medical director, Dr Peter Oliver, asking her to rejoin the ship as the Senior Sister. Cashier Stephen Ward, who had signed off the ship when she returned from Philadelphia, received a telephone call at home two days later informing him that the relief chief cashier had not volunteered to sail. Stephen offered to return. He later said he felt a sense of ownership in *QE2* and did not feel he could walk away from this voyage then sit at home and learn what she was doing from the media. As he drove back to Southampton, he passed RAF Abingdon, which was far busier than usual with grey military aircraft. On the roads there were several Army trucks moving south in small convoys. When he arrived at Southampton Docks, he observed more Army trucks vying for quayside space with vehicles delivering stores for loading on board. Stewardess Sue Crozier was one of the crew members who was able to grab a few days' leave. As she drove home to Devon, she noticed Army trucks heading to the east and remembers thinking to herself she had a good idea where they were going. Accounts officer David Luke and his twin brother, hotel officer Jamie Luke, both volunteered to sail. However, it was decided by the fleet personnel manager, Arnie Williams, and the purser, Brian Vickers, that two twin brothers should not sail together to a dangerous war zone. Jamie Luke, who was on leave, stayed home caring for their parents and celebrating their father's ninety-second birthday.

Waiter Kevin Dunn went home to his parents for a few days. His father supported his decision to sail but thought he should be well prepared and took him shopping for outdoor clothing, which included thermal under-wear, thermal socks, woollen sweaters and a thick padded down coat. On the evening before he returned to the ship in Southampton, his father was busy sewing name tags on the new clothing, including his socks. Kevin could not understand this and remarked to his dad, 'Nobody is going to steal my stuff.' Later his father told his son he had wanted his name on his clothing in case he had the difficult task of identifying body parts should disaster strike *QE2*.

At a meeting of ship's heads of department on 4 May, it was emphasised that crew volunteering to sail should be medically fit with any doubtful cases referred to Cunard's principal medical officer. Of those crew signed on the ship's articles, no one was obliged to sail. The ship would be crewed by volunteers only. Crew members under the age of 18 were required to obtain a signed letter of consent from their parents or legal guardian.

A meeting was held in *QE2*'s Theatre where two representatives of the National Union of Seamen (NUS) presented a deal that had been agreed between the union, government and shipping companies. It was agreed that those who volunteered would, if selected, remain on articles but with changed National Maritime Board (NMB) terms and conditions, including a danger allowance of 150 per cent of normal salary while the ship was in a defined area of 'warlike operations'. It was also agreed that one of the union representatives, Malcolm Bailey, would sail with the ship in the expectation that he would disembark on the way south if the opportunity arose.

The NMB agreements were amended to show that shipowners of requisitioned ships agreed to underwrite personal life insurance policies that would be invalidated if the insured person was serving in an area of warlike operations. Compensation payable to next of kin in the event of death was increased to £43,000 for officers, £35,000 for petty officers and £26,000 for ratings and cadets. The amended NMB Warlike Operations Agreement would apply until there was a cessation of hostilities. The estate of any member of the ship's company who died during the conflict would be exempt from death duties. The Cunard memorandum to crew on the amended NMB agreements concluded by saying, 'The Board of Cunard Line fully appreciate the dedication shown by those personnel who will be sailing in the ship and wish you all God speed and a safe return.'[54]

QE2 employed a large number of non-UK nationals, the majority of whom did not sail with the ship. Only eleven non-British crew, all of them ratings, sailed. Four were from Ireland, and one each from Australia, Canada, Italy, Japan, Malta, New Zealand and Spain.

The ship's laundry was operated as a concession and staffed by Singaporean and Malaysian men. The NUS lobbied Cunard for the laundry to be manned by British crew for this voyage. The company agreed to the proposal and so the staff were signed off and flown home to Singapore. The laundry was then run by a group of British stewardesses. Many were from the Merchant Navy 'pool' in Liverpool, some of whom were signing on *QE2* for the first time. They were a lively and hardworking group who ran the laundry effectively during the voyage. On board they became known affectionately as the 'steam queens'. With the ship due to sail with a record number of people, it was inevitable that the demand for laundry services would increase. This was eased by the installation of a washing machine in room service pantries on every passenger deck.

The laundry stewardesses were among just thirty-five women who went to war on *QE2*. Some of the women found themselves doing jobs they would not normally do. For example, Susan Hogg, who normally prepared passenger manifests and handled queries at the passenger bureau on Two Deck, was assigned as personal secretary to the commander of 5 Infantry Brigade, Brigadier M.J.A. Wilson. Her work involved taking meeting minutes, typing memoranda and passing messages and documents from the brigadier to others on board. Jacqui White was a stewardess who volunteered to do computer and accounts work in the finance department to cover a staffing gap.

Paul Uglow, a 20-year-old waiter, had been working on the ship for just four weeks when he volunteered. His father encouraged him to go. One of the youngest members of crew was 17-year-old Stephen Easter. He had signed on as a commis waiter and was promoted to waiter shortly before the ship was requisitioned. When he went to volunteer at the Writers' Office on Six Deck, he was told crew under 18 years of age needed written parental consent. He telephoned his parents from one of the coin-operated payphones that were connected to the UK's terrestrial telephone network when the ship was alongside in Southampton. He spoke to his mother, who then wrote to the company's fleet personnel office giving permission for her son to sail. Another crew member who had only recently joined Cunard was 18-year-old Alan Flewers, also one of the youngest on board. He was optimistic about the safety of the ship and before sailing said, 'As soon as we leave the Solent, we will be closely guarded.' Another young man, 17-year-old Des Sweeny, wished to sail but his parents would not give their permission.

The Volunteers

The Cunard Fleet Personnel Department in the Southampton office played a very important role from the moment the liner was requisitioned. They were the main link between the ship and families ashore, many of whom came from the Southampton area. Sandra Godden, who worked in the department, remembers they witnessed many wills before the ship sailed. Cruise director Tim Castle recalls, 'I didn't make a will but I did ask my neighbours to hold a letter for delivery to my mother and sisters in the event that I didn't return.'

The requisitioning of the ship led to one couple bringing forward their marriage plans. Martin Boatwright, the personal steward to the captain, married his girlfriend Tina from Shrewton the weekend before the ship sailed. 'We talked about it and decided to get married before I went to war,' said Martin.[55] Captain Jackson was surprised when Martin asked him for time off to walk down the aisle but willingly approved the request. The captain's steward was known as the 'captain's tiger', the Merchant Navy equivalent of a batman.

As the ship was converted, crew members would ask each other whether they were volunteering. 'Are you going?' was a common question. Some of those who decided not to go were concerned for those who were volunteering, asking questions such as 'Are you sure about this?' and 'Have you thought this through?' Many crew were of the opinion that, while war is never desirable, military action was justified in this case as the invasion of the Falkland Islands was unprovoked and unwarranted. A view common among the crew was that the government was right in trying to resolve the crisis diplomatically and peacefully, resorting to military force only when it became clear the diplomatic route had failed.

Most crew members had conversations with families on whether they should volunteer. When hairdresser Timothy Williams told his mother he was volunteering, she replied, 'Oh my, you're the last of my sons I thought would go to war.' Tim had two brothers. Clive Dalley was eager to volunteer. His father was a Merchant Navy veteran from the Second World War who had sailed on the Arctic convoys. Terry Foskett's father had served in the Second World War at Dunkirk and Normandy. Brian Gosney, a leading gloryhole steward, was one of many crew members who faced family pressure. His daughter Cheryl tried to persuade him not to volunteer, to which Brian replied that he had been on *QE2* since her maiden voyage and could not stay at home while she went to war. Nicola Wright, 9-year-old daughter of contractor Geoffrey Wright, whispered, 'I did not want him to go – I just didn't.' Commodore William E. Warwick, former captain of *QE2* and the father of the Chief Officer, had survived the sinking of the armed merchant cruiser HMS *Andania* in the Second World War. He never questioned his son's decision to sail. David Humphreys received support from his father, who had served in the Royal Artillery in the Second World War, and his mother, who had served with the Women's Royal Naval Service.

When sailing on a passenger voyage, *QE2* carried an average of 1,015 crew members. Of these, about 355 provided services that were not required on a liner performing a military role. They included the concessionaire personnel, who worked for businesses that rented space on *QE2* from Cunard. Steiners provided the hairdresser concession, Mecca Sportsman ran the casino, Ocean Trading operated the shops and Ocean Pictures provided the photography studio. The concessionaires decided their own arrangements for staffing. No casino staff sailed on the voyage. Two hairdressers, one photographer and six shop staff volunteered to sail. Anthony Dance, who was celebrating his transfer to another ship when he heard *QE2* had been requisitioned, volunteered to sail. Another Ocean Trading employee, Kent Frazer, had signed off the P&O ship *Sea Princess* a few days earlier. He recalls, 'When I learned that the *QE2* was to follow the same path *Canberra* had taken, I immediately called the Ocean Trading office in Southampton and volunteered to be part of the crew.' Two other *Sea Princess* shop staff volunteered and were accepted, namely Martin Broughton and Anthony Butts. Others laid off included singers, dancers, musicians, librarians, beauticians, kennel maids, casino croupiers and florists. Dancer Christine Dare was not required to sail and before disembarking said, 'I would like to be going – I expect the troops would have liked it!' The liner sailed with a total of 660 crew members, although many more than that volunteered.

Cunard also received offers to volunteer from members of the public. One such example was this telegram dated 4 May from an address in Hockley, Birmingham:

> Sir As an ex-serviceman may I request permission to join your ships crew for voluntary service.
> Sir I remain your obedient servant.[56]

Captain Hutcheson replied, saying that the offer to sail 'is sincerely appreciated and both Cunard and myself thank you for it. At present we are very much over-subscribed with crew and these must be our first consideration as I am sure you understand. Nevertheless, thank you again.'

The shipboard communications for the voyage involved effective collaboration between three officers. They were Allan Holmes, *QE2*'s chief radio officer; Lieutenant Robin Swaine RN, who was the NP1980 officer in charge of radio and satellite communications; and David MacKenzie, an RFA radio officer with responsibility for codes and ciphers. Allan Holmes recalls an excellent working relationship between the three men. There were new requirements in the sending of signals for the ship's radio officers. All outgoing messages had to be given a classification by NP1980, these being top secret, secret, official and unclassified. Some messages needed to be encrypted. *QE2* was not permitted to send signals direct to other merchant ships. If it was necessary to do so, they were sent first to the Ministry of Defence (Navy) for vetting and approval prior to onward transmission. The *QE2* radio officers were required to sign the Official Secrets Act, given the sensitivity and secrecy surrounding the communications and equipment they were working with. Other *QE2* officers with access to classified information also had to sign the Official Secrets Act.

Internal communications could be made using the telephone fitted in every passenger and officer's cabin. However, this was not a secure system because calls made between passenger cabins had to be routed through a manned telephone exchange. Three female telephonists, Kathleen Nilsen, Janet Ryan and Janice Wood, staffed the exchange throughout the working day. The nightshift was covered by David Sharpe.

Although the crew were not classified as combatants, they fell under the revised Geneva Convention Relative to the Treatment of Prisoners of War of 1949. This revision extended prisoner-of-war status to 'Members of crews, including Masters, pilots and apprentices of the merchant marine' (Article 4).[57] Everyone who volunteered to sail was issued with a British Forces card which had name, rank and date of birth. A statement on the card read:

> If you are captured you are required, under the provisions of Article 17 of the Prisoner of War Convention, 1949, to give your captors the information set out overleaf so that your capture may be reported to your next-of-kin. When you are interrogated, but not before, tear off the duplicate portion and give it to the interrogator. GIVE NO OTHER INFORMATION.[58]

The Hague Convention VII relating to the Conversion of Merchant Ships into Warships of 1907 was relevant to *QE2*. The convention aims at greater humanitarian protection for merchant seafarers. *QE2* was not designated as a warship, the ship was not authorised to carry out an offensive role and its crew were not classed as combatants, so the Hague Convention VII did not apply in its entirety to *QE2* and other merchant ships engaged in the Falkland conflict. However, it offered some guidance on how STUFTs should operate. For example, Article 1 of the convention requires that a ship be placed 'under the direct authority, immediate control, and responsibility of the Power whose flag it flies', while Article 5 requires that a ship 'must observe in its operations the laws and customs of war'.[59]

Like the crew of other STUFTs, the *QE2* crew came under the Naval Discipline Act 1957, which governed discipline in the Royal Navy (before being replaced by the Armed Forces Act 2006). The Act established tighter laws for the conduct of personnel serving in the Royal Navy than the civilian laws of the land. Article 1 of the Act provided the legal basis for strategic command of *QE2* passing to Captain James RN of NP1980. Captain James would take orders from the commander of the task force on where the ship went and the timing of her movements, and he would be responsible for taking on-board operational decisions should circumstances suddenly change. Any order from Captain James to Captain Jackson would have binding effect even if it were against the expressed wishes of the latter. But while strategic command passed to the Royal Navy, Captain Jackson retained responsibility for navigation and the safe passage of the ship. There could be times when the immediate obedience of orders might be necessary for the safety of the ship, so all personnel were thus subject to one overriding code of conduct. Captain James or a naval officer nominated by him could commence disciplinary action against a crew member under the Act in order to ensure safety and effectiveness of operations. Meanwhile, Staff Captain Alexander Hutcheson retained responsibility for day-to-day discipline of the crew in accordance with Merchant Navy Discipline Organisation (MNDO) procedures. The ship's crew thus came under two disciplinary codes, although the Naval Discipline Act was paramount.

All the crew of *QE2* remained in their own cabins with the exception of some female crew. There were thirty-five females sailing (thirty-four crew plus war artist Linda Kitson). Some were berthed in the luxury cabins on Two Deck amidships near the Rotunda close to the Military Police office.

The Volunteers

This made it easy for the women to summon assistance should they receive any unwanted attentions from the predominantly male complement. Stewardess Lorna Le Peuple was interviewed by the press before the ship sailed. When asked if she had any concern, she replied, 'I've bought myself a sailing anorak and some boots in case we have to take to the boats.'

7

5 Infantry Brigade

After eight whirlwind days of structural alterations and offloading and loading of equipment and stores, *QE2* was ready to receive the three battalions of 5 Infantry Brigade: the 1st Battalion the Welsh Guards, the 2nd Battalion the Scots Guards and the 1st Battalion the 7th Duke of Edinburgh's Own Gurkha Rifles. The formal embarkation of troops began at 0545 hours on 12 May, led by the Welsh Guards with a regimental band from the Household Brigade on the quayside piping the men aboard. The troops entered the ship on Five Deck forward, walking up the wide metal ramps that were usually used to drive cars on board. The troops carried anti-tank weapons and radio apparatus, in addition to their bergens, rifles and brown suitcases.

The embarkation was an emotive time with some unexpected scenes on board. A soldier from the Scots Guards sat playing Beethoven's melodic 'Für Elise' on the piano in the Rotunda on Two Deck. Most of the pianos had been offloaded from the ship, but this one had remained in place. Soldiers crowded around, enjoying the impromptu recital.

The commander of 5 Infantry Brigade was Brigadier M.J.A. (Tony) Wilson. He had been commissioned into the King's Own Yorkshire Light Infantry in 1956. His extensive experience as an infantry officer[60] and as an instructor at the Royal Naval College at Greenwich[61] provided key knowledge of naval tactics and operational procedures. He was promoted to brigadier and appointed the commander of 5 Infantry Brigade in 1980. Brigadier Wilson was assisted by the brigade major, Major Brendon Lambe.

Immediately after the invasion of the Falklands, military units started to receive new instructions. Two battalions under Wilson's command, namely 2nd Parachute Battalion and 3rd Parachute Battalion, were detached from the Brigade and sent south on board *Canberra* and *Norland* attached to 3 Commando Brigade, commanded by Brigadier Julian Thompson.[62] This left the Brigade with just one battalion: the 1st Battalion the 7th Duke of Edinburgh's Own Gurkha Rifles. Wilson then reconstituted the Brigade by adding the 2nd Battalion the Scots Guards and the 1st Battalion the Welsh Guards. The two Guards battalions had been due to take part in the Trooping of the Colour on Horse Guards Parade in June. The ceremony to celebrate the Queen's official birthday went ahead with six battalions instead of the usual eight.[63]

The Gurkhas are troops from Nepal who have chosen to serve the British Crown and possess a legendary fighting reputation. There was some doubt they might not be allowed to sail on *QE2* for political reasons. However, the government of Nepal gave the British government its support for the deployment of Nepali citizens to the South Atlantic.[64] In 1982, the commanding officer of 1st Battalion 7th Duke of Edinburgh's Own Gurkha Rifles was Lieutenant Colonel David Morgan. He said, 'The morale is very high – in twenty-two years with the battalion, I have never seen it higher.'

5 Infantry Brigade deployed to the South Atlantic in four ships. All the troops and much of the equipment sailed on board *QE2*. The Brigade's heavy weapons and the bulk of its military stores were loaded on board two Townsend Thoreson roll-on, roll-off ferry ships, *Baltic Ferry* (Captain E. Harrison) and *Nordic Ferry* (Captain R. Jenkins). After helicopter decks were fitted and stores loaded, the two ships sailed from Portsmouth on 9 May. A third ferry, *Tor Caledonia* (Captain A. Scott), carried Brigade stores but in the event was not needed, arriving in the war area after the Argentines had surrendered.[65]

As the Brigade had been speedily reconstituted following the detachment of the two parachute regiments, an intensive training exercise was organised in Wales. This was Exercise Welsh Falcon, the word 'Falcon' being chosen due to its phonetic similarity to 'Falkland'. This two-week exercise was mounted in the Welsh Guards' regular training area of Sennybridge and the nearby Brecon Beacons, an area chosen as the terrain resembles that of the Falkland Islands. For the purposes of the exercise, Sennybridge was an occupied British territory, named Falconia. The exercise was used to bring the Brigade up to operational standard. It involved battalion attack training, intensive live-firing exercises, helicopter movements and training in amphibious assaults.[66] Some mock battles were held with air raids simulated by Royal Air Force (RAF) fighter aircraft. The exercise gave the Brigade staff the opportunity to gain team experience working together. Exercise Welsh Falcon was the only opportunity for the Brigade to train together before it boarded *QE2*.

In their book *The Battle for the Falklands*, Max Hastings and Simon Jenkins suggest that the Ministry of Defence did not initially take seriously enough the prospect of 5 Infantry Brigade going to war. The Brigade had struggled to obtain equipment such as bergen rucksacks, cold weather clothing and ammunition.[67] Welsh Guardsman Simon Weston notes that more resources were available during Welsh Falcon:

> It suddenly seemed that we could have any stores we wanted, and any facilities. We practised with our mortars on ranges that normally we would never have been able to get on to, with ammunition that we would never have been able to procure. I'd never seen so many helicopters in my life.[68]

After the exercise both the Welsh Guards and Scots Guards returned to London on 29 April. But the 7th Gurkha Rifles remained at Sennybridge to carry out more field training until 3 May. This included a defence live-firing exercise, which was the largest exercise of this type at Sennybridge since the training that took place there for the Normandy D-Day landings. 5 Infantry Brigade eventually boarded *QE2* on 12 May. Simon Weston recalls, 'It was surreal. It felt like we were in a movie from the Second World War. We all thought the fighting would be over before we got there.'[69] He remembers, 'There was almost a carnival atmosphere below decks. You'd have thought everyone had just been de-mobbed, not mobilised for war.'[70] Welsh Guardsman Tracy Evans, who was 18 years old when he boarded the liner, remembers:

> A once in a lifetime journey. Despite not having all the luxury trappings of a paying passenger I was totally in awe of the *QE2*. We tossed a coin to see which one of us would be sleeping on the camp bed. A two-bed cabin and three men … and I lost. In a luxury ship and I got a camp bed.

Just being on a luxury ship was a new experience for many of the soldiers. Sergeant Danny McDermid of the Scots Guards grew up near the shipyards on the River Clyde. He watched the liner being built, never thinking that he might sail on her one day. Many of the men in 5 Infantry Brigade were very young. Ian Holt of the Royal Corps of Transport was only 17 when he boarded. At first, the Army was reluctant to let him go, but it relented when he said he would be 18 when he arrived in the war zone. Ian celebrated his eighteenth birthday on 2 June, the day he landed at Blue Beach 2, San Carlos, East Falkland.

An amusing incident between two brothers took place on the dockside just before embarkation commenced. Lance Corporal Garry Hearn of the Welsh Guards was with his wife, Faye. His older brother, Michael, was with his girlfriend, Sandra. As the couples embraced and said goodbye to each other, a press photographer captured the moment. The image featured in the *Daily Telegraph* and other newspapers. It was wrongly captioned as husbands and wives bidding farewell to each other. The soldiers were hugging each other's partner!

Pipe Major Meherman Tamang played his bagpipes as the Gurkhas boarded the ship and the regimental Pandit (priest) was on hand to offer the troops a blessing. The battalion consisted of 751 men, the largest unit in the British task force. B Company's Rifleman Baliprasad Rai's was astounded when confronted with the size of *QE2* for the first time at Southampton's Queen Elizabeth II Terminal:

> Such a ship had to be seen to be believed. Why, it was larger than any building I'd seen back home. Never had I slept in such beautiful surroundings or in such a big-soft bed, nor perhaps I ever will? If I was to go to war, then there was no better way to go.[71]

Much was made of whether these mountain men would be able to adjust well to life at sea, as most had never been on a ship before. In stormy weather the higher decks on a ship suffer more from lateral movement. The closer a deck is to the waterline, the less movement there is. The Gurkhas were assigned accommodation on Five Deck, the most stable passenger accommodation on the liner and less likely to cause motion sickness. Although the cabins on Five Deck were some of the smallest on the ship, they were able to accommodate four or five Gurkhas.

A number of meetings of senior officers were held in Southampton while the ship was preparing for war service. At one of the meetings, it was decided the ship would not carry any media reporters. By now there was some unease at media reports revealing details of ship movements and on-board personnel, thus disclosing information that could prove useful to the enemy. However, the Artistic Records Committee of the Imperial War Museum and Fleet Air Arm Museum were keen to have an artist in the field. Linda Kitson, a professional artist who had trained as a commercial graphic artist and worked as a drawing tutor at the Royal College of Art, was considered to be the most suitable person to fill this role and was offered the position of official war artist. The secretary of the Imperial War Museum was confident she was the best artist for the job, commenting, 'She draws very quickly. She's an on-the-spot artist who can capture atmosphere fast and she's prolific.'[72] An official photographer was also appointed by the Imperial War Museum to record the conflict on camera.

Linda Kitson was not permitted to sail on a Royal Navy ship as rules in force at the time permitted only men to work at sea. However, no such restriction existed in the Merchant Navy, so joining 5 Infantry Brigade on board *QE2* provided the ideal solution. The artist initially experienced some difficulty boarding the ship. She told a policeman on the quayside she was the official war artist, to which he responded, 'For all I know you're an out of work punk rocker.'[73] Soon after boarding *QE2*, Linda familiarised herself with the layout of the liner and it was not long before she started work. Before sailing she commented, 'War horrifies me. I would like to think I could bring back drawings which would make people think we should not fight ever again.'[74] Linda Kitson became the first British female official war artist to be sent with frontline troops and the only war artist to witness the conflict in the Falklands.

Although civilians, the artist and photographer enjoyed officer status, which gave them the freedom to go anywhere on the ship and mix with all ranks. During the voyage each would record events from a different perspective. The official war photographer, Paul Haley, worked for the Ministry of Defence as a civilian photographer. He joined *Soldier Magazine*, an MoD publication run by professional civilian journalists and photographers and administered by a team of civil servants, as a senior photographer in 1974. The job description required him 'to be ready to go anywhere in the world at 24 hours notice'. When Argentina invaded the islands, the magazine made a request to send a team to cover the conflict, but unfortunately permission was not granted by the government. However, Paul was assigned to cover preparations for the war, including the Sennybridge training exercise carried out in Wales by 5 Infantry Brigade. Here he met Brigadier Tony Wilson and gave him the photographs he had taken.

Paul Haley was at Southampton Docks the day before *QE2* sailed, taking photographs of visiting dignitaries and of the ship being loaded with ammunition and stores. At 1715 hours that day, he was contacted by *Soldier Magazine* and instructed to prepare to sail on *QE2* the following day. His baggage included about fifty rolls of black and white film and twenty rolls of colour film. It later transpired that Brigadier Wilson had asked for him to sail as part of the Brigade with the only stipulation being that his photographs would be pooled to the press worldwide.

On joining the ship, Paul was assigned a cabin sharing with a corporal in the Royal Signals. Dropping off his kit, he grabbed his cameras and began photographing scenes around the ship as she prepared to sail. He felt he should make contact with Brigadier Wilson, whom he thought might be on the Bridge. Upon gaining entry he was enthusiastically welcomed by the brigadier, who was in conversation with Captain Peter Jackson. The latter gave him a warm welcome and authorisation to visit the Bridge at any time.

Sorting out the sleeping arrangements for the troops was a big job, given the insufficient beds in the passenger cabins to accommodate all hands. This task fell to the staff of Major R.G. Cocking of the 29 Transport and Movement Regiment. Hotel officer Terry Foskett, whose normal job was passenger berthing officer, worked with Major Cocking's team in allocating troops to cabins. The most senior officers were given the penthouse suites. Less senior officers were accommodated on Boat Deck. Junior officers shared cabins on One Deck and other ranks were berthed on decks Two to Five. Except for the most senior officers, everyone in the Brigade had to share. Terry recalls guiding an Army non-commissioned officer (NCO) from cabin to cabin. They went into one cabin that Terry suggested could accommodate three or four passengers, to which the NCO replied, 'It could take five or six.' Second Lieutenant Paddy Redding of the Gurkha Rifles recalls sharing a cabin with two other officers. The most senior officer took one side of the double bed, while the two juniors took turns, one sleeping on the other side of the bed and the other on a camp bed.

Not every soldier who wanted to sail on *QE2* did so. Keith Dobson, of the Royal Signals, arrived at the docks in his Land Rover on the day of departure. As his vehicle lined up to board the ship, he could already 'smell the chefs cooking the evening meal' and imagined himself 'being served caviar and smoked salmon'. His thoughts were shattered when his superior

5 Infantry Brigade

told him of a last-minute change of plan; he had to drive to another dock and board the transport ship *Baltic Ferry*.

Now, with the 2,988 soldiers of 5 Infantry Brigade embarked, the ship was nearly ready to put to sea. At this stage it was unclear what part the Brigade would play in the conflict. If the war was swiftly concluded in the UK's favour, the Brigade would only be needed in a garrison role. But as the days went on, this option seemed less likely. The likelihood grew that 5 Infantry Brigade would have an active role in the fight.

8

The Voyage South
to Freetown

Crew members were in high spirits as departure day approached, going ashore in the evenings to pubs that were popular with ships' crew. Some went to the Alliance Hotel in Oxford Street where the manager, Norman McCowen, discounted all drinks by 20p. Others went to the Red Lion on the High Street and the Cricketers in Bedford Place. The night before departure, *QE2* crew could be found in the Grapes, a famous maritime watering hole near dock gate four. There was a buoyant atmosphere and the pub stayed open late. No crew member missed *QE2*. All those who had volunteered to sail did so. The time of departure had been clearly signposted by the crew gangway on Five Deck, on which a crew member had added 'Don't cry for me Argentina', a reference to a song title from the musical *Evita* about Argentine political figure Eva Perón.

Cunard senior management came to bid farewell to *QE2* on Wednesday, 12 May. Representing the owners, Lord Matthews, chairman, and Ralph Bahna, president of Cunard Line, were hosting the mayor of Southampton and senior military personnel, including Flag Officer Portsmouth, Rear Admiral Anthony S. Tippet RN, General Sir John E. Bramwell, Lieutenant General Sir Frank Kitson, Lieutenant R.B. Trant, Major General H.D.A. Langley and Major General N.J. Withal. The Right Hon. John Nott MP, Secretary of State for Defence, arrived at 1430 hours for a quick tour of the Bridge and made a short address to the troops, naval personnel and ship's crew. Mr Nott was very positive with his remarks. He said the Royal Navy was a superb service and he was sure it would look after

The QE2 in the Falklands War

QE2 and her troops. Captain Jackson spoke briefly to the press, noting that morale was very high among the volunteer crew with a feeling of 'electrical expectancy' among them.[75]

Departure time was scheduled for 1600 hours. That afternoon there was a buzz of activity around the ship as the final jobs were completed. At 1530 hours the flag of 5 Infantry Brigade was raised on the masthead. Shortly before the ship sailed, there were hectic last-minute goodbyes as Cunard shore staff and crew not sailing disembarked, some just minutes before the gangway was landed.

Before the mooring lines were cast off, an accommodating crane driver lifted an item of clothing belonging to Dawn Leyman onto the ship for her husband, Peter. The incident caught the attention of the press and was featured in a number of newspapers. It was also noted by the popular *Daily Express* artist, Raymond Allen Jackson, known better as the cartoonist JAK. He sketched the clothing flying from the ship's masthead in a cartoon which appeared in the paper following day. A singing telegram girl, Sandra Goodrick, also attracted a lot of attention from both ashore and on board as she bid the troops farewell.

Prior to departure, the ship received some highly appreciated messages of support from the public. A tele-message sent to Captain Jackson:

God Speed our prayers are with you
Staff and children of St James School Grimsby[76]

Another read:

To all on board QE2 good luck and God Bless you
A Grandmother[77]

This telex message was received in the ship's Radio Room:

To all who are sailing QE2 good luck and come back soon and safely.
We are with you all the way.
From the staff of Southampton County Court.[78]

Some of the ship's officers watched the departure from a penthouse suite balcony normally occupied by first-class passengers. Many of the ship's petty officers and ratings made their way to Boat Deck, a passenger area where they were not normally allowed. Crew member Jacqui White recalls that the decks, usually full of colourfully dressed passengers, were now covered in khaki. The view from Boat Deck aft had been completely transformed. The sunbathing decks and swimming pools were gone, replaced by the sheet metal of the newly fitted helicopter deck. The deck was full of soldiers three to four deep at the ship's rail.

Both soldiers and crew were seeking out the best vantage points from where they could watch the ship sail. Soldiers climbed into the lifeboats, always out of bounds. Some of the crew followed their example. Petty officer David Humphreys and a shipmate climbed one of the steep metal ladders that led to the lifeboats and found themselves in the company of a group of Scots Guards. The more experienced crew half expected an announcement to be made ordering the lifeboats to be cleared. But the Bridge turned a blind eye and for the only time in its history *QE2* sailed with her lifeboats full. One of the homemade banners said 'Good luck lads'. Many Union Jacks were visible. A kilted Scots guard stood in a lifeboat, waving a yellow Scottish flag with a red lion. One of the banners hung by the troops read, 'Argentina mind your own Falkland business'. On the quayside, thousands of family and friends waved off their husbands, fathers, sons and friends. Crowds of well-wishers lined the viewing balcony of the Queen Elizabeth II Terminal, many of them holding banners, posters and flags.

Under the command of Captain Peter Jackson and assisted by harbour pilot Captain Peter Driver, the liner prepared to sail. At 1603 hours, with tugs *Albert*, *Calshot* and *Clausentum* made fast forward and *Romsey* and *Brockenhurst* fast astern, the mooring lines were let go and the liner, now a troopship, was pulled away from the dock. *QE2* then steamed a little way upstream, to turn.

Within twenty-three minutes the turn had been completed, despite a force 4 to 5 east-south-easterly wind. *QE2* proceeded to sail past the passenger terminal, still crowded with family, well-wishers and the sound of the Scots Guards playing 'Sailing', 'Super Trooper' and 'Rule Britannia'.

As *QE2* moved slowly ahead, it was impossible for those on board not to notice the sheer number of people who had come to see the ship off, with large crowds on both sides of Southampton Water. Thousands watched from Hythe and Weston Shore. Southampton Water was quite choppy, but despite this a variety of small craft followed the ship. The departure was reminiscent of *Queen Mary* and *Queen Elizabeth* sailing from Southampton as troop carriers. Cunard was once again helping the nation with its fleet. All on board were aware that the eyes of the nation were upon the ship as helicopters, some carrying television cameras, flew overhead. It was an emotional departure for all, both on shore and on board.

Pamela Jackson, the wife of the captain, and his daughter Marilyn were among the many watching as *QE2* slipped her moorings and commenced her journey. Of the occasion Marilyn said:

> I remember there were many banners, and the ship's decks were lined with servicemen. Our feelings were a mixture of anxiety for their future, and huge pride in their undertaking. Our journey back to my parents' house in Southampton was subdued, and it was hard to imagine that unlike previous departures when my father had been setting off on a cruise itinerary, on this occasion we had no idea of exactly where they would be and when. Everything felt very uncertain as it must have been for the crew and troops.

What the immediate future held for *QE2* and those on board was unclear. The destination of the ship was unknown. The crew knew the ship was going to the South Atlantic, but would she proceed direct to the Falklands or transfer 5 Infantry Brigade elsewhere? Where, if anywhere, would the ship stop on the way south? How long would she be away? So many questions.

The departure was majestic but not without anxiety on the Bridge and in the Engine Room as maintenance work on two of the three boilers had not been completed. Before her conversion in 1987 from a steam ship to a diesel motor ship, *QE2*'s propulsion machinery comprised three boilers that powered steam turbines. She could travel at a speed of 30 knots with all three boilers operational, around 21 knots on two, but much less, only 6–10 knots, on one. One boiler was already out of action for planned maintenance when the ship sailed. This was not a problem as it was quite normal for the ship to sail with only two boilers in use. But then it transpired that there was a loss of boiler feed-water at a much higher rate than normal, so a second boiler was shut down before departure to investigate the problem. *QE2* produced her own distilled water. Normal consumption was approximately 10 tonnes an hour, but on departure day consumption had more than doubled.

The Voyage South to Freetown

CUNARD

To: Captain Peter Jackson
     RMS QUEEN ELIZABETH 2

Ship RMS QUEEN ELIZABETH 2   Date 12th May 1982

Dear Captain Jackson

Following the requisitioning of your ship QUEEN ELIZABETH 2 by HM Government we are given to understand that your sailing orders will be relayed to you through the Senior Naval Officer on board as instructed by the Commander in Chief Fleet.

We are further advised that your authority as Master in respect to the safety of the ship continues in the normal way and it is your ultimate responsibility.

To further clarify the position, the Department of Trade have confirmed that the Task Force Commander will be responsible for the direction of the ship when you enter the War Zone, however, as the Master you remain at all times the ultimate judge in matters concerning the safety of the ship.

In the event that during the period of the current operation you are superceded at any time for any purpose the contents of this letter will apply to your successor and should be included in the handover procedure.

On behalf of everyone in Cunard Line I wish you and your ship's company God's speed and a safe return.

Good luck.

Yours sincerely

R. m. Bahna

R M BAHNA
Managing Director

Memorandum sent to Captain Jackson clarifying his working relationship with the senior Royal Naval officer appointed to sail on the ship. (Captain P. Jackson)

The QE2 in the Falklands War

Troops assembled on the lower level of the Ocean Terminal waiting to board the liner. (Patrick Hewetson)

Embarkation commenced via the Five Deck ramps usually used for driving cars on board. (Captain P. Jackson)

Shortly before departure all hands are on deck to watch the ship sail. (R.W. Warwick)

A singing telegraph girl (centre of photo) delivering a farewell message to the troops attracted a lot of attention from those ashore and afloat. (R.W. Warwick)

As *QE2* pulled away from the quay, the 'passengers' manned the lifeboats – a sight that had never been seen before and which would never be repeated. (Captain P. Jackson)

By now the flight deck aft had been painted and provided a good spot to witness the departure. (Captain P. Jackson)

The Voyage South to Freetown

A military brass band added to the fanfare of the departure. (R. Smith)

Soldiers wave to well-wishers on the quayside as *QE2* departs for the South Atlantic. (R. Smith)

The QE2 in the Falklands War

QE2 always attracted media coverage and her requisitioning provided no exception. (R.W. Warwick)

The Voyage South to Freetown

Probably the most famous sailing day ever for *QE2* was immortalised on a postage stamp issued by Guernsey on the twenty-fifth anniversary in 2007. (R.W. Warwick)

Small boats accompanied the liner as she made her way down Southampton Water. (R. Smith)

Sea King helicopters from 825 Naval Air Squadron landed on board *QE2* as she cleared the Solent. (R.W. Warwick)

The Cunard fleet personnel office in Southampton was very supportive of the volunteers. This letter was received by Nursing Sister Wendy Marshall. (Wendy Marshall)

The Voyage South to Freetown

While in port for an overnight stay or longer, only one boiler would be in use, but it was highly unusual for the ship to sail with just one boiler operational. However, because of the wartime propaganda value of a scheduled departure it was decided *QE2* would sail on time so the world's media and, more importantly, the Argentine government could see that everything was proceeding according to plan. The ship's departure was being reported live on the BBC and there was live coverage on television channels in the USA. *QE2* sailed down Southampton Water at just 7 knots, considerably slower than usual. With only one boiler in service, she was not capable of speed, quick manoeuvres or sudden stops. One of the tugs stayed with the ship longer than normal, ready to be of assistance if required. The final tug was dismissed when the ship had rounded Bramble Bank. Usually known as the Brambles, this is a sandbar in the central Solent off Calshot Spit that has often proved a navigational hazard for large ships entering or leaving the port.

The ship then steamed slowly down the eastern Solent, passing Cowes and the coast of the Isle of Wight. Jacqui White, who kept a diary throughout the voyage, recalls that at 1800 hours the first Tannoy announcement was made calling 'Hands to flying stations'. She noted that there were no longer any Tannoy announcements for passengers to collect an incoming telegram from the passenger bureau. Shortly after the announcement, two Sea King helicopters from the Royal Naval Air Station (RNAS) at Culdrose, Cornwall, approached the ship and touched down upon the aft helicopter platform. The first Sea King, no. 595 piloted by Lieutenant Commander Hugh Clark RN, landed at 1830 hours. The second, no. 597 piloted by Lieutenant Commander R.H.S. Everall RN, touched down shortly after at 1850. Both landings were smooth despite the strong wind. Members of NP1980 speedily folded the rotor blades back and secured the helicopters with lashings. The two helicopters were part of 825 Naval Air Squadron of the Fleet Air Arm.[79]

QE2 anchored south of the Isle of Wight outside normal shipping lanes while the necessary boiler repairs were made under the leadership of Chief Engineer John Grant. Senior mechanic Paul Fisher remembers that for the Engine Room crew it was a very long night. The anchorage position was well out of the way of curious onlookers, television and press cameras. Neither the boiler problems nor information about the repairs were picked up by the media. As far as people in the UK knew, *QE2* had sailed on time and was on her way.

The QE2 in the Falklands War

Early the next morning on 13 May, the tug *Bustler* made a brief visit to the ship to deliver stores. She was alongside and away between 0120 and 0130 hours. Hotel officer Rupert Ballantyne's diary for the day starts, 'Woken up at 6.30 a.m. by Gurkhas outside my cabin, training. Quite amazing seeing these soldiers running up and down Boat Deck.' By breakfast, the work on the boilers had been completed, and at 0911 hours, the Engine Room telegraph was rung to put the engines on standby. The anchor was aweigh at 0928 hours and the liner was under way.

Before the ship had sailed, the national press was reporting that *QE2* had taken on board 1 million Mars bars. However, the actual number was significantly less. About 200,000 Mars bars were loaded along with other confectionery brands. One of the empty shops was used to store several thousand *QE2* Falklands T-shirts and sweatshirts that had been designed and ordered by two petty officers from NP1980 while the ship was converted in Southampton. The design showed a map with the ship sailing direct to the Falklands. The clothing arrived shortly before the ship sailed. The presence on board of these items was kept a secret during the early part of the voyage.

Shortly after the ship departed from Southampton, the shop filled with troops within minutes of opening its doors. The staff closed the doors and admitted new customers only as people left. Shortly afterwards, manager Anthony Dance was approached by a senior NCO. The NCO said he wanted the shop opened from 0700 to 2200 hours every day so that all troops could shop irrespective of their training hours.

Anthony replied that this was not possible as there were only six staff serving far more customers than normal.

The NCO replied, 'I'm not asking you. I'm telling you.'

Rather than continue the conversation in front of crew and troops, Anthony invited the NCO to join him in the privacy of the shop's office. He closed the door then offered the NCO a drink.

'I never drink on duty' was the immediate reply.

Anthony offered again, receiving the same stern reply. Anthony opened a drawer and produced bottles of whiskey and gin, which he placed on the desk.

The NCO relented and asked, 'Got any brandy?'

Anthony produced a bottle of brandy and the two shared a drink. They agreed opening from 0800 to 2100 hours.

The Voyage South to Freetown

In Port Stanley, the Falkland Islanders now living under Argentine occupation heard about *QE2*'s departure when listening to the BBC World Service. In his book *74 Days: A Diary of the Occupation*, islander John Smith noted on 13 May:

> Very encouraging news bulletin tonight from the BBC, a splendid eye-witness report on the departure of the *QE2* yesterday. Thousands of people; bands of the Scots and Welsh Guards, the pipes and drums of the Gurkhas. The most moving event ever seen in Southampton. It moved us down here as well. To think that all this is happening because of us. Would love to have been there, though would have been quite unable to control my emotions.[80]

The local Falkland Islands radio station was taken off the air on 29 April. By then the BBC World Service was broadcasting an evening programme *Calling the Falklands*.[81] Citizens of the islands relied heavily on the BBC for news throughout the conflict, as would the crew of *QE2* as she steamed south.

With the boiler repairs completed throughout the night of 12–13 May, *QE2* set course for Freetown, Sierra Leone, where she would take on board fuel and fresh water. She would be the third Cunard *Queen* to visit Freetown in wartime with *Queen Mary* and *Queen Elizabeth* both having visited during the Second World War. Freetown was an important stopover during the Falklands War with several task force merchant vessels calling there on the way south. The *Canberra* (Captain W. Scott-Masson) and the Cunard container ship *Atlantic Conveyor* (Captain Ian North) also stopped there on their voyage south.

Soon after the voyage commenced, new daily routines rapidly became established. With nearly 3,000 soldiers, training space was very limited, particularly on the outside decks. Most areas on the ship, such as the public rooms, passageways and stairwells, were designated as training spaces. Those in charge of training held group meetings most days to co-ordinate the timings and locations of training. This applied to both military and fitness training. Training usually started at 0630 hours through to 2130 hours. Any later and the noise would disturb watchkeepers' routines.

Every day a liaison meeting was held, and these continued until arrival at Grytviken. Those attending were *QE2*'s Chief Officer Ronald Warwick,

A flight exercise from the forward landing platform. (Patrick Hewetson)

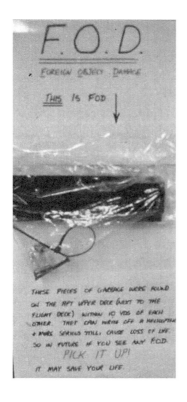

Dozens of Foreign Object Damage (FOD) notices were posted to remind everyone of the dangers of leaving loose objects lying about that could endanger flight operations. (R.W. Warwick)

The two Sea King helicopters positioned athwartships on the aft helicopter deck. (R.W. Warwick)

The two Sea King helicopters have been securely lashed to the aft helicopter deck. The rotor blades were folded back for shipboard stowage. The forward Sea King is fitted with anti-icing strips. (R.W. Warwick)

When the helicopters were not in use, they were firmly secured with rotor blades folded back. Note the Land Rovers stored on the Upper Deck aft. (John Chillingworth)

Flight deck operations were carried out in all weather conditions including, as in this photograph, periods of low visibility. (Stephen Hallam)

the Brigade major, Major Brendon Lambe, and, from NP1980, Flight Deck Officer Lieutenant Roger F. Bevan RN, First Lieutenant, Lieutenant Commander David A.C. Poole RN and Amphibious Operations Officer Major Hugh E. Affleck-Graves RM. The daily meeting was of particular importance as it was the main interface between the ship, Brigade and Naval Party. The meetings focused on information sharing, planning and coordinating activities to ensure that ship's crew and military personnel carried out their duties without disrupting each other. Any issues such as wear and tear on the fabric of the ship or damage due to firing practice were discussed.

As he was now on RNR service, Philip Rentell formally answered to Captain James of NP1980 and not to Captain Jackson. He became, in effect, a staff officer or aide de camp to Captain James, acting at the interface between *QE2* officers and the embarked Royal Navy party. His role was never formally defined but evolved in response to the changing circumstances of the voyage. One of his first jobs was meeting with First Officer Robert Hayward to plan a new lifeboat drill. The existing plan needed to be modified to accommodate the additional people on board.

The first lifeboat drill for all on board was held before the Isle of Wight had receded from view. All hands were required to muster at their designated stations, wearing life jackets. Apart from those on duty watch in the Engine Room, Radio Room and Bridge, there were no exemptions. In every cabin is a sign posted on the inside of the door, showing passengers the muster station where they should assemble in an emergency. However, a normal passenger drill would not work on this voyage, given the increased number of souls. Cabins that normally held two passengers now accommodated four or more soldiers. A reassignment of the number of persons at each muster station was needed as *QE2* had never previously sailed with so many people. Parts of the ship had never previously been used as muster stations, such as the aft helicopter deck. Second Officer Chris Haughton found himself standing on a chair in the Q4 Room, briefing a room full of soldiers. Army officers were briefed on where they should go, and were given responsibility for assembling and mustering their troops.

The mustering process continued with the able assistance of Regimental Sergeant Major Hunt, whose voice had considerable carrying power. Each muster station had an officer or NCO in charge, and each group of twenty-five men had a designated leader. In a real emergency, each group would be directed to a lifeboat or a raft which would have been swung out into the embarkation position by the ship's crew. While the first lifeboat muster proceeded slightly chaotically, things were running more smoothly and effectively a few days later. The lifeboats were swung out to embarkation level so that everyone could observe the procedure. Survival lectures and boat drills became a part of everyday routine.

While the ship was at sea during a cruise, the officer of the watch or captain traditionally made an announcement at midday over the Tannoy. The announcement gave the noon position, distance travelled, speed, air temperature, weather conditions and any other information that might be of interest to the passengers. Second Officer Chris Haughton continued the tradition and made the first announcement of the voyage by saying, 'I would like to take this opportunity to welcome all troops on board and I hope that you enjoy your stay on the ship as we cruise south to the Falklands.'

The noon announcement was followed by one made by a military officer. He announced that the motto for the voyage was 'FOD' or 'Foreign Object Damage'. This meant that loose items should not be left lying around the decks as they could put helicopter operations at risk. He stressed that everyone on board had a responsibility to remain vigilant while on the open deck and should not hesitate to report any unusual sightings in the ocean or sky, as there was always a risk of attack from enemy aircraft, missiles, mines or torpedoes.

Later in the day, it became necessary to transfer two members of the Brigade to a shoreside medical facility for treatment. One soldier had suffered a seizure, while a second had a strained Achilles tendon. At 1745 hours, a Sea King helicopter took off. The two patients were accompanied by an Army doctor and QE2's senior nurse, Sister Jane Yelland. The helicopter transferred the patients to Treliske Hospital, Truro. On the return journey, the helicopter refuelled at RNAS Culdrose to help conserve the ship's limited helicopter fuel stocks. The helicopter landed back on board just after 2000 hours. Those returning brought copies of the daily newspapers covering the war and QE2's departure. These were greatly appreciated by their shipmates. The liner proceeded in a southerly direction, avoiding the main shipping lanes. Jane Yelland recalls:

> The next day I was at the bar in the Wardroom and a pilot was sitting on a bar stool. He turned around and said to me, 'Ah, you must be the

The Voyage South to Freetown

lady we gave a lift to yesterday. It is not often we have the smell of Rive Gauche in our helicopter!' Very smooth, knowing the name of my perfume!

Earlier that day, a French Bréguet Atlantic maritime reconnaissance aircraft had buzzed the liner and wished her well. Various news media quoted American intelligence reports that some of the twelve Soviet radar, photographic and communication satellites were being used to search for the liner as she steamed south. An area of uncertainty was whether the Soviet Union would pass to Argentina any intelligence it might gain from spy satellites. In a television interview, former US chief of naval operations, Admiral Elmo Zumwalt, said that he fully expected the Argentinians to attempt to destroy *QE2*. Meanwhile, in Paris the naval attaché at the Argentinian Embassy stated before *QE2* sailed from Southampton that it was Argentina's intention to sink her. Under international law, the Argentine forces would have been entitled to attack *QE2*. Although she was a merchant ship crewed by civilians with non-combatant status, she had been requisitioned to support the British war effort and was therefore a legitimate military target.

In the evening of the first full day out of Southampton, the principal job was to test *QE2*'s refuelling at sea capability. The amount of fuel on board when the ship left Southampton would be insufficient for a South Atlantic return journey, even allowing for a call at Freetown. The ship headed to a rendezvous point in the Channel with the RFA tanker *Grey Rover* (Captain J.W. Pratt) to carry out a trial replenishment at sea. *QE2* would be the second Cunard ship with which *Grey Rover* had carried out a trial RAS, the first being *Atlantic Conveyor* on 25 April.[82]

Grey Rover approached *QE2* from astern on the starboard quarter and the two ships took up position sailing in parallel, about 150ft apart. The normal RAS procedure is for the RFA ship to use a specially adapted rifle to fire a gunline, a pneumatic line thrower, over the bow or midships of the ship being replenished. Deck hands on the ship being refuelled then grab the gunline, which is attached to a messenger line. The messenger is attached to a winch, which is used to haul the line over to the receiving ship. The fuel pipe is attached to the end of the messenger.

With *QE2* a different system was required. The fuelling point on *QE2* was through a shell door amidships on Two Deck, high above the waterline and nowhere near the bow of the ship. The open door would have been far too small a target for the gunline to be aimed at. So the gunline was fired from the Boat Deck of *QE2* across to the *Grey Rover*. The shipboard end of the gunline was attached to a messenger that led down to the shell door. Those on the *Grey Rover* then attached a heavier line to their end of the messenger, which in turn was attached to the 8in flexible refuelling pipe. The pipe was suspended over the sea from a crane on the *Grey Rover*.

The usual operating procedure when refuelling at sea is for the smaller ship to sail a parallel course alongside the bigger ship. The larger vessel will maintain her course and speed, and if the two ships diverge, it is the responsibility of the smaller ship to correct the situation. This is because a smaller ship can manoeuvre more easily than a larger ship. Usually the receiving ship, such as a navy frigate or destroyer, is smaller than the RFA tanker. However, there are exceptions such as aircraft carriers and, in these most unusual of circumstances, *QE2*. In addition to providing the fuel, *Grey Rover* now had the added responsibility of keeping station with the liner.

As *QE2* was not designed for refuelling at sea, it had no winches for hauling in a supply pipe, so an alternative form of traction power was required. This came in the form of manpower. Approximately 100 soldiers of the Scots Guards took up position along Two Deck near the shell door. Once the messenger line between the two ships was securely established, the soldiers, hand over hand, hauled in the slack on the line followed by the fuel pipe. Crew member Jacqui White observed the procedure and noted 'the term "tug of war" took on a whole new meaning'! With considerable effort the hose was connected to *QE2*'s new bunker line, although there was one amusing incident when part of the line of soldiers fell over skittles style, leading to some cursing and much laughter.

The ship's engineers operated the valves to the fuel ring main pneumatically from the Safety Control Room (SCR) on Two Deck. Centrally placed within the ship, the SCR is manned twenty-four hours a day at sea and in port. Master plans showing all the safety systems of the ship are on display. All liquid transfers, such as ballast water, fresh water, bilges pumping and fuel, are operated from the SCR. The engineer on duty was responsible for ensuring the fuel ring main valve was open once the RAS pipe from *Grey Rover* was secured and before fuel pumping commenced, and then ensuring the valve was closed when pumping was complete. In the event that pneumatic operation was not possible, the valve could

RFA *Grey Rover* approaches *QE2*'s starboard side to carry out her first fuel transfer at sea. (Captain P. Jackson)

View of *QE2* from RFA *Grey Rover*. (RFA Nostalgia)

RFA *Grey Rover*'s fuel pipe is hoisted up on a crane in readiness for the fuel transfer. (R.W. Warwick)

Many hands were on deck to witness the fuel transfer with *Grey Rover*. The fuel pipe was hauled aboard by soldiers through the Two Deck midships shell door. (R.W. Warwick)

be operated manually. A small token quantity of fuel was pumped over while the two ships sailed a parallel course at 12 knots. This was a brief experimental RAS to check the equipment was working properly.

With the success of the exercise, the line was cleared, disconnected and paid back out to *Grey Rover* for retrieval. The refuelling system fitted in Southampton had now been proven to work in an operational situation. This was the first time a Cunard liner had received fuel while under way at sea. *QE2* could now remain at sea virtually indefinitely, providing, of course, that RFA tankers were available to refuel her. As the two ships peeled away from each other, their horns thundered the traditional three-blast salute to signal a job well done by both ships. *QE2* would not need to refuel again at sea until she was returning home from the South Atlantic. The ship now set a southerly course at a speed of 23 knots in calm seas with little swell, avoiding normal sea-lanes for the 3,000-mile passage to Freetown.

The dangerous nature of the voyage and the exceptional increase in the number of people on board led to a change in working routine for many crew members. On a normal voyage, bosun's mate Frank Parkinson would allocate work details for the able seamen (AB) with the bosun, Charlie Thomas. While the ship was at sea, this work would include maintenance of the decks, painting, repair of equipment and safety duties, such as ensuring the secure stowage of any loose items. On this voyage, Frank Parkinson was relieved of these duties during the morning and reassigned to training military personnel in how to launch the ship's lifeboats and life rafts.

An attack on the liner could result in a large number of casualties to the ship's deck officers and ABs, leading to a shortage of crew experienced in the launching of lifeboats and life rafts. To cater for this possibility, as many military personnel as possible needed to be trained to take their place in an emergency. Every day after the ship left Southampton, Frank Parkinson would report to the Bridge at 0800 hours to meet with a small group of Army NCOs. They would then go down to the lee side of the Boat Deck (the less windy side), where Frank would instruct the NCOs how to launch the lifeboats and life rafts. The emphasis was on intensive instruction and practice. The first instruction was how to release the securing arrangements to prepare for the boat to be lowered. The soldiers were then shown how to lift the brake handle and allow gravity to lower the davit down, stopping when the boat reached the level of the deck. The next task was to use tackle to secure the boat firmly alongside the hull. This was necessary to prevent the boat swinging freely on the fall wires when the ship was rolling in a seaway. The tackle would also prevent any movement when getting into the boat. Frank Parkinson monitored the soldiers performing this task, checking to see that the right procedures were being followed. He ended the training session only when he was confident that the day's group would be able to launch the boats and rafts in an emergency without supervision.

With the ship carrying nearly 4,000 souls, additional inflatable life rafts had been loaded on board in Southampton. Only a limited amount of practical instruction and training was possible with the life rafts, as they were contained in cylindrical containers. A rope attached to the container would, when pulled, activate the inflation process. The raft was also fitted with a hydrostatic release unit which would inflate the raft if the ship sank and it had not been activated manually. The life rafts were stowed on Quarter Deck forward and Two Deck aft.

When the morning training sessions were finished, Frank Parkinson carried out regular inspections, paying particular attention to fire hoses, ensuring the connections worked and the equipment functioned effectively. He recalls how focused the deck ratings were during the voyage, with an attitude of 'We're going to do this properly!'

About a week after the ship had sailed, Frank Parkinson remembers going to the Bridge shortly before 0800 hours. As there were numerous *QE2* and naval officers already there, he discreetly made his way to the port bridge wing. Captain Jackson spotted him and came out to talk. He first asked Frank how he was, before asking, 'And how are the men bearing up?'

Frank was able to assure the captain that morale was good. Years later Frank recalled of Captain Jackson, 'What a gentleman. He had time for everyone.'

Many crew members were cross trained to carry out a wide range of duties. With the ship sailing into a war zone, there was the risk of shrapnel damage from bomb explosions and the possibility of the ship being holed near the waterline. To prepare for such an eventuality, the ship's carpenters, plumbers and security petty officers were formed into a damage control team. They received training and instruction from an NP1980 petty officer. For small holes, the damage control team were shown how to hammer wooden wedges into holes to minimise water seepage. Mattresses were to be forced and jammed into larger holes. The team was also trained in how to use splinter boxes, the heavy-duty metal boxes designed to cover a hole in a vessel. The splinter boxes were about 18 square inches in area and 8in deep. The damage control team were taught to fold the angle bar of a splinter box through a hole in the ship's side and then to tighten the box against the ship's interior to prevent water ingress. Those tasked with blocking holes were also taught to use breathing apparatus. Security petty officers were to be stationed on Two Deck aft, filling breathing apparatus sets with air and taking them down to those team members tasked with filling holes.

The operations and training officer for the Gurkhas was Major Mike Seear. His task was to plan and coordinate the Gurkhas' daily training programme during the 5 Brigade training conference held each afternoon in the Double Down Bar. In an emergency, the Five Deck cabins accommodating the Gurkhas had the disadvantage of being the furthest away from the lifeboats. The cabins were just above the waterline of the hull and those in the forward part of the ship were close to the cargo holds which housed tons of ammunition. The Gurkhas would be particularly at risk in the event of an attack from an Exocet, a missile that is programmed to hit a vessel just above the waterline. There was the risk that if *QE2* was struck by a missile or torpedo, the Gurkhas would need to evacuate in darkness and dense smoke, so they trained intensively on how to reach their muster stations in zero visibility. They took part in evacuation drills in the form of orienteering competitions, wearing blindfolds to simulate total darkness.[83] They trained until they were satisfied they could find their way from Five Deck to their lifeboats without lighting. On one occasion, a small group of Gurkhas were seen wandering through a restaurant having taken a wrong turn. The Gurkhas also practised jumping into the swimming pool on Seven Deck, fully dressed and carrying backpacks to simulate an amphibious landing.

Head waiter Andrew Nelder recalls watching Gurkhas carrying out fire drills while blindfolded. 'I had nothing but respect and admiration for the Gurkhas,' he commented over forty years later. Wilfred Whitehead, a public room steward, later told his family he felt sorry for the Gurkhas when the weather was rough, and he would do what he could to make their lives as comfortable as possible. However, he risked getting into trouble if he interfered with their training routines.

When dressed in full battle rig with their faces smeared in camouflage cream, the Gurkhas looked fearsome. At one lecture, an officer was talking about the routine to be followed when taking prisoners of war. Some Gurkhas smiled at this as if to say they didn't take prisoners. The Gurkhas carried a kukri, a curved knife. One of the crew asked a Gurkha about his kukri knife and was told, 'We find them very useful in close quarter combat.' Gurkha officer, Major David Willis remembers that almost all Gurkhas carried a bayonet through a loop on the left ammo pouch. The kukri was carried in a scabbard attached to the man's belt and was regarded as a secondary weapon.

Deck officers and radio officers worked closely with the naval party while the ship's doctors and nursing sisters worked closely with the Brigade's medical personnel, who were made very welcome in the hospital. It was decided that rather than having one of *QE2*'s nurses appointed to the nightshift, this duty would be carried out by a military medic. Two Mobile Army Surgical Hospital (MASH) units were on board, each of which had a surgeon and anaesthetist. The Welsh Guards, Scots Guards and 7th Gurkha Rifles each had a medical officer who held daily clinics for their troops in the hospital. The MASH units held regular training exercises throughout the ship. Treatment of inpatients was provided by the Brigade's doctors. They worked in conjunction with the ship's medical officers, Dr Alan Kirwin and Dr Patrick Hewetson, who before joining Cunard had served with the Royal Navy and Army respectively.

On a normal commercial voyage, the officer who managed the public rooms had a staff of forty crew. The job entailed making sure the public rooms were meticulously clean, staff were present and smartly dressed, and the bars and catering facilities were efficiently run. Public rooms officer Rupert Ballantyne discussed his role with the hotel manager, Ron Kelly. There was no guidance on how the ship's public spaces should be used for the embarked Brigade. It was clear the management of them would change as the voyage progressed.

During the day the Queens and Double Down rooms were used for instruction and training. For the evening, trestle tables and chairs were moved into place to provide an area for the troops to relax and socialise. The troops could purchase two cans of beer a day. The sale each evening of about 6,000 cans of beer and 3,500 cans of mineral and soft drinks indicate the scale of the cleaning task that needed to be carried out by the liner's crew after the evening's recreation was over. The only time the rooms could be cleaned was at night, so a large night gang of stewards was formed for that purpose. The night gang also had to stow away the chairs and tables by early the following morning, ready for instruction and training once more.

The Theatre was in constant use during the voyage for training lectures and briefings on a wide variety of subjects. There were lectures on survival and basic first aid, including treating burn injuries and the use of morphine. All soldiers carried one ampoule of morphine, while those trained in first aid carried five. Lectures and training took place on weapon handling, enemy aircraft recognition, enemy equipment, battlefield first aid, intelligence matters and handling prisoners. There were also lectures about the islands and basic Spanish phrases. A selection of films were shown in the Theatre, mainly in the evenings. The Theatre was also used for the Sunday church services and the occasional show or musical performance.

One job that was very different during this voyage was that of the cruise director, Tim Castle. The job of a cruise director is to run the on-board entertainment, including acting as the master of ceremonies for evening entertainment programmes. Under normal circumstances, the cruise director managed a staff of seventy. These included the cruise hosts, who looked after the passengers on board and hosted shoreside excursions, and entertainers, some of whom would sail on a voyage-by-voyage basis, such as dancers, musicians, golf instructors and lecturers. Nearly all of these staff had been laid off, as passenger entertainment would not be part of the ship's daily routine.

On a typical day, Tim would start work in the passenger bureau on Two Deck, helping the purser, Brian Vickers, with whatever tasks needed completing that day. As lunchtime approached, he would make his way to the kitchen for the Tables of the World restaurant. This kitchen was known to *QE2* crew as the 'Brit kit' (a shorthand for Britannia Kitchen). The ship's Britannia restaurant had been renamed the Tables of the World some years earlier, but the name 'Brit kit' continued to be used by crew. The restaurant was now a very busy mess area with a self-service buffet, thus freeing up waiters for other duties. Tim carried out 'traffic cop' duties, directing the troops and making sure they didn't linger after their meals so there was a steady flow of troops between sittings. He also helped the kitchen staff in ensuring that clean plates and food were flowing to the service counters. The ship's cooks and catering crew worked extremely hard due to the increased number of sittings and the extra meals to be cooked and served. There was a change in the type of meals prepared, with more emphasis on the carbohydrate-rich food many soldiers like. Meanwhile, the *QE2* crew and petty officers' cafeterias and the officers' Wardroom operated on normal sea routine.

The discipline that servicemen learn early in their careers was apparent. NCOs and troops were responsible for cleaning their own accommodation. The cabins on One Deck aft, for which stewardess Elena Littlehales was responsible, were occupied by Scots Guards. Elena recalls the guardsmen made their own beds and cleaned their own cabins. 'There wasn't much for us to do. They were very clean and tidy.' Officers received a steward service, either a *QE2* steward or, for those senior enough, a personal batman. Second Lieutenant Paddy Redding of the Gurkhas recalls, 'The stewards were marvellous and we could get many things from them.' The ship's stewards left tea, coffee and cocoa in the deck pantries, so the troops could make themselves hot drinks. Troops were not permitted in the galleys as foodstuffs were government issue stores. Military Police were

The Voyage South to Freetown

placed on guard to prevent soldiers and non-catering crew members entering these areas.[84]

From the start of the voyage, it was made clear that ship's crew and troops should not enter each other's social areas. On the day that the ship sailed from Southampton, Staff Captain Alexander Hutcheson issued a Notice to Ship's Company which read:

> It is to be clearly understood members of HM Forces are not allowed into crew bars and recreation areas at any time. It is also to be clearly understood that crew members are not allowed into military recreation areas except on duty.

The import of this message was that there was to be no socialising between the Merchant Navy crew and military personnel. Ship's crew were permitted to pass through military areas but not to loiter.

On board there were three separate groups of senior officers: *QE2*, NP 1980 and 5 Infantry Brigade. If the ship was to be operationally efficient, these three groups needed to function effectively as an integrated team, yet they had never previously worked together. Close working relations within teams usually depend upon some degree of social interaction, so the Cunard officers and their military counterparts hosted receptions for each other. The day after the exercise with *Grey Rover*, Captain Jimmy James of NP1980 held a small informal reception for *QE2*'s senior officers to meet Brigadier Tony Wilson, Major Brendon Lambe and other senior officers of the regiments comprising 5 Infantry Brigade. The Cunard officers who attended were Captain Peter Jackson, Staff Captain Alexander Hutcheson, Chief Engineer John Grant and Hotel Manager Ron Kelly.

On another occasion, Brigadier Wilson hosted an evening gathering in the Q4 Room. The principal entertainment was ten minutes of Gurkha bagpipes followed by the pipes and drums of the Welsh Guards and the Bagpiper Band of the Scots Guards. One officer described the programme as 'excellent stuff, but a little hard on the ears within the comparatively small room'.

Captain James had established a good working relationship with senior Cunard officers before *QE2* left Southampton. He described having a 'marvellous relationship' with Captain Peter Jackson and Staff Captain

Alexander Hutcheson, and later recalled, 'Each night the three of us had dinner together – the rapport between us could not have been better.'

As the Naval Party was assigned to *QE2* for as long as the liner was requisitioned, the NP1980 officers were elected to temporary membership of the officers' Wardroom. However, Army officers embarked with 5 Infantry Brigade were not elected as Wardroom members, as they had their own dining and recreation areas. In any case, the Wardroom was simply not big enough to accommodate all officers of the Brigade.

The established dress code in the Wardroom continued to be observed. On a passenger voyage, the evening rig was designated each day as informal or formal. On a normal voyage, passengers were notified of this information in the daily programme. For officers, on informal nights the rig would be the uniform worn throughout the day. On formal nights, all officers would dress in a white mess jacket, white shirt, black bow tie, black cummerbund and dark navy trousers. Most of the officers dined in the Wardroom, while others would occasionally host a passenger table in one of the main restaurants. For passengers, a seat at the captain's table was highly sought after.

For this voyage, Red Sea rig was adopted. This rig was introduced by the Royal Navy in the nineteenth century and later adopted by the Merchant Navy. The rig consisted of a short-sleeved white shirt, dark navy trousers and a cummerbund. Many of the armed forces officers wore cummerbunds embroidered with the crest of their regiment or ship. During the extended refit that followed the ship's requisitioning, the Wardroom ordered a customised batch of cummerbunds with *QE2*'s insignia of the Cunard golden lion. These were worn proudly by many *QE2* officers over the following years. In those days, Cunard did not have an evening dress code for female officers, so hotel officer Frances Milroy and the four nursing sisters wore a dress of their choice. Senior Sister Jane Yelland recalls that the *QE2* medical team became great friends with the MASH teams: 'We had lots of drinks parties and a very busy social life.'

The Wardroom hosted at least two social gatherings on the journey south: one for officers and one for NCOs. The NCOs reciprocated with an invitation to the officers to attend a gathering in the NCOs' mess in the Theatre Bar. The evening ended with the NCOs challenging the *QE2* officers to a 'boat race'. Two teams of eight were formed, each in a queue. Each man in the boat race was given a pint of beer. The man at the front had to drink his pint as quickly as possible and, when he had finished, place the pint pot on his head. Only then could the man behind start drinking. The winning team was the first to have all men with a pint pot on their head. Engineer officer Martin Harrison was a member of the *QE2* team. The race was won by the Army team.

The troops were determined to keep physically fit, both to improve themselves as fighting soldiers and as a means of reducing nervous energy. Every unit was given an assigned time slot for jogging around the Boat Deck, starting at 0630 hours. For passengers the Boat Deck was normally a place for leisurely walks and romantic evening strolls. Now troops ran around the deck all day, five laps to the mile, with NCOs keeping their eyes open for any stragglers, whom they would cajole, often loudly. The Welsh Guards put up a banner on the Boat Deck that read 'All our luv Maggie. Thanks for the cruise.' The noise of hundreds of men in full kit and boots jogging around the open deck formed part of the soundtrack of the voyage, especially for those on Upper Deck, which was one deck below Boat Deck. As the terrain on the Falklands was hilly, troops also ran up and down the stairways to maintain their fitness. The forward passenger staircase was the most popular as this went from Boat Deck down to Five Deck; eight flights in all.

Sometimes the troops jogged while carrying another man on their back in a fireman's lift. Others would be seen wearing full uniform, carrying a heavy backpack and their rifle. The noise was omnipresent and thunderous. Within a short time the vibration from thousands of heavy footfalls began to lift the caulking out of the teak wood deck. The ship's carpenters regularly carried out repairs to the deck when troop exercising was not taking place. The carpenters also had to repair the port and starboard stairs at the forward end of the Boat Deck. The stairs led up to the Signal Deck, which continued around forward of the captain's quarters. It was estimated that in the region of 70,000 laps were run on the Boat Deck every day. Long after *QE2* returned to commercial service, caulking continued to lift out of the deck.

The members of NP1980 and 825 Naval Air Squadron were also expected to keep fit. Their exercise area was the aft flight deck, commencing at 0730 hours every morning. An indication of how seriously daily exercise was taken by the Royal Navy appeared in the daily orders: 'If you don't go voluntarily, you will be going involuntarily.'

On Friday, 14 May, the ship increased speed to 25 knots. The training programme that day included first aid and a lecture in the Theatre on the Geneva Convention. There was plenty of activity on the forward and aft flight decks as the drills and communications between the Bridge and the flight deck teams were practised and tested. An anemometer, a device used to measure air direction and velocity, was fitted. Flight deck floodlights were also installed in readiness for night flying. That same day, the staff captain issued a notice to the ship's company saying that there would be no opportunities for receiving or sending mail once the ship was south of Ascension Island. The announcement reinforced a sense on board that the ship was increasingly isolated. At 1700 hours, Brigadier Wilson chaired the Commander's Conference. The conference would be held every day, during which the latest intelligence would be shared with the Brigade's senior officers.

By the next day, Saturday, 15 May, the weather was warmer and personnel changed into tropical rig for the first time. On this day the first edition of the Brigade newsletter was published. Copies of the newsletter were run off in the print shop on Six Deck, a facility manned by three operatives. The news bulletin was produced every day by crew member Susan Hogg. She would listen to the BBC World Service news in the Radio Room and then type out a summary, which was published on the first page of the daily newsletter. The newsletter included messages from the Brigade commander and other senior officers, followed by announcements to the troops. There was information about daily training, such as map reading, weapon cleaning and measures to be taken in the event of an emergency. Other contributions included a 'Know your enemy' feature with images of Argentine aircraft, armoured vehicles, helicopters and weaponry.

The first edition reported on the efforts of the United Nations to mediate a solution to the Falklands crisis. United Nations Secretary General Javier Pérez de Cuéllar commented that there was 'a clear indication that Britain was genuinely interested in achieving a peaceful solution within the framework of the UN'. He urged further progress or what had been achieved so far would be lost.

The Brigade padre, Alfred Hayes, had his own column, 'Thought for the Day', and wrote some kind comments about the ship's crew: 'who would have believed it would be quite like this – luxury not dreamed of, food fit for a banquet and a highly cooperative staff to help in every instance.'

The Voyage South to Freetown

Another daily routine as *QE2* steamed south was flying practice for the crews of the Sea Kings. The Royal Navy officially designated *QE2* an LPLL (Landing Platform Luxury Liner). On 15 May, the ship went to flying stations for the first organised flying serial. From then on several hours a day were devoted to intensive flight practice. At this stage of the voyage, it was unclear where the helicopters would operate and whether they would be required to disembark troops. Every ship is different and even veteran pilots have to become accustomed to learning where the air pockets and down draughts are that might make manoeuvring more challenging when landing and taking off. As *QE2*, unlike most ships, had two flight decks, it was necessary to agree and practise flight-path protocols for when both decks were operational, with helicopter movements taking place simultaneously at the fore and aft of the ship.

The expertise of the helicopter pilots of 825 Naval Air Squadron was unquestioned. The pilots had to practise not only fore and aft landings but also athwartship touchdowns; in other words, where a helicopter moves across a ship at right angles to the keel. If both the aft landing pads were in use at once, then one helicopter might come in from one direction while another used a different flight approach. The No. 1 landing position forward of the Bridge was in some ways the most difficult because air currents slamming into the front of the ship were deflected upwards and sideways, while the bow area was also subject to more pitching. As one Cunard officer commented, 'One can appreciate that to land on a heaving deck in rough, rainy weather, with a ship doing 25 knots, would be difficult enough. However, to land sideways is a whole new ball game.' The pilots had to match speed with *QE2*, maintain their position and ignore the sea rushing by the hull. The South Atlantic would have proved an icy and unforgiving environment had there been any accidents. Thanks to the skill and expertise of the pilots there were none.

Some of the ammunition on the ship was intended for daily firing practice. Cartons of kitchen waste made the best targets. However, a trail of cartons could reveal a ship's direction of travel and they could only be dumped with the permission of the officer of the watch. Machine-gun fire certainly disturbed the watchkeepers' sleep and strong protests had to be lodged on one occasion about random shots damaging the ship's railings. The davit fall wire of No. 5 Raft was damaged by gunshot and had to be replaced. Years later the ship still had a rail stanchion with a hole in it. On occasion there were some bizarre juxtapositions of noise during firing exercises. One officer recalled the Welsh Guards firing a Browning heavy machine gun from the stern while at the same time a band of pipers played the traditional Scottish song 'Blue Bonnets Over the Border'. Shortly before he passed away, Queens Grill waiter Paul Mason shared a memory: 'My claim to fame is that I was the first *QE2* crew member to be injured on the voyage. I was struck by a small piece of shrapnel when the soldiers were carrying out firing practice at the aft end of the ship.'

Every part of the ship was utilised for some form of training. Giant wall maps of the Falklands and the South Atlantic were spread across the bulkhead outside the Columbia Restaurant on Quarter Deck. This is where the tapestries of the launching of the ship had hung before being removed during the conversion. Passing crew members and particularly soldiers developed a newfound interest in South Atlantic geography.

Hotel officer Terry Foskett had a keen interest in military history and modern warfare. He carried his books on military aircraft and naval warships with him whenever he went away to sea. On the voyage to the South Atlantic, he decided to make 'threat boards' of the Argentine Navy by photocopying photographs from his books and placing them on boards in the Purser's Office. A day or two later, one of the Royal Navy petty officers saw the boards and asked if he would share them. The following day Terry Foskett made his way to the barn behind the Bridge, where an area had been sectioned off with plywood and turned into a classified South Atlantic map-plotting room. The door to the room said 'Classified Area – Royal Navy Only'. Despite the room being a restricted area, Terry was admitted after explaining the reason for his visit.

Inside the room was a large map of the South Atlantic covered in blue, red and green dots, next to which were dates and times. Terry was told that the blue dots were British, the red were Argentine and the green were Soviet intelligence ships. He was interested to observe the positions of various submarines marked on the map. A few days later, Terry supplied to the 5 Infantry Brigade Intelligence Unit a photograph of an Argentine Air Force Pucara close support aircraft. He also lent other military books to officers from the Brigade and NP1980, describing this as his 'small OSINT (Open-Source Intelligence)' contribution to the Falklands War.

By 1800 hours on 15 May, the ship was passing Madeira on the starboard side at a distance of 60 miles – well out of view of the islands. The following day, four church services was held in the Theatre: a service for Roman Catholics, an interdenominational service officiated by Captain Peter Jackson, an Anglican Communion service officiated by Reverend Peter Brooke of the Welsh Guards and a Church of Scotland service. Everyone was invited to the services, which were well attended. The final hymn for the interdenominational service was one traditionally associated with seafarers: 'Eternal Father, Strong to Save'.

After leaving Southampton, lifeboat drill routines continued for all the ship's crew and members of the Brigade. To simulate an attack on the ship, some lifeboat drills were accompanied by mock fires, with army personnel and the deck ratings practising firefighting dressed in fireproof clothing and emergency breathing apparatus. The watertight doors, normally tested once a week during a passenger voyage, were now tested every day. In addition, the watertight doors on Five, Six, Seven and Eight Decks were closed every night during the voyage, which made walking from one end of the ship to the other on the lower decks a cumbersome affair that involved climbing up and down stairways. The ship was divided into fifteen watertight compartments. Anyone in a watertight compartment on Five Deck or below could, when the doors were closed, escape upwards by a stairway to Four Deck.

The ship had sailed with three engineer officers and two electrical officers more than the normal complement to deal with essential maintenance requirements. These included ensuring that watertight doors functioned correctly at all times. The number of plumbers sailing on the voyage was also above normal in order to address any issues that might arise due to the extra demand on the ship's water supply and sewage systems.

The ambience of the ship was very different from a normal voyage. With hardboard sheeting covering all carpets, there was constant noise when walking the corridors, with the clump-clump of footsteps especially loud from the heavy boots of the soldiers. When several soldiers walked down a corridor together, their footsteps would punch out a hard rhythm that was quite loud. The captain's secretary, Judy Carpenter, remembers:

The atmosphere on the way down was very positive and we all went about our daily duties much as normal, though this time we were honoured to carry very special and exceptionally well-behaved passengers, in fact the best passengers we'd ever carried during my service on board QE2.

The public rooms were assigned to different units of the Brigade. Army ratings were accommodated over two sittings, sometimes three, for every meal. The Columbia Restaurant, normally a first-class restaurant, was now the mess room for the Scots and Welsh Guards. The Gurkhas ate in the Tables of the World Restaurant. The Queens Grill was the officers' restaurant with waiter service. The Princess Grill was an NCOs' dining room, with other NCOs eating in a section of the Columbia Restaurant, also with waiter service. Recreation areas were the Queens Grill Lounge and Q4 Room for officers, the Theatre Bar for NCOs, and the Queens Room and Double Room for other ranks. The Casino became a dormitory with camp beds taking up most of the floor space. The Brigade Intelligence Office was set up in the synagogue, a remote location on Three Deck forward. It is believed that some films were shown in this room during evenings.

The Children's Playroom on Sports Deck became another dormitory accommodating about forty men. The ship's engineer officers also had their quarters on Sports Deck. One of them, Eddie Cripps, recalls being woken suddenly from his sleep by a banging sound. Like many others on board, his mind had become programmed to operating in a war zone and he first thought that the vessel was under attack. It turned out that the heavy lift machinery doors had not been secured and were swinging to and fro with the motion of the ship.

Prior to departure from Southampton, a lot of food was offloaded and replaced with foodstuffs to provide a more balanced diet for the troops. It was described by the military as good, simple fare that was appreciated by the troops. Charles Carty, one of the soldiers, remarked, 'We sometimes had prawn cocktail for starters.' Guardsman Tracy Evans praised the food on board, noting that the breakfast was excellent and 'Our slop jockey chef could learn a lot from the *QE2* chefs'. One of his platoon, Nigel O'Keefe, liked *QE2* so much that after leaving the Army he became a *QE2* crew member.

Ship's baker and confectioner Stephen Hallam had his role somewhat redefined. He usually made soufflés, pies and appetising cakes for the passengers' afternoon tea. Now most of his time was taken up making slab cake. Together with fellow confectioner Vic Day, they would cut the cake into slices that were offered to the soldiers every evening. Some of the soldiers were assigned to assist in the bakery.

Stephen recollects the occasion when one young soldier came into the bakery and plonked his rifle on the work surface where they were making apple pies. One of the 'feckies', the nickname given to confectioners, made a remark about the soldier committing a hygiene violation by putting the weapon on the sanitised surface.

The soldier responded by saying, 'Wherever I go my weapon must go with me. If I lost it, it would be better to jump overboard than face the wrath of my sergeant major.'

Before the ship was requisitioned, Stephen had become acquainted with telephonist Janet Ryan. They volunteered for the voyage. When they married in 1983, they became one of the few married couples both of whom held the South Atlantic Medal with rosette.

The Gurkhas had specialist chefs who were given access to the ship's kitchens so that they could cook the hot and spicy Bhat meals that the soldiers appreciated. They also had a choice of regular Western food if they wished. Crew members were occasionally invited to eat Bhat dinners with the Gurkhas on the journey south, including waiter Pierre Cornlouer, Sister Wendy Marshall and hotel officer Rupert Ballantyne. The Bhat food was popular with other troops. Corporal John Stevens tried to sneak into the Gurkhas' part of the galley to get one meal but was caught and told in no uncertain terms to leave.

A number of spaces around the ship served as offices. The Card Room on Quarter Deck became the Brigade Headquarters, the Library on Quarter Deck was the Brigadier's Office and the Reading Room on Boat Deck became battalion offices. A conference room was established in the Double Down suite on the Upper Deck. Barclays Bank on Two Deck housed a very large safe and became the Paymaster's Office. It did a brisk trade, cashing cheques for the soldiers, some of whom wanted to repay debts they had run up playing cards in the evenings. The Royal Navy took over the Manifest Office. Military offices were set up in the Security Office, Tour Office and Quiet Room. One of the more unusual changes of function was the ladies' toilet on Quarter Deck forward near the Midships Bar, put to use as a map room. This type of arrangement was typical of how space on board the ship was reallocated and used for functions for which it was never intended. Another example was the Steiners hairdressing salon on One Deck, which was designated the education office and became the base for 81 Intelligence Section.

The crew bars stayed open in the normal way. While the military were limited to two cans of beer, no such limits were imposed on *QE2* crew. Although crew and troops were not permitted in each other's social areas, most crew made welcome any soldiers who found their way to a crew bar. Able seaman Tom Young recalls crew inviting troops to the crew bars. There were many occasions when troops and crew interacted together over a drink in the evenings.

Mechanic Paul Fisher recalls some soldiers coming into the Three Deck Pig crew bar disguised as waiters, cooks and kitchen porters. They had approached *QE2* crew members and asked to borrow crew clothing. The crew obliged and lent them waiters' jackets and kitchen working gear. The disguises were not intended to fool crew members but to evade the attentions of the Brigade's Military Police, who regularly patrolled crew bars with the ship's security petty officers on the lookout for troops. Crew members would warn soldiers when a patrol was approaching a bar, so that the soldiers could leave or hide. However, some soldiers were caught by the Military Police and were assigned punishment details such as jogging around the Boat Deck with extra weight.

Waiter John Davies recalls sharing a drink with some of the sergeants he served in the NCOs' mess on Quarter Deck. Carpenter Bill Bailey met two officers from NP1980 and sometimes invited them to the Petty Officers' Club. The ship's security petty officers, who also drank in this bar, ignored what was strictly speaking an infraction. Some socialising between crew and troops occasionally took part in cabins. One crew member invited some soldiers to his cabin for a drinks party. The occasion ended after a visit from the ship's security petty officers. A neighbouring crew member had complained about loud music. On this occasion, no action was taken against anyone involved.

Some Scots Guards officers invited the ship's nurses to dine with them in the Queens Grill one evening. The reply from Senior Sister Jane Yelland was that unfortunately they could not accept the invitation as they were not permitted to dine in military areas. The officers replied that they would ask one of the Brigade's padres to make the request to Captain Jackson. Captain Jackson then agreed that the three off-duty nursing sisters could accept the invitation. They dressed in evening clothes and enjoyed a lovely evening in the Queens Grill.

Engineer officer Rod Fair remembers that when one of the Scots Guards found that he had a grinder in his workshop, he asked for his bayonet to be sharpened: 'When his mates found out, I got buckets of them. All those shiny bayonets fresh from duty at Buckingham Palace.'

The Voyage South to Freetown

The troops had access to only one shop, which sold chocolate, crisps, cigarettes, canned drinks, suntan lotion, camera film and some souvenirs, such as T-shirts. The troops referred to the shop as the NAAFI: the Navy, Army and Air Force Institutes (NAAFI) company supplies to armed forces personnel recreational goods and facilities that are not provided by military authorities. NAAFI establishments can be found on almost all UK military bases and Royal Navy ships. However, the *QE2* shop had no formal association with the NAAFI and continued to be run by Ocean Trading staff. As the shop was now in a wartime situation, it ceased to be a commercial entity and could not make a profit. The shop staff repriced all items at cost plus a 10 per cent mark-up to cover the cost of staff wages.

The on-board shop staff split into two shifts. They had far more passengers to serve and less time for restocking, but Anthony Dance and the NCO with whom he had discussed shop opening hours on sailing from Southampton got on well for the rest of the voyage after their initial discussion. The relationship was always friendly and each respected the other's position. The NCO invited shop staff to the Brigade's lectures and briefings, saying, 'We're all on the same side here.'

After the shop closed at 2100 hours, the staff worked an extra two hours restocking the shelves. On one occasion, the staff found handwritten messages wishing good luck to all on board *QE2* inside cartons of chocolates from Rowntree Mackintosh. Aware of the destination of the confectionery they were packing, the chocolate company staff had used the opportunity to send good wishes.

The shop staff received help from an unexpected quarter. Before joining Ocean Trading, Anthony Dance had worked in shoreside supermarket retail, where one of his colleagues was Steve Davison. Early in the voyage they were astonished to meet one another on the ship. Steve Davison was a soldier with the Brigade's Signals Squadron. He was sharing a cabin with three other soldiers. The four of them would help the Ocean Trading shop staff restock the shop every evening in exchange for a crate or two of beer.

The shop became one of the places on board where the troops could relax and interact socially. Shop assistant Kent Frazer recalls:

I remember one of the Scots Guards, a fair-haired chap about the same age as myself. He had been in the store several times and was always pleasant. He had been playing cards and must have had a bad day. He asked if I would lend him £10. I did. I wouldn't have done that under normal circumstances but I thought about what he would be going through in just a few days. I loaned him the money but never expected to see him again. The next morning he walked into the shop with a big smile on his face, told me that he had won all his money back plus more and that he couldn't have done it without me. I often wonder if he remained lucky and survived the conflict.

The early part of the voyage saw the ship's crew working hard to adjust to the needs of their new passengers. One area concerned the small gymnasium and swimming pool on Seven Deck, 'C' Stairway. The facilities in the gymnasium comprised weights, dumbbells, floor mats, benches and a few cycling machines. The gym could accommodate no more than twenty-five people. The ship's regular health and fitness instructor was not sailing on this voyage, so crew member Clive Dalley volunteered to manage the gym.

The day after the departure from Southampton, the gym space was crowded and chaotic with soldiers queuing up the stairway. Clive spoke with officers from the Brigade and they worked out a rota system for the gym. The gym opened at 0700 and closed at 2200 hours with the facilities in constant use throughout the day. Clive suggested that an Army Physical Training Instructor (PTI) help him manage the gym. This was arranged. Clive found the troops were always respectful and polite. On some occasions after the gym had closed, Clive would invite some of the NCOs for a beer before locking up. He worked closely with the instructors, who showed their appreciation by presenting him with an Army PTI shirt before they disembarked.

The Wardroom Social Committee organised an equestrian meeting for the evening of Saturday, 15 May. It was titled Saturday Night at the Races. A length of canvas on which a race track had been painted was rolled out over the Wardroom deck. The track was divided into several segments. Six small wooden horses numbered from 1 to 6 had been made. The horses' names included Bunkers Built (by Galtieri out of Sheer Terror), Ascension Missed (by QE2 out of Radar) and Queen Serviced (by RAS out of Rover). The players rolled a large dice. The horse whose number came up when the dice was rolled moved forward one segment on the track. Races held that evening included the Sierra Leone Selling Plate, the Freetown Frolic, the Galtieri Gallop and the Mid-Atlantic Marathon. Bets were made with the odds shown on a blackboard. Jacqui White was one of the crew invited to the event. She recalls an evening of good humour and loud cheering. The evening was an enjoyable event for all who attended and a further opportunity for the officers of the ship, the naval party and the Brigade to become acquainted and form amicable working relationships.

On Sunday, 16 May, the BBC World Service carried news that the Secretary of State for Defence, John Nott, had warned that if the UN negotiations did not settle the crisis by the end of the week, then Britain would pursue military action. That day the Theatre was almost full for the church service. After the service Captain Jackson hosted a lunchtime cocktail party to which senior officers from *QE2*, NP 1980 and 5 Infantry Brigade were invited. The 1700 hour Commanders' Conference that day included a briefing by the Brigade's air liaison officer on Argentine aircraft.

One of the main exercises that commenced on 17 May was helicopter embarking and disembarking drills. All the troops wearing full kit took it in turns to carry out this exercise. The Sea Kings accommodated between about twenty and twenty-four men. Soldiers were instructed on how to put on an inflatable life jacket and were given a strict warning not to activate this during the drill. For some, it was a new experience as this was the first time they had been inside a helicopter. Some were disappointed that the exercise did not include a flight.

Some Hindu films were shown for the Gurkhas. The Gurkhas had brought video cassette tapes of Indian films that they hoped to watch, but they struggled to find a video player. However, a crew member was able to help. Carpenter Bill Bailey occupied passenger cabin 5044 on Five Deck. He had used his carpentry skills to fit the cabin with a television and video machine that he had bought in Hong Kong during a world cruise. He also fitted a refrigerator for his beer. His neighbours in adjoining cabins were Gurkha soldiers. One day a Gurkha officer asked Bill if some Gurkhas could watch films in his cabin. Bill agreed and opened his cabin one evening, saying to the Gurkhas that they should help themselves to beer. Then he went to the Petty Officers' Club to socialise. When he returned, about twenty soldiers were crammed into his tiny cabin. They immediately stood up when Bill returned and offered to leave. Bill insisted they stay and finish the film. It was nearly one o'clock by the time he got to bed that night. Some Gurkha soldiers later invited Bill to join them for a Bhat dinner.

On one occasion, Chief Engineer John Grant shared a lift with some soldiers. The soldiers noticed the purple stripes on the chief engineer's shoulder epaulettes and asked him about the ship's engines. The outcome of the conversation was that the chief engineer gave a guided tour of the Engine Room to the soldiers.

Most of 5 Brigade were assigned to passenger accommodation, but with the ship sailing with only two-thirds of her normal crew complement, some troops were allocated to empty crew cabins. Two Welsh Guards were assigned to a cabin on Five Deck aft. Their next-door neighbours were two ship's waiters, Jeremy Letherbarrow and Kevin Dunn. Also on board was Jeremy's uncle, Clifford Letherbarrow, a head waiter. The two would sometimes socialise together. Jeremy Letherbarrow and Kevin Dunn had a refrigerator in their cabin where they kept their beer. They told the two guardsmen that they could enter the cabins and help themselves to beer whenever they wanted. Jeremy and Kevin hid their cabin key on a small ledge by the stopcock to a water drinking fountain outside their cabin. After the guardsmen had helped themselves to beer, the two waiters would replenish the fridge.

While the ship was in Southampton, it had been decided that a senior cruise staff officer should sail to help organise officers' and ratings' entertainment. Tim Castle was selected due to his familiarity with the sound and light systems in the public rooms. He hosted a nightly radio show called *Falkland Island Discs*, a title inspired by the long-running BBC radio programme *Desert Island Discs*, which was first broadcast in 1942. The show was broadcast from the ship's Sound and Reproduction Equipment (SRE) room on Three Deck. The SRE room was the ship's internal communications hub, through which Tannoy announcements and in-cabin music stations were routed.

During the voyage, some NCOs from the Welsh Guards offered to help Tim as guest DJs. The ship did not stock new or recent records, so many of the song requests from the Brigade could not be played. A frequent request from guardsmen who had spent part of the day jogging around the Boat Deck was the Olivia Newton-John song 'Physical'. Unfortunately, this record was not on board. When it was requested, Tim Castle sometimes replaced it with a 1959 Chuck Berry B-side called 'Too Pooped to Pop'. A room steward lent Tim his record collection to supplement the ship's own.

Some tasks carried out by the soldiers on the voyage south were important but not always joyous. Paul Ackerman of the Royal Army Pay Corps remembers, 'We spent most of our time on the way south setting up Army Dependants Assurance Trust to financially protect families if their loved ones did not return.'

The day before the ship arrived at Freetown, Captain Peter Jackson received a message from another Captain Jackson, with whom he had worked at Port Everglades in Florida. This was a regular port of call for *QE2* when sailing between New York and the Caribbean Sea:

> To: Captain Peter Jackson commanding RMS *Queen Elizabeth 2*.
> We at Port Everglades wish you, your officer, your crew and the troops you carry every success in your worthy effort. We pray for your safe and swift return.
> Captain Robert Jackson
> Port Everglades Pilots Association[85]

That same day, *QE2*'s captain received a kind handwritten letter from the Reverend Peter Brooke, the chaplain of the 1st Battalion Welsh Guards. The letter ended with the words, 'I have been very impressed by the welcome and generosity of all your staff. I know I can say this without affectation because so many people have said as much to me.'[86]

A loading trial was carried out with a detail of soldiers carrying ammunition up several flights of stairs at the forward end of the ship from No. 1 Hatch. Two companies of the Brigade – 81 Ordnance Company and 91 Ordnance Company – combined to form a chain gang, which they jokingly called 'Queen Elizabeth the Second's Own'. Some of the ammunition was used for firing practice.

Later that day, a briefing for *QE2* crew was given in the Theatre. Staff Captain Alexander Hutcheson started off by saying, 'Well, what a little adventure we've got ourselves into this time.' He then joked that 'The ship will not be painted grey' and 'Crew will not be expected to dress in full kit and jog around the Boat Deck with the Army.' Brigadier Wilson then made a speech and the crew also heard from the head of the Royal Navy detachment, Captain James.

The military officers explained some of the problems and dangers that had already been experienced and others that might lie ahead. The brigadier gave a breakdown of Argentine forces at sea, on land and in the air. Slides were shown of aircraft and ships used by enemy forces, some of which had been sold to Argentina by the British. It was noted that the

Argentine Air Force had purchased some C130 Hercules aircraft from the USA that could be used to search for *QE2*.

Brigadier Wilson asked if anyone in the audience had visited the Falklands. Steward Pierre Cornlouer raised his hand. Brigadier Wilson said he would like to speak with Pierre at the end of the meeting. The Brigadier rounded off his speech by thanking the *QE2* crew for volunteering, noting that of all the personnel on board, the crew were the only ones who had chosen to be there and they were respected by the Brigade for this. This unnecessary but kind gesture was appreciated and generated good feeling between the military and the *QE2* crew, with the latter now more aware of the dangers that might lay ahead.

After the meeting, as requested, Pierre Cornlouer approached Brigadier Wilson, who said he needed to know what Pierre knew about the islands. The two of them made their way to the education office located in the Steiners hair salon on One Deck. Pierre was asked by Brigade intelligence officers to say everything he knew from his visits to the Falklands. He told them he had served as a catering crew member on board the RRS *Bransfield*, a small ice-strengthened ship of the British Antarctic Survey. As well as visiting Port Stanley, the *Bransfield* had visited ports and scientific stations in the Falklands, South Georgia and Antarctica, transporting scientists and their equipment. Pierre was shown a film of the Falklands and asked by the intelligence officers to talk about the places he recognised and to give any information that might be of use to the Brigade. Pierre was asked if he had anything else to add. 'There's four pubs in Stanley,' he replied. For part of the voyage Pierre served as a personal steward to Captain Jimmy James.

One day, hotel officer Terry Foskett asked a Scots Guards officer what would happen when British troops landed on the islands. The reply in a cultured English accent was 'No problem at all. My chaps will knock them off.' Terry was assigned a group of ten soldiers to inspect the ship to ensure that the carpet protection boards remained securely in place. Each morning a sergeant major would march ten guardsmen into the Double Down Room, stand them to attention, then turn to Terry and say, 'Ten-man detail reporting for duty sir'. Terry would then lead the group around the ship to secure and repair any loose or damaged hardboard. Repairing and, if necessary, replacing the hardboard required several man-hours every day to keep the coverings in shipshape condition. As the voyage progressed, it became apparent that the hardboard was experiencing heavy erosion and was effective only in areas experiencing relatively light usage. It was necessary to remove the hardboard in the vicinity of 'D' Stairway near the Columbia Restaurant because the boards were deteriorating and the deep-blue carpet on the stairway was becoming eroded. With Captain Jackson's permission, the carpet was lifted, exposing the steel deck, which could better withstand troop movements.

Timothy Williams' job as a hairdresser changed significantly. As the Steiners hair salon on One Deck had been taken over by the Brigade, Timothy worked in another space on One Deck, which on passenger cruises functioned as a combined beauty salon and chiropodist. On this voyage, the space was used by Timothy as a barber shop. Timothy was an instantly recognisable crew member with a pink fringe and three diamonds set in one ear. On passenger cruises, women provided most of his custom with hair-styling appointments lasting up to an hour. On this voyage, he dealt only with male customers with haircuts lasting just a few minutes.

At the start of the voyage, Timothy needed a period to adjust, joking, 'I'm more used to blow dry and set, not short back and sides.' There were no appointments and at times a queue formed outside. Those passing the barber shop would hear Timothy joking with the soldiers, 'Leave your weapons outside, boys.' He charged 75p a haircut, much less than it would have cost a fare-paying passenger in 1982. Unlike on a passenger voyage, most members of the Brigade did not offer tips, but Timothy did not mind. He took the time to chat with the soldiers as he would have with any other customer. He remembers some of the Brigade admitting to him that they were a bit scared of what might lie ahead, an understandable emotion.

Early in the voyage, Timothy had used his key to go into the main Steiners salon, not realising that it was now a military area. Fortunately, no Army personnel were there at the time. Timothy had gone there looking for some hairdressing equipment but quickly left when he saw maps and charts spread out on tables. This was the only occasion he entered the main salon during the voyage.

Monday, 17 May ended with some evening entertainment in the Queens Room provided by the choir of the Welsh Guards and the pipes and drums of the Scots Guards. This was followed by some traditional dancing by the 7th Gurkha Rifles. As the days went by, other events took place to keep the troops entertained. The crew contributed when they could, sometimes in small ways, such as the occasion when Signalman Garry Parr from Leicester was summoned to the Bridge on his 18th birthday to be greeted and congratulated by Captain Jackson.

After six days at sea, at 0900 hours on Tuesday, 18 May, the officer of the watch sighted Cape Sierra Leone Light. Soon after, the liner approached the harbour entrance and Freetown harbour pilots Kenokai and Jones boarded. By 1145 hours *QE2*, with the assistance of tugs *Sena* and *Intermani*, was docked port side to the berth with mooring lines secure fore and aft.

This was *QE2*'s maiden call at Freetown and under normal circumstances the arrival would have been ceremonial. Local dignitaries would have been invited to an on-board reception hosted by the captain and an exchange of gifts made. No such event took place in order to keep the liner's southerly passage plan as secret as possible. The Sierra Leone authorities helped by waiving customs, immigration and port health requirements. This was on the strict understanding that there was no shore leave for troops and crew.

The passage from Southampton to Freetown had taken five days, one hour and twenty-four minutes over a distance of 2,956 miles, and had been accomplished at an average speed of 24.35 knots. Even at that economical reduced speed, the engines had consumed 1,919 tons of oil, leaving 4,050 tons remaining in the bunkers. This would be the last time that the ship was alongside a dock until she arrived home in Southampton. The climate in the port was hot and humid with a cloudy sky and virtually no breeze. Some of the troops exercising on the upper decks were sunburnt.

From the ship it was possible to see some of the local shanty towns with rusty corrugated roofs and wooden shacks, behind which were hills covered in tropical vegetation. The jetty area had been cordoned off by containers and fencing for security and to stop local traders from setting up sales stalls. Outside the cordon, a crowd of about 100 local people gathered, some of whom shouted at the soldiers on deck to throw down money. Some soldiers and crew threw down coins and packets of cigarettes from the Boat Deck. Some old mattresses were thrown down from Two Deck aft. Eventually, an announcement was made from the Bridge by First Officer David Pope: 'This is a military order. All members of the armed forces must immediately cease throwing coins and other objects to members of the local population. Military Police have been instructed to enforce this order.'

The Voyage South to Freetown

A gangway was placed in the shell door opening on Five Deck port side to enable officials and the ship's agent to board. *QE2*, along with all other STUFTs, had been formally advised that no one on board was permitted to contact a ship's agent directly but had to submit any orders for fuel or other supplies through the Ministry of Defence (Navy), London. The agent in Freetown was the Sierra Leone Shipping Agency, which had been appointed by MoD (Navy) to assist all STUFT ships.

Most local boat traffic was kept clear of the ship but a few enterprising traders slipped through. They offered fruit, coconuts and wooden carvings. They attempted to do business through the portholes on the lower decks, throwing up lines of string to which baskets were attached. Mail was received on board for crew and military.

A total of 1,867 tons of fuel were taken on and as much fresh water as possible. There had been concerns at the start of the voyage that with the extra number of passengers the ship might experience a shortage of fresh water. However, the ship's evaporators that make fresh water from seawater were working well. Although water consumption from Southampton to Freetown was high, the problem did not become critical. The evaporators were producing an average of 1,000 tons of fresh water per day with a deficit of about 200 tons daily. About 1,500 tons of water were taken on board while the ship was in the port. Some fresh food provisions were also loaded. Fuel was supplied simultaneously from the quayside and from a barge moored on the starboard side. However, the pumping rate for fuel was slower than anticipated, with the result that sailing was delayed until 2300 hours.

The ship departed from Freetown with two crew members fewer than when she arrived. A Lloyd's marine surveyor, David Yeardley, had signed on articles in Southampton. His brief was to keep an eye on the main turbine alignment. The liner was sailing under 'a condition of class', which meant that Lloyd's had restricted the engines to a maximum of 144rpm. His work complete, the surveyor signed off and was repatriated to the UK. Despite shore leave being prohibited, a kitchen porter managed to slip ashore and failed to return before sailing time.

The stop at Freetown was a calculated risk, but it meant *QE2* could now proceed non-stop to the war zone without the risk of running low on fuel. The liner put to sea shortly after fuelling was completed and was clear of the harbour by midnight. Security was such that *QE2* slipped in and out of Freetown unnoticed by the world's press.

Freetown, Sierra Leone, was the first port of call on the voyage south. (Patrick Hewetson)

Troops gathered on the Boat Deck, probably disappointed that no shore leave was permitted in Freetown. (R. Smith)

9

Freetown to South Georgia

From Sierra Leone, QE2 sailed almost due south for a day and a half towards Ascension Island, a British Overseas Territory in the equatorial regions of the Atlantic Ocean. The QE2 radio officers had been permitted to transmit messages up until now, but this stopped after leaving Freetown when complete radio silence was observed. However, in accordance with maritime law the ship's radio officers continued to keep listening watches for distress signals from other vessels.

When QE2 entered service in 1969, she was fitted with degaussing equipment. This consisted of copper cables installed around the circumference of the ship's hull on Three Deck. When an electric current is introduced into the cables, it cancels out the ship's magnetic field and reduces the possibility of activating a magnetic mine. The system had been checked a couple of times near Portland and Portsmouth, but it had never been activated other than for testing. During preparations for the voyage in Southampton technicians from the Ministry of Defence visited the ship to check the system. Electrical engineer officer John Griffin remembers the system being activated on the way south and having to change the settings periodically when requested to do so by the ministry. The settings had to be adjusted due to the difference in the Earth's magnetic field north and south of the equator.

The most important task after leaving Freetown was the creation of a total blackout so that no light would be visible from the ship during the hours of darkness. In the words of Captain James RN, the giant liner would be converted from 'the brightest star on the ocean, to the darkest'. Lieutenant Rentell was given the task of supervising the operation. Chief

The 'mermaids' (two nursing sisters) lie alongside the recently constructed swimming pool to await the arrival of King Neptune for the 'crossing the line' ceremony on the voyage south. (Patrick Hewetson)

Officer Warwick circulated a memorandum defining which groups would take responsibility for various areas of the ship.

There are hundreds of portholes on *QE2* as well as large floor-to-ceiling public room windows on the upper decks. The four ship's carpenters led by senior carpenter Bill Bailey set up trestle tables on Two Deck forward. Here they made wooden templates which they used to cut out hundreds of circular black plastic pieces in the sizes of the various portholes and windows. The two most common sizes were nicknamed after black vinyl record sizes, with the smaller size referred to as 45s and the larger size referred to as LPs. The ship's Tannoy system was used to call the troops in turn by deck to collect their blackout coverings. Two Army officers were assigned to each passenger deck to supervise the securing of the coverings in cabins.

Most of the crew cabins and many of the passenger cabins had a deadlight, a round heavy steel plate hinged at the top and with two screen bolts at the bottom. The carpenters locked tight many of the deadlights. Darkening of the large public room windows was assigned to various

Freetown to South Georgia

work groups. By concentrated effort the job was completed in three days. However, in the tropics the black plastic tended to crinkle when subjected to the sun's rays and the blackened windows created a greenhouse effect within the ship, placing added stress on the air conditioning. A regular job for the carpenters was a daily inspection of blackouts to secure any covering that was peeling away. The ship's doctor, Alan Kirwin, advised crew to try to spend time on the open decks every day to help alleviate the effects of the absence of natural daylight.

From now on, every night on the journey south, the officer of the watch would make the same announcement when it got dark: 'Blackout now in force. All members of the forces and ship's company are to co-operate to ensure that the ship is effectively blacked out.' At first there was a certain laxness from a minority of personnel. Often light would be showing after the first announcement, and a second or even third announcement would be necessary. The helicopters flew after sunset, partly for night flying practice and partly to observe whether any light was visible from the ship. Troops would regularly go out on deck to watch the evening flying exercises. Some of them had brought cameras and had to be asked not to use the flash as this not only affected the pilots' night vision but violated the darken ship requirement.

One evening, Lieutenant Rentell was assigned to inspect the ship's blackout from a helicopter. He flew from the aft of the ship in a Sea King, which made a hovering circuit to identify areas where chinks of light were visible. He recorded the locations of light leakage so that the offending cabin or public room could be visited and remedial measures taken. For the first two or three nights some light was visible, but soon all hands accepted the importance of the blackout. It was observed from the helicopter that the ship was difficult to spot from a mile or so away, except for the navigation lights, but even these were not used after Ascension Island.

Other crew members were also given the opportunity to fly in a helicopter. Electrical engineer officer John Griffin was one of them:

> We took off and landed and flew round *QE2* many times. I was able to take photographs out of the open door, tethered of course. It felt very safe. However, in the Wardroom that night the pilots were there and I asked why we did so many landings and circuit. One of the Fleet Air Arm pilots said until *QE2* he had not landed on a ship before! It brought the house down! I think he was joking!

Captain Jackson handed over the command of the ship temporarily while he made a flight to take some photographs. Chief Officer Warwick also flew in a Sea King. He remembers how strange it was to see the ship steaming along at 25 knots in the middle of the ocean with no land in sight.

Inspection of the blackout took place daily. One evening, shortly after the ship had departed from Ascension Island, carpenter Bill Bailey was walking along Boat Deck checking for chinks of light when he saw a beam of light shining from the Sports Deck. It was clear it was coming from one of the of the starboard penthouse suites occupied by a senior Army officer. Bill went to the offending cabin and found the door unlocked and the cabin unoccupied. The officer occupying the room had developed the habit of peeling his blackout down during daylight hours and on this day had neglected to replace it. Bill removed almost all the lightbulbs from the suite, leaving just a bathroom light so that the occupant had sufficient light to find his way around. The next day, the officer mentioned at the daily meeting of senior officers that something puzzling had happened: the lightbulbs in his cabin had been taken! He was told the bulbs had been removed due to a blackout violation. There were no further problems with light leakage from the penthouse suites after this incident.

The blackout, alongside covering of the carpets with hardboard, resulted in a total change of the ambience of the ship. The public rooms, normally light and airy, were now dismal places, permanently blacked out with the large rectangular windows covered in boards and sheeting. The atmosphere and mood on board was different from a passenger voyage in every respect. But the morale of the crew remained good. As accounts officer David Luke recalls:

> We were a band of brothers who knew we were sailing into imminent danger as we were the target for the Argentinians. Over time, heading south, we developed a very special bond with our shipmates and this comradeship remains with us to this day.

Most of the crew made preparations for an emergency evacuation. They were encouraged to pack a 'grab bag' with essential items they did not wish to leave behind if the ship had to be abandoned. Decisions on what to put in a grab bag varied from person to person. Popular items included torch, passport, bank card, family photos and possessions of sentimental value. One crew member joked that all he had in his grab bag was a bottle

Freetown to South Georgia

Keeping fit was of paramount importance and exercises were carried out throughout the day, every day. (R.W. Warwick)

QE2's helicopter deck was exclusively reserved for exercising. (R. Smith)

Troops trained on stairways around the ship, which broke the rhythm of physical exercise routines. (R. Smith)

The bergen backpacks that soldiers exercised with were sometimes replaced by a comrade carried in a fireman's lift. (R.W. Warwick)

With the day's training exercises over, the Boat Deck reverted to its intended use, as an area to relax and enjoy the view. (R.W. Warwick)

Runners had to use the stairways at the forward end of the Boat Deck to complete a full circuit. The stairways required regular maintenance from the ship's carpenters due to the heavy wear to which they were subjected. (Patrick Hewetson)

The QE2 in the Falklands War

Each unit was allocated a time slot for physical exercise on the Boat Deck. Unit leaders would give instructions on the form of exercise to be carried out. (R.W. Warwick)

On days with a calm sea, the forward flight deck was used for rifle practice. (R.W. Warwick)

Gurkhas training with Carl Gustav 84mm anti-tank launcher. Each weapon was manned by two men: a loader and a firer. (Stephen Hallam)

Troops line up on the Boat Deck awaiting for orders from their sergeant major. (Malcolm Scanlan)

Military training was carried out wherever a convenient space could be found. On this occasion, the troops are outside the library on Quarter Deck. (Stephen Hallam)

The Brigade was equipped with a variety of weapons. On most days during the voyage exercises were held to familiarise the soldiers with the use of them. (Stephen Hallam)

The underside of the flight deck aft became a popular place for training outside. (R.W. Warwick)

The constant activity soon took its toll on the formerly pristine Boat Deck. (R.W. Warwick)

Some of the crew had the opportunity to view their ship steaming along in the ocean from a Sea King helicopter. (R.W. Warwick)

Freetown to South Georgia

The noticeboard on Quarter Deck, D Stairway, was used to update crew and troops with the latest information about the conflict. Hardboard protection of the carpet in this much used area failed, so the carpets were rolled up and put aside. (R. Smith)

Prior to taking their turn jogging on deck, soldiers would have to climb several flights of stairs to reach the Boat Deck. (R.W. Warwick)

The QE2 in the Falklands War

The Queens Room on Quarter Deck was one of the most elegant rooms afloat. (R.W. Warwick)

All the lounge chairs were taken ashore and the dance floor protected by hardboard. (R.W. Warwick)

In the evening, the Double Down Room served as a recreation area. (R.W. Warwick)

A liaison meeting between department heads was held daily. From left to right: Ronald Warwick (chief officer of *QE2*) and Brendan Lambe (brigade major of 5 Infantry Brigade). And from NP1980: Lt Roger Bevan, Lt Cdr David Poole and Major Hugh Affleck-Graves. (Paul Haley)

of vodka and a carton of 200 cigarettes, asking, 'Well, what else am I going to need?' Many crew laid out their life jacket, their clothing and what they would take with them so that they could easily find things in the dark if power failed during an emergency. Tim Castle decided that if it was necessary to abandon ship, he would take all his cold weather gear with him. He would wear as much as he could and take the rest in a carry-on bag so that he could offer clothing to others in the lifeboat. He arranged all the clothes he planned to wear on his day bed.

War artist Linda Kitson was an easily recognisable figure around the ship, clutching her sketchpad and with her shirt pockets bulging with pencils. She had an earnest and rather intense air about her. She later recalled:

> Travelling to the other side of the globe to sub-zero temperatures via the Equator, I had no idea what to wear at all. Not helpful was a kindly relative saying 'You will need to be very smart as you will be eating in the Officers' Mess.' The 'what to wear' had its funny side. By the time I got to the Quartermaster's store on board *QE2* the Gurkhas had taken everything in my size and I was left with combat trousers that fitted the tallest Scots Guards.[87]

Like Paul Haley, the official war photographer, Linda Kitson, was allowed to roam the ship. She could sketch wherever and whatever she wanted. There were some unusual sights for her to draw, such as heavy artillery, vehicles stowed on the open decks, helicopters landing and taking off and soldiers attending meetings. She was frequently seen on the Bridge, the flight deck, the galley and in any location where troops were active. She positioned herself as inconspicuously as possible, often sitting on the floor. She preferred not to engage with the crew as she sketched and would avoid conversation with onlookers. She would immerse herself in drawing and did not like to be interrupted or have her presence acknowledged. While sketching, Linda Kitson wanted personnel to carry out their duties as if she was not there. She would often work with several sketchpads at a time, moving between them as personnel moved about their duties. If the officer moved away, she worked on another drawing. When he returned, she would revert to the original sketch.

War photographer Paul Haley documented activities around the ship with his camera. He soon met *QE2* photographer Paul Guest and they became firm friends. He also became acquainted with some of the

Brigade's photographers, who had set up an intelligence cell darkroom. In case he was killed or his films went missing, Paul started each roll with an image of his press card. He would package completed rolls of film in batches of five, ready to dispatch when the opportunity arose. On his first day at sea, he had just finished packing the first five rolls of film when a Tannoy called hands to flying stations. A Sea King was being mobilised to take an injured man off to hospital. He gave the films to Senior Sister Jane Yelland, who was accompanying the patient, giving her instructions on how to send them to the *Soldier Magazine* office. In Freetown, Sierra Leone, he followed a similar routine with a clergyman from the Mission to Seamen, who was one of the few people allowed to board. He asked him to take the films to the airport and to give them to a pilot to carry back to the UK. It was a system often used at the time called 'By Hand of Pilot', which he had successfully used a few times previously in various places around the world.

A few days before the ship arrived at Ascension Island, Paul Haley discussed his future plans with Brigadier Wilson. The brigadier replied, 'As far as I am concerned, you are part of 5 Infantry Brigade and you can come with us wherever we are going. Obviously you can leave at Ascension and go home but it's up to you.' Paul had no intention of leaving the ship and missing the opportunity to document the war.

Each day, weapons training was held around the ship with guns being dismantled and reassembled. Soldiers practised stripping and reassembling weapons in the most unlikely locations – the shopping mall, public rooms, passageways, stairwells or wherever they could find space. With the crowded cabins accommodating far more passengers than normal, many soldiers took to cleaning their boots and weapons in the passageways.

The ship's health and fitness instructor Clive Dalley had met a Scots Guards officer who asked him if he would like to help service some weapons. As a result, Clive found himself on Five Deck degreasing heavy machine guns. When he noted an ammunition box dated 1949, Clive made a comment about the year. The reply was 'Don't worry about the date – they're still lethal'. The Scots Guards officer showed his appreciation for Clive's help by allowing him to fire a range of weaponry from the stern of the ship. Wearing ear defenders, he fired a Browning heavy machine gun, a self-loading rifle (SLR) and a Sterling sub-machine gun.

In 1982, *QE2* was equipped with an early generation satellite navigation system known as NAVSAT. The liner was one of the first commercial

The day's events concluded with the inevitable paperwork. (R. Smith)

Executive chef Victor Coward made sure his team did their best to enhance the ingredients supplied by the military. (R.W. Warwick)

The chefs on board allowed the Gurkhas to prepare curries, which were very popular with others in the Brigade. (R.W. Warwick)

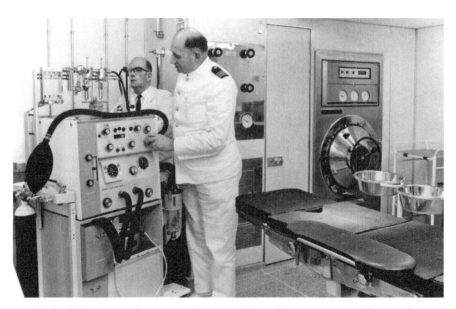

QE2 had a fully equipped operating theatre and dental surgery manned by two doctors and three nursing sisters. Over the years it was the scene of many operations, such as appendix removal, childbirth and amputation. (R.W. Warwick)

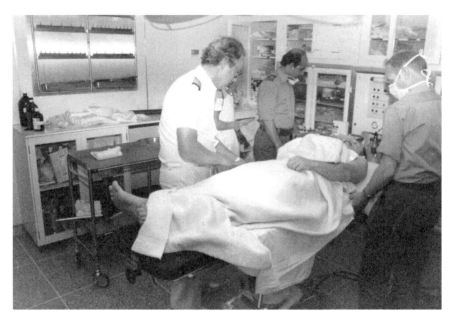

QE2 and Brigade medics shared their expertise and held emergency exercises in the hospital. (Patrick Hewetson)

War artist Linda Kitson sketched scenes and activities all around the liner. She made her presence as unobtrusive as possible. (M. Scanlan)

This sketch from Linda Kitson records a variety of activities being carried out in the Double Down Room. (Imperial War Museum)

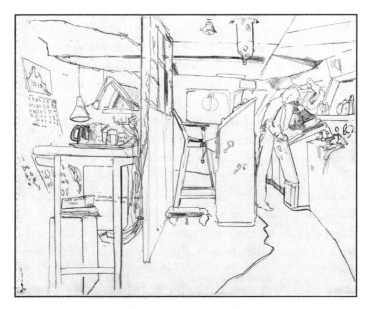

Linda Kitson's sketch of the Bridge portrays the scene with great accuracy. Many of her sketches were accompanied by side notes giving further information on the scenes she sketched. (Imperial War Museum)

ships to use satellite navigation. An orbiting satellite would rise over the horizon and transit across the sky before setting below the horizon a few minutes later. During this period, *QE2* was able to obtain an accurate fix of her latitude and longitude. The NAVSAT system comprised several satellites positioned about 600 nautical miles above the Earth's surface in polar orbits spread out at the equator. This meant the nearer the ship was to the poles, the more frequently positions could be obtained. This method of navigation provided a significant advantage because an accurate position could be obtained every few hours around the clock in any weather conditions. If the satellite system had not been available, the ship's position would have been obtained by celestial navigation, if conditions were favourable. This entailed a sextant to measure the angular height of the sun or stars, requiring a cloudless sky and a clear, sharp horizon, which frequently was not the case in the Atlantic Ocean.

The day after departing from Freetown, *QE2* crossed the equator on 19 May. For a few days previously, it had been rumoured that a VIP would visit the ship on this day. Jacqui White recalls conversations going around on who the VIP could be. There was speculation that a senior political figure would arrive by helicopter from Ascension Island on a 'rally the troops' visit. All was revealed when the noon Tannoy announced that the reigning monarch of the area would arrive that afternoon. Crew and soldiers were asked to muster on the forward helicopter deck. The VIP was 'King Neptune', who was visiting for the traditional 'crossing the line' ceremony. Most of the ship's crew had sailed across the equator several times and were familiar with this passenger ship ritual, which involved subjecting those crossing the line for the first time to an initiation ceremony such as kissing a fish and being covered with an unpleasant mixture of flour and water before being ceremoniously thrown into a swimming pool.

Several days previously, the chief officer had asked the carpenter and bosun to construct a makeshift swimming pool for crew and troops to use on warm days. The pool was erected forward of the cargo hatch and supported each side by the two crane bearers. The frame was made of timber with a canvas insert to hold the sea water. This pool was used for the ceremony.

Cruise director Tim Castle set up a microphone with loudspeakers. A member of the ship's crew was dressed as King Neptune. Two nurses, Jane Yelland and Wendy Marshall, set the scene dressed as mermaids complete with tails. Crew patrolled the deck, searching for volunteers who wished to take part in the ceremony, although not everyone who ended up in the pool had volunteered. Many paid homage to the King whether they wanted to or not. The *QE2* crew who were not involved with the ceremony watched warily from a distance in case they were singled out as victims. Some Army officers were unceremoniously dunked by their men. Photographer Paul Haley went to the Bridge to photograph the ceremony rather than risk being chucked in the pool with his camera equipment. Members of 5 Infantry Brigade crowded every vantage point to watch the proceedings, including the Bridge wings and its unprotected roof. Many of the Gurkhas found the ceremony amusing, being unaware of the custom on board ships of celebrating crossing the equator. The occasion was a light-hearted break in routine for soldiers and crew alike.

The arrival of the liner in tropical latitudes led to crew members seeking out deck space to sunbathe. Senior Sister Jane Yelland recalls:

Once we reached warmer waters, it was a problem as to where we nursing sisters could sunbathe! It was not feasible or appropriate to lie on the open decks while the troops were exercising. We were informed that a penthouse suite was empty, so we went out from the central corridor and climbed over the wall on to the sun deck of the suite.

But the suite in question was not empty! A few days later, Jane was sunbathing with her colleague Wendy Marshall:

Suddenly the door of the suite slid open and Brigadier Wilson appeared. He said, 'Ladies, I am most impressed with your athleticism but please in future do just knock on the door and my batman will let you in so that you can walk through to the sundeck!'

The nurses were kept busy most of the time. One day it became necessary to perform an emergency appendectomy operation on a Scots Guardsman. The *QE2* crew were preparing to operate when Major James Ryan RAMC asked if his team could help in the operation; the offer was accepted. One of the team was Ian Fletcher, who became an Army nurse when he was 18. He and his colleagues were very complimentary about the ship's medical equipment and operating theatre.

The two ships transporting 5 Infantry Brigade's heavy weapons and military stores, *Baltic Ferry* (Captain E. Harrison) and *Nordic Ferry* (Captain

R. Jenkins), arrived at Ascension Island a day ahead of *QE2*. The ships had taken a course to the island that was well to the east to minimise potential detection by Argentine Boeing 707s, which, it was now known, were patrolling the South Atlantic searching for task force vessels.[88]

QE2 approached Ascension Island on 20 May, two days after leaving Freetown. The island, located approximately halfway along the 8,000-mile supply chain between the UK and the Falklands, was the focal point of British logistical operations during the conflict, with the island a hive of activity as stores and personnel were flown out from the UK and then transferred onto ships. There was some concern shortly before her arrival as the liner had been sighted by a Soviet Primor'ye class navy spy ship, known in intelligence circles as an alien intelligence gatherer. The vessel was small but heavily equipped with antennae and sophisticated radar, and it was unlikely she was there by coincidence. One of the ship's helicopters flew out to have a look at the vessel, which stayed about 2 miles away from *QE2*. There was little doubt the spy ship would report the presence of *QE2* to Soviet authorities in Moscow. There was speculation on board whether the Kremlin would then notify the Argentine government *QE2* had arrived at Ascension. To date no information has come to light on whether Moscow alerted Buenos Aires.

Captain Jackson's orders were to stay 25 miles away from the island, the nearest British territory to the Falklands with a port and major airport. *QE2* did not anchor at Ascension but kept on the move, frequently changing course. This continuous movement meant she was less at risk from any Argentine submarines that might have been operating in the area. A Nimrod aircraft from the RAF base at the island's Wideawake Airfield surveilled the ocean in the vicinity of the island and around *QE2*. The Nimrod had reported an Argentine cargo ship 200 miles south-west of Ascension, but this did not interfere with *QE2*. On one occasion, the Nimrod saluted *QE2* by dipping its wings as it passed overhead.

The Soviet spy ship ultimately departed and a rendezvous was made with HMS *Dumbarton Castle* (Lieutenant Commander N.D. Wood RN), a Royal Navy North Sea oil rig protection vessel with helicopter landing capabilities. Between 1330 and 1600 hours, live firing practice was cancelled and helicopter operations were carried out. A Sea King from *QE2* and a yellow RAF Sea King rescue helicopter based at Ascension shuttled stores from *Dumbarton Castle* while the vessel maintained station off the liner's starboard side. Some ammunition was transported from *QE2*'s forward hold to other ships in the area, using helicopters operating from the forward flight deck. The process was slow due to limited deck space on the naval vessel. An officer and six soldiers from 81 Ordnance Company were cross-decked to *QE2*.

In the early hours of 21 May, *QE2* reversed her course and spent most of the day steaming northwards to rendezvous with the Cunard container vessel *Atlantic Causeway* to transfer stores. The vessel was also transporting air crew and helicopters south in support of the Brigade. Unfortunately, *Atlantic Causeway* did not receive the signal giving details about the rendezvous and was now positioned further south.

Some personnel left the ship at Ascension Island. Two mechanics, Harold Burton and Frank Pollard, along with contractor John McMullan were signed off for personal reasons. Malcolm Bailey, the NUS representative, was withdrawn. All four were repatriated to the UK. The two Marconi technicians who had embarked at Southampton to work on the SCOT communication system also left the ship. Three soldiers were medically evacuated. One had a heart condition, another a lung condition, while the third was a soldier whose appendix had been removed a few days earlier.

Those who embarked at Ascension on 21 May included Major General Jeremy Moore RM, Commander Land Forces Falkland Islands, and his command staff who had flown out from RAF Brize Norton the night before. From the Bridge, Second Officer Paul Jowett remembers Moore's helicopter landing sideways on the forward helicopter deck. A member of the Royal Marines, Major General Moore was appointed Commander Land Forces Falkland Islands due to the amphibious nature of Operation Corporate. Before boarding *QE2* he had been the Land Deputy Commander in the Royal Navy Headquarters at Northwood, Middlesex, which was commanded by Sir John Fieldhouse.

Royal Marine Andrew Jackson was part of the headquarters group. The night before joining the ship, he camped out among the volcanic ash of Ascension Island. All on board the helicopter were expecting a short, easy flight, but it was longer than envisaged. The ship, having been warned that an Argentine submarine might be in local waters, was carrying out anti-submarine manoeuvres. The helicopter was running low on fuel and just before the flight was to be aborted *QE2* was 'found' and everyone was safely landed. Jackson was allocated a cabin next to the noisy propeller shafts, but a Royal Marine is trained to sleep anywhere.

In 2011 Ascension Island issued this stamp to celebrate the seventieth anniversary of RAF Search and Rescue. The stamp depicts *QE2* and a yellow RAF Sea King. (R.W. Warwick)

Unfortunately, there were no comfortable cabins for some of those who joined the ship at Ascension Island. This group bunked down in one of the shell door recesses used for gangways when the ship was in port. (Ken Henderson)

Freetown to South Georgia

Members of 132 Field Battery Royal Artillery used a *QE2* postcard to inform Lt Col R. Middlemass that they had arrived on board safely. (Ken Henderson)

Major General Moore was assigned the Queen Mary Suite, one of the ship's luxury penthouses. Other senior Army officers were assigned suites nearby. Lieutenant Philip Rentell was asked to give up his suite for an officer, so after Ascension Island he bunked down in another suite with two members of NP1980, Lieutenant Commander Shaw and the flight deck officer, Lieutenant Roger Bevan. Commanded by Major Mike Fallon, sixteen gunners from the 132 Field Battery, 'The Bengal Rocket Troop' of Support Company, the Royal School of Artillery, Larkhill, also joined the ship.

Bombardier Ken Henderson was in good hands because he was accompanied by his father-in-law, Bombardier J. Jackson. With most accommodation now allocated to the Brigade, many of the men bunked down in camp beds in a shell door recess. A Wessex and a Chinook were kept busy loading a large quantity of stores sent to Ascension from the UK. Soldiers then moved the stores from the flight deck into one of the public rooms for sorting.

By 0140 hours on 22 May, contact had been established with *Atlantic Causeway* and *QE2* reversed course and headed south. By 0656 hours, the two ships were in sight of each other, and the flight crews were called to flying stations. The transfer of stores and equipment by helicopter lasted from 0710 hours to 1040 hours. *QE2* responded positively to a request from *Atlantic Causeway* for spare parts for its 3cm radar and the loan of a transceiver. The flight crews were called to stations again in the afternoon to return some stores to Ascension Island that had been received the day before and were now required elsewhere. More bags of mail were received, most destined for other ships serving in the South Atlantic.

During the second day off Ascension, the helicopters were primarily involved in airlifting to the ship from the island about 5 tons of high-priority stores, some of which were for transfer to other ships later in the voyage. In addition to the ship's two Sea Kings, assistance in moving stores was provided by two Wessex helicopters and a Chinook based on the island. The stores received on board were welcomed by the Brigade and NP1980. However, unifoxers ordered in Southampton did not arrive. A unifoxer is a towed anti-submarine device that emits noise to distract incoming torpedoes.

There was some very impressive flying at times, with three helicopters stacked up off the stern waiting to land supplies. The Royal Navy flight coordinator on the Bridge, Lieutenant Roger Bevan, and his men worked hard to ensure the landing and take-off routines ran smoothly, while the deck and landing pad crews moved tons of cargo under hot and arduous conditions. On one occasion, a Sea King conducted a highly skilled manoeuvre, landing an underslung load on the aft deck of *QE2* while simultaneously executing a neat 180-degree turn. The pilot of a Chinook, based on Ascension, also showed impressive flying skill when he brought his big twin-rotor helicopter level with the Bridge and kept pace for a while so that his crew could take pictures of the ship slicing through the South Atlantic. The big Chinook was a breathtaking sight with flight crew leaning out of every available opening, including the tailgate, with cameras to capture the moment on film. As a bit of bravado, the Chinook turned 90 degrees and flew sideways, briefly keeping pace ahead of the Bridge of the onrushing *QE2*.

QE2 received an estimated 10 tons of mail at Ascension, some of which bore postmarks only four days old. The receipt of mail from home is important in sustaining the morale of the armed forces and those who support them. When she was requisitioned, *QE2* joined the British Forces Post Office (BFPO) mail system. Family and friends writing to those on board had to use the address 'BFPO Ships'. Because ships are movable rather than static entities, whose location during an operational situation changes often at short notice, the use of a land-based address is impossible. In 1982, mail using the BFPO system was delivered to the forces mail centre at Mill Hill Barracks for sorting. Based on the latest classified information on the known or anticipated destination of a ship, the mail was then sent to a British military base or other establishment for onward delivery. During the war, Ascension Island was the central hub for processing mail after it left the UK.

Like members of the armed forces, *QE2* crew were entitled to send blue aerogrammes. These were single sheets of lightweight paper with adhesive borders that could be folded into an envelope. Known as 'blueys', these aerogrammes were free for UK addresses providing there was no enclosure. For all other envelopes, it was necessary to affix postage stamps with normal inland letter rates applying. The *QE2* Cashiers' Office had ordered a large supply of stamps for members of the crew and armed forces who wished to send larger envelopes or parcels. A temporary Army post office was set up in the Theatre Bar with responsibility for managing all BFPO mail movements. A notice from Staff Captain Hutcheson was circulated to the ship's company, informing them that after the ship left Ascension

The QE2 in the Falklands War

Island there would be no mail posting opportunity for at least ten days. Crew were able to send a message of up to thirty words free of charge to their families 'when restrictions permit' – in other words, when the ship was not observing radio silence and could transmit messages. Urgent telegrams of twelve words of a compassionate nature could be sent free of charge under similar rules.

Many crew and soldiers received welcome letters from friends and family at Ascension. Some of the mail was not addressed to an individual but was sent, for example, to 'Soldier', 'Officer' or 'Scots Guard'. These were usually messages of good wishes. Several letters were sent by young schoolchildren. There were requests for pen friendships from those back home, sometimes children but often ladies who wanted to offer support to the troops. Eighteen-year-old Andy Butterworth was one of the soldiers assigned to sort the mail. He noticed a letter from Weston-super-Mare, the hometown of some of his relatives. Andy was captivated by the letter, which had been written by a lady named Ruth, and he replied to her on *QE2* stationery. The pen friendship continued throughout the conflict. When Andy returned home, he contacted Ruth and they agreed to meet. They married a couple of years later. Andy returned to *QE2* with his wife, Ruth, to enjoy a very different cruise to the one he had made in 1982.

Newspapers were received with some of the British tabloids having sent free copies. A recent edition of the *Daily Mirror* showed a picture of the aft end of *QE2* with the new helicopter deck. The newspaper described how the Argentines had said they would sink *QE2* on Argentine National Day, 25 May. This is an important day in the Argentinian calendar, marking the anniversary of the May Revolution of 1810. Copies of the article appeared on some bulkheads around the ship with dismissive comments added!

QE2 departed from Ascension Island on 21 May. That day the first British landings took place at San Carlos on East Falkland. By the end of the day, a secure bridgehead had been established by 3 Commando Brigade, which had travelled to the islands on board *Canberra* and *Norland*.

On boarding *QE2*, Major General Jeremy Moore learned to his dismay that the SCOT satellite communication system was not functioning. The intention had been that as the ship headed into the South Atlantic, the SCOT system would enable Moore to receive confidential updates from Northwood and the Falklands on the latest disposition of land-based and naval forces. It was essential that the deployment of 5 Infantry Brigade complement the advances made by British forces after the San Carlos

Freetown to South Georgia

landings. Unfortunately, however, the two Marconi technicians who had sailed with the ship to work on the SCOT satellite terminal had been unable to get the equipment operational before they disembarked at Ascension.

Chief radio officer Allan Holmes then offered the services of three of his staff to try to rectify the problem. Allan and radio officer Phillip Marriott took over the listening watches in the Radio Room while radio officers Peter Hughes, Thomas May and Brian Martin set about working on the equipment. They received a lot of encouragement from the newly arrived signal corps, but despite their best efforts the satellite terminal was not fully operational before the ship's arrival in South Georgia. Meanwhile, with the assistance of Lieutenant Swain from NP 1980 and RFA radio officer David MacKenzie, some unclassified messages were transmitted from the ship's Radio Room.

A mock headquarters was set up for training exercises. The Midships Bar was reconfigured to represent as best as possible the operations room on HMS *Fearless*, the Royal Navy ship where Major General Moore was due to set up his operational headquarters in the waters around the Falkland Islands. From here procedures for the command and coordination of the land forces were developed and intensively rehearsed. However, this was largely a paper exercise as secure communications could not be made outside the ship. The training continued daily for the period that the headquarters staff were embarked.

With Major General Moore unable to communicate securely with Army and Royal Navy forces in the Falklands, he could not, unfortunately, influence events on the ground.[89] Planning between Major General Moore and Brigadier Wilson for the deployment of 5 Infantry Brigade now took place without full knowledge of the disposition of British forces in the field, other than the sketchy details gleaned from the BBC World Service.

After the ship had passed Ascension, a group of hotel officers began to meet every evening at 1800 hours in a cabin on One Deck for a convivial drink. They had not previously done this during peacetime service. As Terry Foskett noted, 'For an hour or so we just wanted to relax with our peers to help us deal with our fears as we all realised that this was no longer a game but a real and dangerous war with uncertainty on what the future would hold for us.' These sentiments were echoed by hotel officer Rupert Ballantyne, who recalled, 'When we heard the news that the *Canberra* went in close to make her first landing, the seriousness of the situation was hammered home to everyone, including myself.' War artist Linda Kitson observed a change in the mood on the ship: 'It got increasingly alarming when our super cruise ship became more evidently a troopship. On passing Ascension Island it came over the tannoys that we were in the arena of warfare and I can tell you that the atmosphere really changed.'[90] As the Cunard flagship steamed deeper into the South Atlantic, there was among the crew some edginess and excitement at being deployed in a theatre of operations. However, despite a more serious and determined air, morale on the ship remained high.

QE2 received protection from the RAF after she departed Ascension Island. RAF Nimrod aircraft reconnoitred the South Atlantic south of Ascension, searching for any Argentine ships or submarines that might pose a threat. None were detected. There is some uncertainty on whether *QE2* was escorted south by a Royal Navy submarine. It is known that Royal Navy submarines were deployed in the South Atlantic during Operation Corporate.[91] However, details of their whereabouts during the campaign remain secret. The authors made a Freedom of Information request on whether *QE2* received a submarine escort between Ascension Island and South Georgia, but the reply from the Ministry of Defence neither confirmed nor denied this.[92] If the ship did receive submarine protection, it could only have been for part of the journey to South Georgia. The ship's impressive speed would have made it difficult for a submarine to escort the ship for the entire journey.

The 5 Brigade staff posted maps of the Falkland Islands on noticeboards on Quarter Deck by 'D' Stairway with a tally of the aircraft, ships and submarines lost and damaged. Although there was a serious feeling on board as *QE2* steamed south, there was lightheartedness too. One of the main sources of amusement was the snippets the troops added to the boards. They included jokes and comments, some of them rather rude about officers and NCOs, witty poems and trivial rhymes. The information board and Falklands map were an invaluable source of information for all on board. An amusing cartoon drawn by a member of the Scots Guards showed two guardsmen relaxing in full combat gear on a beach, being served a drink by a smartly dressed waiter with a tray. A group of penguins are stood nearby. The caption read, 'Good idea to bring Bob along, Jock!'

After the ship had left Ascension Island, a BBC documentary video that had been flown from the UK was screened in the Queens Room. It was called *A Queen Goes to War* and covered *QE2*'s sailing from Southampton.

Hundreds of troops and crew watched the video. Many were very vocal in expressing their opinions of the commentary. The BBC World Service radio was listened to attentively as the ship sailed into the South Atlantic. Reception of the service was excellent throughout the voyage and it became the main source of news of the conflict. The news was relayed daily to the Theatre Bar, Queens Room, Double Room, Columbia Restaurant and the Tables of the World Restaurant at 0900, 1100, 1300 and 1600 hours. The service was also available in cabins on the music channel. For those on board, the BBC provided a valued connection across the sea to home. Many found the precise tones of the newsreaders welcome and reassuring. The bulletins were a lifeline reminding everyone that although they were a long way from home, they were not alone. People back home were supporting them and wishing them well.

Back home, Captain Jackson's daughter Marilyn remembers:

One evening I was at my parents' house with Pamela watching the 6 o'clock news, and suddenly we heard my father's voice being transmitted from 'somewhere' below the equator. It seemed odd although perfectly understandable for the mission to be shrouded in secrecy. We followed the news bulletins avidly but with trepidation, knowing what a large target *QE2* might be.

To deal with any possible threat from aircraft, men from the embarked RAF Regiment Squadron set up an anti-aircraft defence system. This involved drilling and welding to fit two mountings on the Bridge wings. The construction work was carried out by employees of Harris Pye Marine, who were signed on to the ship's Articles as contractors. The new mountings held 7.62mm general-purpose machine guns (GPMGs) and Browning 0.5in heavy machine guns. Two GPMGs and four Blowpipe Air Defence missiles were located on each side of the funnel. The Browning machine guns, with the capability of firing around 800 rounds a minute, were manned around the clock. These were the only armaments that the 67,000-ton liner carried for her own protection. Under international law these weapons could only be fired in self-defence. As *QE2* was still a Merchant Navy vessel, it was not allowed to carry offensive weapons. Under international law, if a merchant ship carrying defensive weapons were to use those weapons offensively, then its crew could be treated as unlawful combatants. In the event, however, there was no need for the weapons to be fired in anger. The firing exercises nevertheless added to the noise levels. There were now fewer helicopter flights in order to conserve fuel. While the installation of the armament was taking place, military lookouts armed with rifles were posted from dawn to dusk on each wing of the Bridge and on each side of the funnel.

By now the secret had leaked that the ship was carrying a stock of *QE2* Falklands T-shirts and sweatshirts. The shop staff were increasingly asked when they would be available for purchase, so they decided to break open the stock and launch the sale on 22 May. With nearly 4,000 souls on board, demand was high. The entire stock of 10,000 sold out within twenty-four hours.

Sunday, 23 May turned out to be a day of good weather. The sea was calm with just a few ripples. The visibility was exceptionally good and the horizon was very clear. There were scattered fair weather cumulus clouds visible as far as the eye could see. A church service was held in the Theatre but with only about one-third of the previous Sunday's attendance. Most hands were on the open decks enjoying the sunshine. In order to conserve fuel, flying exercises were not carried out, so the silence added to the tranquillity of the day. At lunchtime the officers invited all ladies on board to the Wardroom for drinks.

As *QE2* headed south on the last leg of her outward voyage, more safety precautions were put in place. On the Bridge, the radars were turned off and the ship was electronically silenced. To compensate, extra lookouts were posted on the Bridge wings. Radar is a great boon to navigation and for the detection of other vessels, but transmitted radar waves can be unique to a particular ship and enable it to be identified, so some parts of the radar had been changed to alter the transmission characteristics. This would reduce the chance of *QE2* being detected. With the radars switched off, it would not be easy for the enemy to find the liner.

As another precaution, the ship altered course a number of times when other ships were sighted on the horizon. This was to avoid getting too close and risking the possibility of the whereabouts and direction of the ship being revealed to others.

The watertight doors on Six, Seven and Eight Decks, which previously had been closed only at night, were now shut permanently as the ship steamed closer to the war zone. In addition, the watertight doors along Five Deck passenger accommodation were closed day and night. The doors, which divide the ship into fifteen watertight compartments,

The machine guns mounted on the Bridge wings could be used for defensive purposes only. (Captain P. Jackson)

When the blackout came into force, the Sea King helicopters made night flights around the ship to check that no light could be seen. (R.W. Warwick)

The QE2 in the Falklands War

A Sea King helicopter approaches the stern of *QE2*, which is steaming ahead at 25 knots. (R.W. Warwick)

Capture cards were printed on board and issued to all hands. (R.W. Warwick)

F/Ident/189

If you are captured you are required, under the provisions of Article 17 of the Prisoner of War Convention, 1949, to give your captors the information set out below so that your capture may be reported to your next-of-kin. When you are interrogated, but not before, tear off the duplicate portion and give it to the interrogator. GIVE NO OTHER INFORMATION. *Once this card has been issued to you you must carry it upon you at all times.* In your own interest you must ensure that the particulars of your rank are kept up to date.

(Fill in your particulars in BLOCK LETTERS)

BRITISH FORCES IDENTITY CARD

(Issued in compliance with the provisions of Article 17 of Geneva (POW) Convention, 1949)

SERVICE NUMBER... R892483   RANK... 2ND ENGINEER

SURNAME... CHILLINGWORTH

CHRISTIAN/ FORE NAME(s)... JOHN FRANCIS

DATE OF BIRTH...

BRITISH FORCES IDENTITY CARD

(Issued in compliance with the provisions of Article 17 of Geneva (POW) Convention, 1949)

R892483 (DUPLICATE)

SERVICE NUMBER... RANK... 2ND ENGINEER

SURNAME... CHILLINGWORTH

CHRISTIAN/ FORE NAME(s)... JOHN FRANCIS

DATE OF BIRTH...

St.S.   S50717

All crew members were issued with a British Forces Identity Card to complete and keep in their possession. This image shows the identity card of the second engineer officer. (John Chillingworth)

Brigade officers gather together for a meeting on the helicopter deck. (R. Smith)

With the blackout in force, meetings were held on deck when the weather was favourable. (Captain P. Jackson)

Four members of a Welsh Guards mortar crew on the journey south. From left to right: Simon Weston, 58 Hughes, 11 Hughes and Yorkie. Simon Weston was the only soldier in this photograph to survive the war. Tragically, the other three died in the fire on board RFA *Sir Galahad*. (Republished with the kind permission of Simon Weston)

QE2 engineer officer Steve Arnold shares a few moments with three Gurkha soldiers. (Steve Arnold)

Uniform patch badge with the crest of 5 Infantry Brigade: a key crossed over a bayonet on a red background. (R.W. Warwick)

There were many humorous contributions to the noticeboards around the ship This cartoon was drawn by a Scots Guard as the ship sailed south. (R.W. Warwick)

All hands were encouraged to spend some time on the open deck when the blackout was in force. (Ken Henderson)

A stairwell provided a space for band practice. (R.W. Warwick)

Choir practice in the Two Deck rotunda provided some respite. (Patrick Hewetson)

The crew and members of the Brigade joined forces to entertain each other on the journey south. (R.W. Warwick)

Freetown to South Georgia

A relaxing time for some while on duty: flight deck crew await the landing of the RAF Sea King near Ascension Island. (Stephen Hallam)

Sweatshirts and T-shirts in black, blue, white and beige were offered for sale in the shop. The entire stock was sold out before arrival at Grytviken. (David Luke)

could be operated by the officer of the watch on the Bridge and could also be operated locally or by manual hydraulic pumps on Four Deck.

QE2's twenty lifeboats were swung out by their davits from the stowage position and left lowered at embarkation level with the Boat Deck. In this position, personnel would be able to board the boats very quickly, thus saving valuable time in an emergency.

To maintain a high level of fitness, the troops continued to jog around the Boat Deck daily. NCOs shouted at the troops to motivate and encourage them. Occasionally, an NCO would break the rhythm of the troops' jogging, ordering them to walk before shouting another order to start jogging again. Some of the off-duty crew looked down from their sunbathing deck near the dog kennels, known to the crew as the 'doggy deck'. Some soldiers put in extra roadwork, running after their scheduled training sessions had finished. This period of fitness training in the equatorial latitudes with the sun beating down was very different to the conditions under which the troops would operate on the Falklands during the southern hemisphere's winter.

One evening, the troops hosted a concert in the ship's Theatre comprising a series of acts, including a Scots guitarist and a stand-up comedian from the Welsh Guards. The atmosphere was not one of complete levity, with many in the audience preoccupied with what lay ahead. While some of the laughter was buoyant, some was nervous. But the Welsh Guardsman gave it his best shot and told some good gags. The finale was some bagpipe music from the Scots Guards. That day the menu for the troops was cream of leek soup, brisket of beef with lima beans and potatoes, cold meats, salad and apple pie with custard.

Crew members discussed the course of the conflict and speculated on the ship's future movements. The work routine of many crew was similar to a normal voyage but with some important differences. For example, finance officer David Luke was tasked with accounting for the food and drink consumed during the voyage so that the cost could be charged back to the Ministry of Defence via the Cunard accounts office in Southampton. The special accounting charge code adopted for the voyage was 999.

Hotel officer Terry Foskett processed an order from 5 Infantry Brigade for the printing of 4,000 capture cards for the troops to use if they became prisoners of war. This card required the soldiers to enter their personal details, name of next of kin, the camp or hospital where the prisoner was being held and any health details they might wish to disclose. If the card

Freetown to South Georgia

was used, it was to be sent to the International Committee of the Red Cross in Geneva. The ship's printers, led by Islay Sinclair, were kept busy printing a number of other items for the military, including daily orders for 5 Infantry Brigade, 500 street plans of Port Stanley, 500 copies of twenty different photographs of Argentine aircraft, guns and other equipment, and 1,000 medical forms for the Royal Army Medical Corps. The printers had been unaware of the extra demands that would be placed on them but completed all work in full, and on time.

The weather grew increasingly chilly as *QE2* encountered the winter of the southern hemisphere. No reports had been received of icebergs when the ship departed from Ascension Island. It was anticipated that there would be icebergs in the South Atlantic, but it was not known where or how far south.

Many live-firing exercises were held at the end of the day from the aft flight deck or from One Deck. In the early part of the voyage, soldiers would fire at rubbish thrown over the side of the ship. The shop staff would help by providing used cardboard boxes for targets during the drills. Bosun's mate Frank Parkinson remembers throwing bags of rubbish into the sea from Two Deck aft during shooting practice. As a reward, the shop staff and Frank were allowed supervised sessions firing weapons from the aft helicopter deck.

A long-standing favourite activity for *QE2* passengers was trap shooting. The clay pigeon apparatus was installed at the extreme stern of the ship on One Deck. Shortly after departure from Southampton, carpenter Bill Bailey was talking to some soldiers. One mentioned he had seen the trap catapults, which would be good for target practice if there were any clays available. Fortunately, the clays had not been offloaded in Southampton and Bill knew where they were kept. He provided access to them and the Brigade used them as targets. The troops were thus able to aim at moving aerial targets as well as targets in the water. For helping out the troops, Bill Bailey, an experienced clay shooter, was also allowed a spell firing guns from the aft end of the ship.

Some other crew also managed a spell of target practice. Senior mechanic Paul Fisher recalls observing a firing practice session from Two Deck aft:

The guns were very loud and a sight to see. Every tenth round was a red tracer bullet. When practice was over, they all left except the sergeant who was dismantling one of the guns that had jammed. I went to have a chat with him. After he had reassembled the gun, he handed it to me so I could have a go. I fired a few rounds, an experience I won't forget.

The captain's secretary, Judy Carpenter, remembers firing an SLR which 'had a hell of a kick'.

Tuesday, 25 May saw a change in the weather. It was getting cooler, so the rig of the day was changed from tropical whites to blues. Jogging around the Boat Deck continued even when there were heavy rain squalls, with soldiers continuing their circuits in full kit despite getting cold and drenched. There was an increase in the number of crew willing to participate in training exercises on lifeboat and raft launching. The engineer officers were instructed to carry out extra checks and servicing on the lifeboat engines. As the day drew to a close, fog patches began to surround the ship.

At noon on 26 May, the ship was in position 47°59' south, 25°20' west and the air temperature which had been steadily falling was now down to 5°C. Soon it was near zero with a wind chill factor far lower than that. The ship's supply of cold weather gear was increasingly in demand. The sky was now overcast, which was an advantage as any Argentine reconnaissance aircraft looking for *QE2* would have difficulties sighting her. However, the risk of Argentine submarines was another danger to be borne in mind. There was speculation on board that the British did not know the exact location of two of the Argentine submarines. Were they in port in Argentina or had they been sent to intercept *QE2*? Would they be waiting for the ship at South Georgia?

Ammunition and stores continued to be unloaded from the holds for distribution to the troops as their personal issue. The holds on *QE2* were designed to carry cars and a small amount of freight and were accessed from the fore deck when the ship was in port. Any movement of stores while the ship was at sea had to be carried out through small internal doors which, in most cases, opened into passenger areas. Because of this, there was a constant stream of trolleys up and down the passageways from the forward holds, which caused unavoidable damage to floor coverings and bulkheads.

The closer *QE2* came to the war zone, the keener was the attention paid to her by the international media. The news as the ship sailed south from Ascension Island was both good and bad. While a bridgehead had been successfully established at San Carlos, the loss of ships was high. Those listening to the BBC World Service heard that air raids against British shipping were intense with the pilots of Argentinian aircraft being taxed to the limit. On 21 May, HMS *Ardent* (Commander A.W.J. West) was bombed in Falkland Sound and sunk with the loss of twenty-two lives. On 23 May, HMS *Antelope* (Commander N.J. Tobin) was destroyed by an Argentine air force bomb in San Carlos water with the loss of two lives. On 25 May, HMS *Coventry* (Captain D. Hart Dyke) was bombed to the north of West Falkland and sunk with the loss of nineteen men.

The Cunard-owned merchant ship *Atlantic Conveyor* (Captain Ian H. North) was destroyed after being struck by two Exocet missiles on 25 May. The casualties were substantial, with the loss of the ship's master and eleven other members of the ship's company – over one third of her total crew complement of thirty-three souls. The loss of *Atlantic Conveyor* caused particular dismay since some *QE2* crew had friends serving on board. Captain North, a highly respected Merchant Navy master mariner, was the last man to leave his ship. The senior Royal Navy officer of embarked NP1840, Captain Michael G. Leyard RN, saw him getting into the water and approaching a life raft. He did not see him again. Captain North was posthumously awarded the Distinguished Service Cross. He is remembered on the new *Atlantic Conveyor*, launched in 1984, with the officers' bar named 'The North Bar'.

Atlantic Conveyor, launched in 1969, was the first British merchant ship lost to enemy action since the Second World War. There was a sharp realisation on board *QE2* that not all Cunard ships and crew would return home. Second Officer Paul Jowett recalls that Captain North had been a mentor to him and many others who had joined the Cunard Line. The ship's loss was both a human tragedy and a huge logistical setback to the military operation to recapture the islands. *Atlantic Conveyor* had been carrying ration packs and tents. She carried Harrier aircraft as well as a mobile airstrip to enable them to land at the beachhead. She was also carrying three Chinook and six Wessex helicopters[93] to transport troops to the front line. Fortunately, the Harriers were offloaded before the attack, but all the helicopters except one Chinook were lost.

This news impressed to all on board the seriousness and danger of the operation as the ship sped south. The crew and the Brigade became increasingly aware of the reality of the situation in which they were immersed. Tim Castle of the cruise staff recalls that as the task force started to lose ships, it became clear that 5 Infantry Brigade might be essential to winning the war, which would make *QE2* an even more valuable target. With these thoughts of danger in mind, he made a point of getting to know the locations of fire-fighting equipment as he walked around the ship.

Back in Southampton, Cunard fleet personnel manager Dennis Shepherd travelled to Gosport to comfort the family of a crew member lost on *Atlantic Conveyor*. The fleet personnel office did their best to keep relatives back home informed of what was happening with all Cunard ships, although inevitably the company was constrained in what it knew and what could be said. A letter signed by personnel manager Arnie Williams was sent to all *QE2* next of kin on 26 May:

> All communications with the ship are in the hands of the Ministry of Defence and in the main we are no better informed about her whereabouts than what one reads in the newspapers. We know however that she has passed the Ascension Islands [*sic*]. We have received a report back from the Ascension Islands that all is proceeding normally on board the ship and that everybody, both crew and military, are in good spirits.[94]

The letter goes on to say:

> We are liaising with the Missions to Seamen who have put their welfare services at our disposal and you will no doubt have a card from them within the next few days ... All of us in Cunard Line are proud that the *Queen Elizabeth 2* is performing such an important role in the Falklands crisis and we ashore have nothing but admiration for those members of our sea staff who so readily agreed to sail with the ship to the South Atlantic.[95]

The Missions to Seamen is a Christian welfare charity dedicated to serving and supporting the seafarers of the Merchant Navy. The Missions to Seamen sent a brief card to all next of kin that read:

> We understand that you may have a relative or friend on a vessel requisitioned for Falklands Islands' duties. If we can be of any help at this time please do not hesitate to contact your local Chaplain or Regional Director.[96]

It was now clear that Grytviken in South Georgia was *QE2*'s destination, where 5 Infantry Brigade would disembark. The decision by the British government to recapture South Georgia before the Falklands surprised many. In the big scheme of things, South Georgia could be seen as unimportant; a remote outpost with no permanent civilian population and irrelevant to the main objective of capturing the Falklands. But, unbeknown to those on board *QE2*, the decision had been taken that the liner would not be allowed to go in close to the Falklands and run the risk of aerial attack. The ship was to stay well outside the range of Argentine fighter aircraft. There was a requirement for a secure harbour where *QE2* could anchor and be sheltered from severe weather as 5 Infantry Brigade was transferred to other ships. There was only one place in the whole of the South Atlantic fitting those requirements and that was South Georgia. So for 5 Infantry Brigade to reach the Falklands, the island of South Georgia first had to be recaptured. British forces reclaimed South Georgia on 25 April.

The second on-board edition of the news magazine *The Leek* was produced by the Welsh Guards. The magazine contained a message from the commanding officer, Lieutenant Colonel John Rickett, who affirmed his full confidence in the troops under his command:

> I know that whatever we are required to do, we will carry it out to the very best of our ability in the finest tradition of our regiment. We are trained and prepared both physically and mentally; our morale is sky high and we are thoroughly confident. I wish you all the very best of luck; do your duty. May God bless us all.[97]

Much of the magazine displayed the humour of the Welsh Guards as they prepared to disembark. One report referred to the recent 'crossing the line' ceremony, noting that No. 3 Platoon had devoted 'considerable energy in throwing their Platoon Commander Second Lieutenant Black into the swimming pool, with guardsman Hunter giggling in the background'. Readers were informed of a change of accommodation for two NCOs: 'Lance Corporal Cordy and Lance Corporal Brinkworth are both very happy now that they have found suitable accommodation in the Dogs Kennels beneath the funnel.' There were phrases to use when encountering Argentine soldiers on the battlefield, along with translations into

Spanish. Useful conversation-openers included 'Take me to your Rugby Officer', 'Have you got a brother living in Cardiff?' and 'Do you want buy a white flag?' There was a reference to the recent FA Cup final that Tottenham Hotspur had won, beating Queens Park Rangers, but without their star Argentine player, Osvaldo Ardiles: 'Tottenham didn't need Ardiles' (with the helpful translation *'Tottenham no nesesitaba Ardiles!'*). The magazine included a prayer contributed by the padre.

As *QE2* sailed closer to the active war zone, the navigators on the Bridge began to vary the course of the ship. While generally heading southerly, they adopted a form of steering known as zig-zagging. This was the practice of frequently and at irregular intervals altering direction to port or starboard. This form of steering was designed to confuse the enemy by disguising the true course.

Carpenter Bill Bailey was approached by a soldier who occupied one of the larger passenger cabins on One Deck. The soldier had loaded ammunition into his gun without first engaging the safety catch. The gun accidentally discharged a bullet, which penetrated the headboard above the bed. The soldier was anxious as the unauthorised discharge of a weapon is a serious offence and he would have been put on a disciplinary charge if an NCO or officer had found out. Could the carpenters help? Bill Bailey and his fellow carpenter Bob Farmer dismantled the headboard and saw that the bullet had gone through the upholstery and its wooden support and was embedded into the aluminium bulkhead. They removed the bullet and then fitted a new wooden support with foam upholstery and silk fabric covering. By the time they had finished, there was no evidence a bullet had been discharged in the cabin.

Below decks, Chief Officer Warwick spent a few hours with military officers planning the disembarkation of troops, equipment and stores in South Georgia. As the ship had been observing radio silence since passing Ascension Island, it was not possible to exchange messages to agree a plan with other ships.

Bosun Charlie Thomas and his team set about preparing to transfer troops using the ship's lifeboats. Four of the larger and more spacious Harding Launches were stripped of some statutory lifesaving equipment to make as much room as possible for troops and their gear. The Hardings had powerful engines and two propellers and were able to travel much faster than the regular lifeboats. Under normal circumstances, these launches were used to ferry passengers ashore when the liner anchored

Freetown to South Georgia

The service elevators were used for the removal of stores from the cargo hold in readiness for transfer to other ships. (R. Smith)

Some of the stores and equipment were moved to the ship's side doors on Five Deck, ready to be passed over to the trawlers when the liner arrived in Grytviken. (R. Smith)

outside a port of call – for instance, if the harbour was too small for *QE2* to enter.

Preparations for the disembarkation of the Brigade were also being made in other departments. The chief cashier Stephen Ward carried out his last official transaction with the Army paymaster, who along with his staff had taken over Barclays Bank on Two Deck. Stephen cashed him a large government cheque so that the troops would have adequate funds available after the cessation of hostilities. In effect, he was giving back to the paymaster cash that the troops had spent on the journey south. Money had flowed into the ship's safe from cash receipts as soldiers purchased their daily allowance of two cans of beer, paid for haircuts and bought snacks and souvenirs from the shop. Stephen recalls:

> A moving transaction was when I cashed a cheque for one of the helicopter pilots just before he departed. The young man didn't say a word, obviously lost in the thoughts of his responsibilities and what was about to come his way.

As the ship approached South Georgia, the ship's crew and the Brigade started the process of saying goodbye and wishing one another well. Sue Crozier and other members of the crew gave black garbage bags to many of the troops to enable them to waterproof their personal effects in their backpacks. Waiter Jeremy Letherbarrow had become friendly with three of the Royal Artillery officers whom he served every day in the Queens Grill. Two days before arrival at Grytviken, the three officers asked Jeremy if he could take possession of their dress uniforms after they disembarked. He agreed and met the officers, giving them a bottle of red wine. The officers gave him a navy-blue Army officer's belt with a crimson stripe which Jeremy has kept to this day. It was agreed that the officers would collect their uniforms after the war from the Letherbarrow family home in the New Forest. The chief officer gave Major Brendon Lambe a bottle of port for his onward journey. Several months after the conflict was over, the officers met up and Brendon said he'd had to guard the port with his life.

Later in the afternoon of 26 May, crew member David Humphreys went on the forecastle head for some fresh air. He made his way underneath the forward helicopter deck to the port bow, where he looked out and saw an iceberg with a tall, jagged edge close to the horizon. It appeared to be an isolated berg and its presence gave no cause for concern. However, as the evening approached it was becoming colder as the temperature continued to fall. No one on board knew it but more ice lay ahead of *QE2*.

That evening after dinner, Brigadier Wilson was presented with a picture of the ship signed by the restaurant manager, head waiters and waiters of the Queens Grill. Brigadier Wilson thanked the crew for volunteering and looking after the troops. The Brigade had brought on board more maps of the Falklands than they needed, so many of the catering staff obtained copies which they then asked Brigade members to sign. Head waiter Andrew Nelder collected 320 signatures on his map. Some of the restaurant crew surreptitiously passed souvenirs to the officers, including *QE2* silverware. Speeches were made by officers dining in the Queens Grill. Major General Jeremy Moore said a few words and then called forward the youngest member of the ship's company, waiter Stephen Easter, and presented him with a wall chart. The chart had been prepared by 81 Intelligence Section and was a map of the Falklands with the words 'Operation Corporate'.

Towards the midnight hour, mist patches set in and visibility was substantially reduced. At midnight the deck officers changed their watch. First Officer Bob Hayward and Second Officer Chris Haughton took over the 12 to 4 watch. At the start of their watch, the radars were on standby. But due to the reduced visibility, every fifteen minutes or so the officers would switch the radars on to do an occasional sweep and see if any targets showed up in the vicinity. If all was clear, the radars were switched back to standby to avoid the risk of the liner being detected. Later during the watch, when Chris Haughton switched on the radar to do a sweep, he observed three faint targets about 12 miles ahead. On the radar they had the same appearance that small ships might present and at first it was thought they could be fishing trawlers, or possibly Russian intelligence vessels masquerading as trawlers. The number of targets soon multiplied and it quickly became apparent that *QE2* was entering a large ice field to the north-east of South Georgia. First Officer Hayward alerted Captain Jackson, who came to the Bridge. The changed conditions meant that *QE2*'s arrival in Grytviken would be delayed. A brief signal was sent advising that due to poor visibility and the presence of ice, the ship was steaming at reduced speed and would be late at the rendezvous.

The risk of hitting an iceberg had now to be weighed against the risk of revealing the position of the ship to the enemy. The risk of attack from a fighter aircraft was slim as no Argentine fighter aircraft could operate so far east and have sufficient fuel to return safely to Argentina without inflight refuelling. However, it was known that Argentina had reconnaissance aircraft with the capability of reaching *QE2*'s position, namely a C130 Hercules and a Boeing 707. Captain Jackson consulted with his officers and judged that navigating through the ice field with the radar switched off was a greater risk than possibly revealing the ship's position because the radar was switched on. They noted that if there were Argentine submarines patrolling the area, they would have to proceed in the ice field with equal caution. Captain James was appraised of the situation and agreed with the decision to activate the radars. This proved to be a wise move as more and more icebergs appeared on the radar screen. They could not be seen visually in the darkness, so the ship continued to move cautiously. At one stage, the ship slowed to a speed of 4 knots as Captain Jackson and his deck officers navigated *QE2* through this formidable natural hazard.

During the rest of the night, numerous icebergs, some of massive proportions, loomed out of the darkness. The ship evaded small icebergs and gave a wide berth to the huge tabular bergs with steep sides and flat tops. If the ship had collided with one of these great masses of ice, it would have suffered considerable damage.

By daylight the imminent danger was past, although one huge berg could still be seen 7 miles from *QE2* towering above the low-lying mist. It was so huge that it looked like the white cliffs of Dover, while other bergs resembled cathedral spires rising from the ocean. It had taken nearly six hours to navigate the ice field. The fog was still thick but patchy. Lieutenant Philip Rentell later wrote, 'When dawn broke we were rewarded with the spectacular sight of huge bergs visible above the mists, the sunrise creating wonderful shades of red, orange and yellow reflected from the normal blue-white ice.'[98] After what those on the Bridge had just experienced in the South Atlantic, it was difficult not to remember the fate of RMS *Titanic* after she struck ice on her maiden voyage in 1912.

Very few people on board had any idea of the peril that *QE2* faced. Most slept through it all. But the drama on the Bridge was real enough. Captain Jackson later commented, 'Never have I known such a harrowing experience.' The following morning, the captain's secretary, Judy Carpenter, wrote in her diary, 'thick fog and icebergs – viewed one iceberg from Two Deck which was much larger than the ship and very close!' Guardsman Simon Weston watched the icebergs on deck with some mates, later recalling, 'the beauty and size and sheer brooding menace of those great white tower-blocks somehow brought home to us what we were involved in, and what we were about to do – nobody spoke'.[99]

Entries in the ship's logbook recorded the hazardous position the ship was in, using mariners' phrases such as 'ice routine' and 'evasive steering in use'. While accurate, these understated logbook entries fail to convey the tension on the Bridge and the peril of the situation.

Expert seamanship saw *QE2* through the ice field that night. Paul Wooller, a waiter, described his emotions:

My enduring memory of my time during the Falklands conflict was the peace and serenity among the icebergs as we made our way through them, especially at night with a billion stars illuminating the sky and thinking not too far away carnage and chaos was happening.

Brigadier Wilson was due to leave the ship that day. He showed his appreciation of the ship's crew by penning a parting message in the newsletter produced daily as the ship steamed south:

Very shortly we shall all transfer to other ships off South Georgia and start on the last phase of our move to the Falkland Islands. It looks as if the Brigade will arrive there by about 1st June, that is early next week. Once there, we shall join 3 Commando Brigade. We shall sort ourselves out; and then start joint operations to recapture the Islands. Orders will be given out on landing … This is the final issue of this newspaper, and to the Master and ship's company of *QE2* I would say 'Thank you' for the way you have looked after us on this voyage. We have come to know you well, we admire you, and we shall always be proud that we sailed with you in your magnificent ship. To the Brigade I would simply say this: we shall start earning our pay as a team shortly; and we are in this game to win.[100]

Upon reading this, some of the ship's catering ratings approached the kitchen clerk, Charles Dunn, and asked him to write a message by way of response to Brigadier Wilson. Charles sat at his desk in the galley office and typed a message to the Brigadier on Cunard notepaper, part of which read:

I can assure you, Sir, that we without reservation, have never during our service with Cunard, and *QE2* in particular, EVER had such well behaved or appreciative 'Passengers' as we have with us at this time. The tokens of appreciation by way of thanks, their cheerfulness, and above all, their awareness of this present difficult situation, does them proud, and indeed confirms your faith in them as a Fighting Force to be reckoned with. Our hearts and prayers go with them and you as you leave us, and we pray for a rapid end to this conflict.[101]

The message illustrated the respect and goodwill of the ship's company towards all in 5 Infantry Brigade. Many soldiers in the Brigade expressed their appreciation of their time on board. Sergeant Rab McQuarrie remembers:

I sailed as a medic. All memories of my time on board were good ones. The staff bent over backwards to be as nice as humanly possible to us. The accommodation and food were absolutely first class. It will be a voyage none of us will ever forget.

The main event for the morning of 27 May was a rendezvous with the Royal Navy destroyer HMS *Antrim* (Captain B.G. Young RN) to transfer Major General Moore, Brigadier Wilson and their headquarters staff officers. It was planned for early morning but was delayed because of the hazards of the previous night. The rendezvous eventually took place in the afternoon in a position near 52°50' south, 34°59' west. It was very cloudy. Indeed, so dense was the cloud bank on the horizon that at first glance it could be mistaken for coastline. As the two ships manoeuvred towards each other, the mist gave welcome cover against the risk of attack. Captain James expressed his relief that there was a now a warship close by with the capability to hit back at an attacker.

By now HMS *Antrim* was a well-travelled veteran of the conflict, having been involved in the battle for South Georgia. Her exterior was distinctly weather beaten and the battles she had fought were highlighted by a line of cannon shell holes down her sides. A large hole was clearly visible in the aft end of the vessel, the result of an unexploded Argentinian bomb during the San Carlos landings. The bomb had lodged in the missile magazine but fortunately did not detonate. Had the bomb exploded, it is likely that *Antrim* would have had her stern blown off and the ship been abandoned.

One of her helicopters had disabled the Argentine submarine *Santa Fe* (Captain Horacio Bicain). *Santa Fe* managed to limp into Grytviken and eventually sank alongside the whaling station jetty. The whereabouts of submarines had been one of the big uncertainties of *QE2*'s journey south. Had *Antrim* not detected and disabled *Santa Fe*, there was the real possibility that the submarine could have remained in the vicinity of South Georgia to attack *QE2* and the other British ships assembled in the anchorage area.

Antrim crew member David Yates described how 'crowds of us poured onto the upper deck to see the ship we had all heard so much about, and yet most of us had never seen'.[102] From *Antrim* the first part of *QE2* that could be seen was her funnel, peering above the low-lying mist. Lieutenant Christopher J. Parry RN, a helicopter observer on board HMS *Antrim*, witnessed the arrival:

> ... the scene was dramatic as the huge, impressive ship just loomed out of a bank of sea fog, funnel and superstructure first, about four miles away ... The whole scene, centred on the most famous, most iconic liner in the world sailing in the depths of the Southern Ocean and off such a strange shore, made you want to pinch yourself to make sure you were not dreaming.[103]

Antrim kept a radar lookout to the west for long-range Argentine aircraft that might pose a threat to the two ships. Major General Moore, Brigadier Wilson and their staff officers left *QE2* by helicopter. The goal was for Major General Moore to be able to communicate with Admiral Sandy Woodward en route to the Falkland Islands so that plans for deploying 5 Infantry Brigade could be finalised. For two hours the Sea King helicopters flew back and forth, transferring personnel and stores between the two ships.

Two of *QE2*'s Harding lifeboats transported men and equipment, with forty people in each. Bosun's mate Frank Parkinson was in charge of the party that lowered the first lifeboat from the Boat Deck. A mechanic was assigned to each launch to deal with any engine problems that might arise. Paul Fisher was the mechanic in the first launch lowered. The sea had been relatively calm when *QE2* and *Antrim* rendezvoused, but by the time the launches were lowered the swell had increased to several feet high, which made casting off the launches from the davit falls a tricky manoeuvre. Disembarkation from the launches onto *Antrim* proved to be treacherous. Paul Fisher recalls that after travelling the short distance between the two ships:

> We manoeuvred the launch alongside *Antrim* where rope ladders had been thrown over the side for our passengers. I was in the wheelhouse of the launch whilst they were getting off. As one lad jumped for the rope ladder, the launch rose with the swell then crashed against the *Antrim* crushing his legs.

The unfortunate warrant officer suffered a broken leg. This incident was also witnessed by *Antrim* crew member David Yates, who saw the soldier miss his footing and slip between lifeboat and warship.[104] The war was over for him and he returned to *QE2* by helicopter, where he was stretchered to the hospital. The remainder of the men were transferred safely. A total of eighty-eight personnel were transferred to the *Antrim*.

During the rendezvous Lieutenant Parry visited *QE2* to liaise with the 5 Infantry Brigade staff officers to make sure that their needs and requirements would be met on board *Antrim* as she sailed back to the battle zone. He noted how *QE2* had been stripped bare of luxury fittings and was struck by the smell of military equipment, noting, 'I wasn't expecting a smell like that on a cruise ship.' In the Queens Grill Lounge, now the Army officers' bar, he met with some Welsh Guards officers who at first mistook him for an NCO. They briefly discussed the role that the Guards might play after they landed on the Falklands.[105] Over forty years after the conflict, Lieutenant Parry recalls how accommodating the crew were. He asked for a cup of tea from a passing crew member, who swiftly returned with a pot of tea. Lieutenant Parry also took advantage of being on the ship to meet briefly with colleagues from 825 Naval Air Squadron on the flight deck.

Word reached *QE2* that *Antrim* was running low on envelopes. Accounts petty officer David Humphreys responded by sending 1,000 foolscap envelopes along with a batch of *QE2* postcards as souvenirs for *Antrim*'s crew. The opportunity was taken to replenish some of *Antrim*'s depleted stocks of food, drink and confectionery. *QE2* also delivered sacks of mail for *Antrim* and other task force ships which had been carried down from Ascension Island. Mail from *Antrim* was received on board *QE2* to be taken north. By 1337 hours all transfers had been completed and the two ships parted company. The recovery of *QE2*'s launches proved difficult with the heavy swell. Considerable stress was placed on the falls as the weight of the launch came on them suddenly between the rise and fall of the swell waves. Stress was transmitted up to the davit head, causing a fracture in the bedding plate.

Brigadier Wilson penned a farewell and thank you message in the final edition of 5 Infantry Brigade *QE2 News*. (R.W. Warwick)

The QE2 in the Falklands War

Waiters and officers from 5 Infantry Brigade at a presentation in the Queens Grill after the Brigade's final dinner on board. Brigadier Tony Wilson was presented with a portrait of *QE2* signed by the restaurant staff and waiters. Brigadier Wilson is to the right of the portrait. Presenting the portrait on the left is head waiter Jonathan Norton. (Andrew Nelder)

Those on board never tired of watching helicopter activities, such as the rendezvous at sea with HMS *Antrim*. (Ken Henderson)

Freetown to South Georgia

R.M.S. Queen Elizabeth 2
Saturday 29th May 1982

Breakfast

Chilled Fruit Juice

Oatmeal Porridge — Assorted Cereals

Boiled and Scrambled Eggs

Breakfast Bacon

Fillet of Smoked Codling

Preserves

Bread — Toast — Scones

Tea or Coffee

This was the final breakfast on board *QE2* for many of the troops. (Andrew Nelder)

The QE2 in the Falklands War

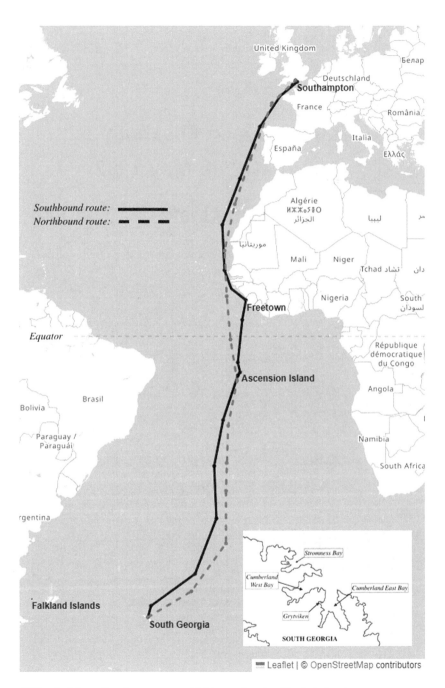

QE2 sailed from Southampton on 12 May and arrived back in her home port twenty-nine days later on 11 June 1982. During her time away, the liner steamed 14,967 nautical miles. (OpenStreetMap)

Captain Peter Jackson, master of *QE2*. (R.W. Warwick)

The day after departure, the Sea King pilots carried out flying exercises to familiarise themselves with the new landing areas. (Patrick Hewetson)

The initiation of those crossing 'the line' is now well under way. (R.W. Warwick)

Witnesses to King Neptune's visit provided one of the most spectacular photographs of the voyage with soldiers cramming every vantage point including the unprotected Bridge roof. (Patrick Hewetson)

On occasions, an instructor would conduct the exercise routines. (Captain P. Jackson)

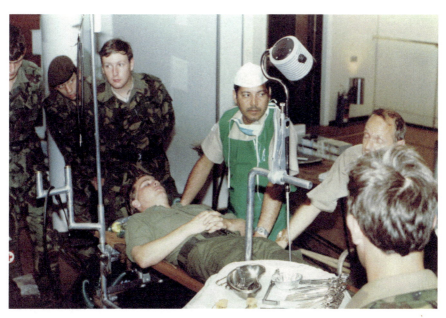
The Brigade's medical teams carried out training exercises at locations around the ship. (Patrick Hewetson)

The rendezvous with HMS *Dumbarton Castle* on the southbound voyage took place near Ascension Island on a hot day with light cloud cover. (Stephen Hallam)

Another delivery of equipment by helicopter in the Ascension Island area. (R.W. Warwick)

QE2's aft helicopter deck had plenty of room for a Chinook helicopter to land, carrying more troops to complement 5 Infantry Brigade. (Captain P. Jackson)

A chain gang was formed to unload mail, stores and equipment from the Chinook helicopter. (R. Smith)

As the liner headed further south, a platform was constructed on each Bridge wing for 7.62mm general-purpose machine guns. Similar equipment was mounted each side of her funnel. (Patrick Hewetson)

A few of the ship's crew were able to take a flight in one of the helicopters and take a unique photograph of their ship. (R.W. Warwick)

Taking in the sun while lying on top of military stores! (R.W. Warwick)

Stores stowed on the helicopter deck are moved down to the flight deck ready for offloading. (R. Smith)

The ammunition stowed on Signal Deck had to be manhandled by chain gang down five decks to the helicopter landing area. (R. Smith)

Icebergs surround the liner as she approaches her destination of Grytviken, South Georgia. (R. Smith)

Troops assemble in the Queens Room for the final time while they await the call to disembark. (R. Smith)

The Sea Kings and ship's launches were used to transfer troops and some equipment to HMS *Antrim*. Major General Moore, Brigadier Wilson and their staff officers joined *Antrim* by helicopter while others were transferred by launch. (R. Smith)

QE2 seen from one of the other ships anchored in Cumberland East Bay. (Bernard Mennell)

RFA *Resource* (left) manoeuvring near the Cunard cargo ship *Saxonia* with red funnel. On the right, the Fortuna Glacier meets the sea. (Stephen Hallam)

One of the Sea Kings of 825 Naval Air Squadron preparing to take off with an underslung load. The two Sea Kings would soon leave *QE2* and join *Canberra*. (R. Smith)

The sun set shortly after 1600 hours during *QE2*'s stay in Grytviken. The low cloud base in the bay provided some protection from aerial surveillance. (Malcolm Scanlan)

As the liner heads home, baker Stephen Hallam takes centre stage on a calm, sunny day on the now disused flight forward deck. (Stephen Hallam)

The tanker RFA *Bayleaf* prepares to transfer fuel to *QE2*. (Stephen Hallam)

The turbulent sea caused the ships to roll and stretched the fuel pipe during the refuelling. (R.W. Warwick)

As *QE2* passes Ascension Island on the northbound passage, the yellow RAF Sea King made a return visit. By now the paint on the aft helicopter deck is showing signs of erosion. (R.W. Warwick)

Ammunition that remained on board when the liner left Grytviken is unloaded at Ascension from the forward helicopter deck. (Stephen Hallam)

On behalf of the Royal Navy, HMS *Londonderry* welcomed *QE2* home with a twenty-one-gun salute. (Captain P. Jackson)

The survivors gather on the forward deck as the liner approaches the dock. (Captain P. Jackson)

Crowds of family, friends and well-wishers gather along the quay to welcome the ship home. (Stephen Hallam)

In 2004, Commodore Warwick and Captain Jackson meet on the Bridge of *Queen Mary 2*. (Kim Warwick)

In March 2024, twenty-seven *QE2* Falklands veterans enjoyed a reunion in Southampton. *Back row, left–right:* Steve Easter, Lee Wilkinson, Martin Harrison, Dennis Clow, Bill Bailey, Frank Parkinson, Gary Pickering, Thomas Harper, David Humphreys, Sue Crozier, Andy Snell, Tessa Dallyn, Kevin Dunn. *Front row:* Ian Burrell, Terry Foskett, David Luke, Stephen Ward, Judy Carpenter, Clive Dalley, Ron Warwick, Phil Rentell, Jane Yelland, Andrew Nelder, Wendy Marshall, Lesley-Ann Tomlinson, Sylvia Leigh, Maria Callaghan. (Gary Bennett)

10

Grytviken, South Georgia Island

Darkness came at 1700 hours in these southern latitudes as the short South Atlantic winter day gave way to night. After the transfers were finished and the launches recovered, *QE2* bid farewell to HMS *Antrim*. At 1745 hours, the engines were put on stand-by and the approach to Cumberland East Bay, South Georgia, commenced. Once again the ship was navigating through icebergs. The fog thickened to near zero visibility. At 1804 hours, Right Whale Rocks was identified on the radar as 4½ miles away. The depth of water where the ship was to anchor was 360ft.[106] Lieutenant Rentell was assigned to take charge of the mooring operations forward. The anchor windlass had been covered over by the forward flight deck, so with the duty carpenter he had to scramble around and under the supporting structure. Two shackles (180ft) of cable on the starboard anchor were walked back in advance of it being let go. At the planned mooring position, the windlass brake was taken off and the cable was allowed to run freely out of the hawse pipe for another eight shackles. By 1922 hours, the vessel was safely at anchor in Cumberland East Bay, approximately 1 mile from the old whaling station at Grytviken. A minute later the engine telegraph rang 'finished with engines', but the engineer officers below were required to keep them available at immediate notice.

The passage time from Freetown to Grytviken was eight days, twenty hours and twelve minutes, during which time *QE2* had travelled a distance of 5,035 nautical miles. This gave an overall average speed of 23.9 knots, despite the ship having slowed down off Ascension, when rendezvousing with other ships and travelling through ice fields. It was too dark that evening to see anything of the old whaling station and the surrounding coast of Grytviken. South Georgia was the closest the ship would come to the war zone, which was some 800 miles to the west. This was the troops' last night on board. *QE2* had brought the troops this far and now they were leaving. There was a sombre mood throughout the ship.

Among the other vessels in Cumberland East Bay when *QE2* arrived was the P&O liner *Canberra*, the North Sea ferry *Norland* (Captain M. Ellerby), HMS *Leeds Castle* (Lieutenant Commander C.F.B. Hamilton) and the bright-red HMS *Endurance* (Captain N.J. Barker RN). There were also five trawlers fitted out at Rosyth Dockyard as mine sweepers with special communications equipment. Their Merchant Navy crews had been replaced by Royal Navy personnel. Four of the trawlers, *Cordella* (Lieutenant M.C.G. Holloway RN), *Northella* (Lieutenant J.P.S. Greenop RN), *Farnella* (Lieutenant R.J. Bishop RN) and *Junella* (Lieutenant M. Rowledge RN), were hired from J. Marr & Son, Hull. *Pict* (Lieutenant Commander D.G. Garwood RN) was hired from British United Trawlers, Hull. The trawlers now became the new 11th Mine Countermeasures Squadron. They were the only STUFTs during the campaign to fly the White Ensign.[107] The tug *Typhoon* (Captain J.N. Morris) was also on hand to assist. *Typhoon* was the first vessel to leave the UK when the task force was assembled. The role of the trawlers was to transfer troops from *QE2* to other ships in the bay.

Soon after anchoring, Captain Nicholas Barker RN of HMS *Endurance* and also the naval commander of South Georgia, and Captain Christopher Burne RN, the head of Naval Party 1710 on board *Canberra*, boarded *QE2* to meet with Captain James, senior officers from 5 Brigade and Chief Officer Warwick. The meeting, held in the Queen Mary Suite, was convened to agree a plan for the disembarkation of the Brigade. Those on *QE2* proposed that the offloading of cargo begin immediately, since this was likely to consume at least forty-eight hours, with the transfer of troops commencing not in the hazardous and freezing conditions of darkness but waiting a few hours until daylight. A counter proposal was made by Captain Barker and Captain Burne, who wanted the transfer of troops to begin immediately, with the movement of cargo going forward simultaneously. It was noted that the ships in South Georgia were at risk of air attack and that the heaviest anti-aircraft weapons were on board *Leeds Castle*.[108] All involved in the discussion had well-thought-out arguments which, as befitted experienced and professional officers, were expressed concisely, calmly and politely. Eventually, agreement was reached to commence disembarkation as soon as possible.

Security dictated that no overside lights were to be used, so the trawlers came alongside with some difficulty in the darkness. The trawler *Cordella* was the first vessel to make it alongside *QE2* successfully at 2120 hours. Soon after, at 2145 hours, the Welsh Guards commenced boarding the trawler. By 2310 hours, they were on their way across to *Canberra*. The Gurkhas followed and were taken to *Norland*. The Gurkhas were carrying impressive loads of equipment. Gurkha officer Major David Willis recalls that the Gurkhas did not have access to vehicles and could not rely on helicopters, so everything had to be carried:

> The scale of ammunition was 100 rounds of 7.62mm calibre carried in five magazines. Everyone carried an additional reserve of 200 rounds in their backpacks including a belt of machine gun ammunition. On top of this men carried their share of grenades, mortar bombs, projectiles for the anti-tank weapons and trip flares.

Both the liner and the trawlers lost some paint during the night. A start was also made on discharging military cargo including ammunition from No. 1 Hatch. But offloading was just too difficult in the darkness, and the bulk of the work had to be put off until daylight. The tug *Typhoon* came alongside next, followed by an attempt by HMS *Leeds Castle*. The plan to use *Leeds Castle* to ferry troops to other ships was fraught with difficulty when her mast made contact with *QE2*'s overhanging bridge wing as she tried to manoeuvre alongside.

For *QE2*'s crew the disembarkation of the soldiers was a moving time. Sue Crozier was in the Queens Room with the Welsh Guards shortly before they disembarked and felt emotional about their departure. She was composed until the orderly quiet was broken by the troops singing. 'I was weeping buckets,' Sue later recalled. Stewardess Elena Littlehales was in the Theatre that evening watching a film. Also watching were some Welsh Guards. Halfway through the film, guardsmen started to leave their seats and exit the Theatre. To Elena this was the first indication that something was up. At the end of the film, the Theatre was nearly empty except for *QE2* crew. It had now become clear that the Welsh Guards were preparing to leave that evening. Elena made her way up to the Boat Deck where

The QE2 in the Falklands War

many of the ship's crew had gathered to watch the Welsh Guards disembark. Hairdresser Timothy Williams recalls the chill cold in the air and the mist around the ship as the soldiers disembarked. He told himself he would have to remember what was happening that night because it would never happen again. Captain's secretary Judy Carpenter recalls the evening:

> It was very dark and foggy. Throughout the night we transferred troops to the *Canberra* and *Norland*. I remember standing on deck, watching all the activity, my heart sinking for our VIP passengers now off to battle.

Able Seaman Tom Young was on duty by the gangway:

> On the night the troops left the *QE2* they were in single file along the alleyway. It was so eerie you could hear a pin drop. Nobody said a word apart from thanks and goodbye as they walked past me to get in the tender. It is something that will always stick with me.

Pierre Cornlouer gave two cans of beer to a Welsh Guard, who replied, 'Thanks. I'll drink these when we get to Stanley.' Clive Dalley gave *QE2* T-shirts, pin badges and cigarettes to some of the soldiers he had formed friendships with in the gymnasium.

On the Boat Deck, shop staff Anthony Dance, Kent Frazer and Tony Butts decided to fetch some cartons of cigarettes and chocolate from the shops. Back on deck they opened the cartons and called down to the Welsh Guards, wishing them well and lobbing down cigarette packets and the occasional Mars bar. In his book *Moving On*, Welsh Guard Simon Weston wrote:

> There was an unexpectedly emotional farewell from the staff and stewards of the Cunard liner … We'd got to know each other well during the two-week trip south. They threw us down carton after carton of cigarettes, and one woman yelled out 'Good luck lads, keep your heads down'.

Anthony recalls throwing one packet of cigarettes that was caught out of the air by a guardsman, who called back, 'How's that!' – the cry cricketers sometimes make if they catch out an opponent.

This incident was a spontaneous display of solidarity and support for the disembarking troops. When faced with the choice of silently watching soldiers head off for war or of displaying friendship and comradeship, the crew on the Boat Deck that night in Grytviken chose the latter option. By now the shop staff were recognisable to the troops, so despite the darkness and mist the Welsh Guards could identify who was responsible for throwing the parting gifts raining down on them. A Welsh Guards officer later contacted Ocean Trading to thank them for the generosity of the staff. As shop manager Anthony Dance recalls, 'I had some uncomfortable questions to answer after the voyage!' Simon Weston recalls that the gift of 'tailor-mades' was very welcome: 'Like most squaddies, I had only my usual rolling tobacco – and trying to make a decent roll-up in a force 10 gale can be a right headache.'[109]

Chief Officer Warwick was at the shell door as the soldiers passed through to board the trawlers. He remembers that despite the late hour, the soldiers were in good spirits and ready to go. He also remembers the disembarkation was quite treacherous at times when the incoming swell widened the gap between the two vessels. Many watching the disembarkation were amazed at the amount of kit the soldiers had to carry. One of the troops who disembarked onto *Junella* was Welsh Guardsman Tracy Evans, who many years later was still complementary about the food on board *QE2*.

The first real view of Cumberland East Bay and South Georgia came with dawn on 28 May. As the sun rose, the transfer of the troops and stores started in earnest. Both 825 Naval Air Squadron Sea Kings were airborne by 0800 hours with the trawlers now plying between *QE2* and other

Snow covered the ship's decks in the morning of her second day at anchor in Cumberland East Bay. A military lookout was maintained while at anchor. The weapons were removed and transferred to another ship before *QE2* departed. (Captain P. Jackson)

The forecastle hatch to the cargo hold is open and the removal of equipment and ammunition is now well under way. (R.W. Warwick)

Suitcases galore are loaded into the trawler. (Stephen Hallam)

Some troops of 5 Infantry Brigade disembark from *QE2* on to a trawler which will transfer them to another ship anchored in the bay. (R. Smith)

The trawlers taking on stores from the hold had to manoeuvre with caution to avoid their masts making contact with the flare of the bow. (Gary White)

The QE2 in the Falklands War

Canberra looks serene against the snow-covered mountains around Grytviken, an image that belies the danger the P&O liner faced from air raids while landing troops in the theatre of war. (Captain P. Jackson)

Although the sea appears calm, a moderate swell existed most of the time that *QE2* was at anchor in Cumberland East Bay, making troop transfers to the trawlers difficult at times. (J. James)

One of the trawlers alongside *QE2*'s starboard side. The contribution made by the four requisitioned Hull trawlers was beyond measure, shortening *QE2*'s stay in Cumberland East Bay by days. (R.W. Warwick)

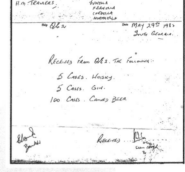

Cunard's accounting procedure required documentation to be provided for the transfer of stores to other ships. (David Luke)

On 4 March 1982, *QE2* arrived at the Kowloon Passenger Terminal in Hong Kong, where the P&O liner *Canberra* was already berthed. Both ships were on their annual world cruise. Less than three months later, the two ships would meet again but in circumstances that could not have been predicted at the time. (Michael DiFore)

ships. The unloading of stores proceeded smoothly. During the loading in Southampton, Army personnel had kept accurate records of what was loaded on board and where it was stowed. These records greatly facilitated the unloading process in Grytviken and ensured that supplies and equipment were transferred to the right ships. Throughout the day, stores were sent over by helicopters from *QE2* to other ships, mainly *Canberra* and *Norland*. The Sea Kings transferred stores and ammunition in underslung cargo nets. The forward helicopter deck by No. 1 Hold, where most of the ammunition was stored, was in almost continuous use with helicopters flying to and fro.

The Army Land Rovers that had been securely stowed on the Upper Deck were transferred by helicopter in underslung lifts to other ships. They were followed by the Rapier Blindfire trailers, other wheeled transport and the steel drums of aviation fuel and oil. The anti-aircraft guns from the Bridge wings and by the funnel were stripped down ready to be offloaded to be used elsewhere. It was estimated that about 250 tons was lifted off *QE2*. The various musical instruments belonging to 5 Brigade were offloaded in Grytviken but did not travel with the troops. They were carried by sea to the Falklands and eventually reunited with their respective owners after the cessation of hostilities.

Throughout the morning, crew made their way outside to check the view. There was an air of surrealism to what they could see. The scenery was bleak but beautiful. Imposing snow-capped mountains spawned glaciers which flowed to the sea, calving small icebergs into the bay. A weather-beaten *Canberra* with rust marks clearly visible on her side was anchored closer to Grytviken, having arrived seven hours before *QE2*. *Canberra* had earned for herself the nickname the 'Great White Whale' during the first landings when she sailed into San Carlos to disembark her troops. Television pictures were beamed around the world of Argentine fighter aircraft screaming down San Carlos and over the ships at anchor, with *Canberra* prominent among them. Also visible was HMS *Leeds Castle* and the North Sea ferry *Norland*. As chief cashier Stephen Ward stood on the aft helicopter deck, he recalled sailing on *Norland* the previous year to visit the Netherlands on a holiday. Another Cunard ship was also in the anchorage, *Saxonia* (Captain H. Evans). *Saxonia* was a refrigerated cargo vessel that had carried food stores to the South Atlantic to replenish RFA ships.[110] Those with binoculars could see the wreck of the Argentine Puma helicopter that had been destroyed near King Edward Point when the UK had recaptured the island.

Grytviken, South Georgia Island

Staff Captain Hutcheson made a Tannoy announcement saying that being in a place such as South Georgia was a strange and new experience for everyone, and that the reality of the situation might be hard to grasp. He stressed that all crew should stick to established procedures when carrying out their duties and be prepared for the situation to change. They should remember to think FOD (foreign object damage). Crew and military personnel should report any FOD hazards on land, sea or air that could pose a risk to *QE2* and in particular to the helicopters.

The Sea Kings took full advantage of the facility on board HMS *Leeds Castle* to refuel, thus enabling *QE2*'s flight decks to remain in continuous use. The work proceeded as fast as possible in uncertain weather conditions. The transfer of baggage, equipment and personnel continued uninterrupted with the flight deck crews manhandling, netting and slinging loads at the rate of fifteen per hour throughout the day.

The *QE2* deck ratings played a vital role in the disembarkation of troops and stores. The ABs were responsible for ensuring that the trawlers were berthed securely alongside the ship so that troops could transfer safely. The two cranes on the forecastle head were operated by four of the more experienced deck crew, namely bosun Charlie Thomas and three bosun's mates: Frank Parkinson, Chris Holter and Brian Denton. Their job was to use the cranes to lift the pallets of ammunition and other stores from the hold and then lower them onto cargo netting spread over the forward flight deck. When the cargo net was full, the crane operators would rotate the cranes away from the flight deck. This allowed a Sea King to move in and hover while the flight deck crew attached the cargo netting to the helicopter as an underslung load. The Sea King would then depart for one of the ships anchored in the bay. Meanwhile, the crane hook was slowly lowered back into the hold where ABs were waiting to attach the next pallet.

Operating the cranes was a difficult job in freezing conditions. Normally, *QE2*'s forecastle head cranes were used to load and unload stores only when the ship was berthed alongside in a major port, such as Southampton or New York. This was the only time in *QE2*'s history that the cranes were used for moving stores by helicopter while the ship was at anchor. These operations were carried out in very cold weather, with the downdraft from hovering helicopters providing an added wind chill that made the task more challenging. The crane operators rotated regularly throughout the day as it was impossible to work for more than an hour in such conditions.

195

Small groups of Gurkhas could be seen singing and performing traditional dances around the ship as they waited to disembark. Before disembarking the Gurkhas presented Captain Peter Jackson with a silver kukri knife. Captain's secretary Judy Carpenter recalls that it 'was indeed a formidable weapon and it was hard to believe that such friendly, polite people could be capable of using it'. One of the 7th Gurkha officers asked if he could use *QE2*'s launches to transport his men to the North Sea ferry. This request was granted and just before noon the ship's launches began to load the Gurkhas and their equipment for the trip across the bay to *Norland*.

When the boats reached *Norland*, they found no pontoon alongside for disembarking. The hatch on *Norland*, which was normally used for disembarking cars to the quayside, was 8ft above the water, considerably higher than the Gurkhas were tall. The troops could not even see the ship's deck, let alone reach it from *QE2*'s launches. This presented a challenge for the soldiers. The solution was for the Gurkhas to climb on to the roof of the cab. The 55 Field Surgical Team also transferred to *Norland* with Major Ryan RAMC noting, 'Our adventure in the luxury liner was over. Oh, how we had come down in the world.'

Some Scots Guards sang 'You'll Never Walk Alone' as they made their way down to Five Deck to disembark. Like the Welsh Guards, the Scots Guards were transferred to *Canberra*. Captain Richard Field of the Blues and Royals remembers the ship-to-ship transfer at Grytviken:

> We awoke one morning to be overawed by the majestic and startling beauty of Grytviken where during the course of the 27th of May, we were transferred to the *Canberra*. Reality was here at last. Not only had the Camembert run out days before and the last bottle of champagne [been] drunk on the *QE2*, but also the *Canberra* was announced to be a dry ship![111]

The transfer of troops and equipment took place under a blanket of grey cloud. As the Brigade disembarked, *QE2* became eerily quiet with something of the air of a ghost ship. However, this lasted only a few hours before she welcomed on board new passengers; the survivors of three Royal Navy ships that had suffered bomb damage while *QE2* was sailing south. The crew of HMS *Antelope* (Commander N.J. Tobin) had travelled to Grytviken on board *Norland*. As *Norland* headed towards Grytviken, her crew donated clothing to *Antelope*'s crew.[112] The *Antelope* crew gave three cheers for *Norland* as they disembarked, remembers *Norland* steward Reg Kemp.[113]

The crew of HMS *Ardent* (Commander A.W.J. West) had arrived at Grytviken on board *Canberra*. The *Ardent* crew had settled into *Canberra* very well and some did not want to leave. When the time came for them to disembark, the decks of *Canberra* were lined with soldiers and crew members to see them off. A group of Army musicians assembled on the promenade and played 'Rule Britannia' and 'Hearts of Oak' as the *Ardent* crew disembarked on to *Leeds Castle*.[114] *Ardent*'s crew responded with the 'Oggie, oggie, oggie' cry beloved by British military personnel and rugby fans. *Leeds Castle* then ferried the sailors across the bay to *QE2*. *Ardent*'s crew had been applauded as they disembarked from *Canberra* and they were applauded again as they boarded *QE2*.[115] Shortly after they embarked, *QE2* received a signal from the 2nd Battalion the Scots Guards on board *Canberra*. It read, 'To HMS *Ardent*. We will avenge you.'[116] The crew of HMS *Coventry* (Captain D. Hart Dyke) arrived the following day on board RFA *Stromness* (Captain J.D. Dickinson).

Some of the Royal Navy crew arriving on board were rather subdued, while others were more buoyant. Some walking wounded who had sustained injuries in the earlier stages of the conflict also embarked. Eight Special Air Service (SAS) men who had survived a helicopter crash came aboard. At the time, nothing was known of the circumstances of the crash.

While the disembarkation of troops and supplies proceeded smoothly, a misunderstanding arose between Naval Party 1980 embarked on *QE2* and Naval Party 1710 embarked on *Canberra*. The *Canberra* officers asked for some of *QE2*'s food stores, claiming that without them the troops they had just embarked would 'be short of food'.[117] The *Canberra* officers argued that *QE2* didn't need her food stores as she was heading 'back home'.[118] It was claimed that *QE2* refused to offer up any food stores. The rivalry between the Cunard and P&O lines has usually been a friendly one, with mutual respect on both sides, so the claim made that the Cunard liner refused to hand over food stocks is disappointing.

At this stage of the conflict, *QE2* had only received the order to head towards Ascension when she departed from Grytviken. No order had been received on what she was to do after that and there was certainly no indication that she would be returning home. On the contrary, there was the very real possibility that *QE2* would disembark the survivors of the three lost naval warships at Ascension, then return to the South Atlantic with additional military personnel and stores. The transfer of significant quantities of supplies between ships engaged in a military campaign is not something that can be decided upon between ships. *QE2* could only transfer cargo and supplies to other ships when authorised to do so by senior military commanders in the field or by the Ministry of Defence in London. No such orders had been received. The late timing of the request was such that even if it had been granted, there was insufficient time to make the transfer, given the near continuous use of helicopters and trawlers for transferring troops and military supplies in deteriorating weather conditions. Major General Moore and his staff had arrived in the region on board *QE2* only hours before, and if they had received a request from *Canberra* for the transfer of urgently needed food stocks to keep 5 Infantry Brigade fed it is difficult to believe this would not have been authorised. *Saxonia* had been requisitioned to carry food supplies and she was anchored nearby, so presumably had food available for distribution.

QE2 responded positively to pre-arranged requests from other ships for victualling and other supplies. The ship's chief barkeeper, Ernie Lamb, arranged for the transfer of five cases of whiskey, five cases of gin and 100 cases of canned beer to the trawlers. In accordance with Cunard's stock-keeping procedures, a signed receipt was obtained for these items. Meanwhile, *Canberra*'s Ocean Trading shop manager visited *QE2* to request supplies. *QE2* shop manager Anthony Dance authorised the transfer of large quantities of confectionery, savoury snacks and soft drinks to *Canberra*. *QE2* also transferred victualling stores to *Norland* and to the Royal Marines shoreside party in Grytviken. Captain Jimmy James later acknowledged the help of *QE2*'s hotel manager Ron Kelly and catering manager John Hewison in handling these arrangements.

War artist Linda Kitson and photographer Paul Haley left the ship in Grytviken. They were transferred to *Canberra* and disembarked when the ship reached San Carlos. After *QE2* had left Ascension Island, Paul had taken several group photographs in order to have a photographic record of all of the troops on board. Before arriving at Grytviken, he had obtained some waterproof clothing and webbing from one of the Gurkhas whose wedding he had photographed earlier in the year. By the time he left the ship, he had taken over 600 images and in the process created a unique historical record of a merchant ship at war.

Before disembarking with the Brigade, Linda Kitson left her sketches on board for safekeeping. This provided an opportunity for some of the senior officers to view them on the return voyage. The margins of the drawings were full of information about each particular scene along with notes about colours and names of personnel. Those who had been sceptical about the need for a war artist on board changed their minds when they saw the quality of the drawings and how events and activities had been meticulously portrayed. The detail was such that many of the people featured could be identified. In some of the general views, such as the flight deck viewed from the higher decks at the aft of the ship, individual staff working with the helicopters could be recognised even though they were tiny relative to the size of the whole picture.

When he transferred to *Canberra*, Major Ronald Clark wrote a letter to his parents on *QE2* notepaper. He told them:

> ... the past few weeks have been unreal, in the sense that once the training for the day was over we would sit and sleep where the famous and the stars of the world pay vast sums to be. The Cunard staff treated us as if we were normal passengers.[119]

At 1655 hours, all flying operations were completed and the two Sea King helicopters and all the hands of 825 Naval Air Squadron took off from *QE2* for the last time and headed for *Canberra*, their new home for the time being. By 2049 hours, *Canberra* had weighed her anchor and set course back to the Falklands. In the darkness, *Norland* followed her out of the bay.

Snow started to fall on 29 May, blanketing the South Georgia landscape and leaving a 2in covering over the decks of *QE2*. By daybreak there was a blue sky, some white cloud and a clear view of the harbour, snow-clad mountains and glaciers. A small iceberg drifted in the harbour; it had probably calved from one of the glaciers that fed into the bay. Those on board were struck by the awesome scenery of this remarkable island. Amidst the beauty of it all, it was hard for those on board to remind themselves why they were here. As the day wore on, the snow turned to slush and it became potentially treacherous on deck.

A lot of military stores remained in the flaps of the hold, so a group of soldiers worked throughout the night. They moved out everything down as far as flap eight, finishing at about 0700 hours. Shortly before noon, RFA *Stromness* arrived in the bay with the crew of HMS *Coventry*, who were transferred to *QE2*. Meanwhile, stores were transferred from *QE2* to *Stromness* by the trawlers. Personal kit and rations had been assembled in the corridors and were moved towards the shell door by chain gangs. The task of loading items onto the trawlers became more difficult as the height of the swell increased. Senior radio officer Allan Holmes and RFA radio officer David MacKenzie made a brief visit to *Stromness* with some information about radio codes. They were treated to a quick drink in the officers' mess before transferring back to *QE2*.

About thirty Royal Marines were garrisoned in Grytviken. They received an invitation to board *QE2* for lunch, where they received a delivery of mail, their first in some weeks. In exchange for lunch, a group from the liner were invited to tour the old whaling station. The chief officer arranged a launch to take them ashore. When the Cunard group landed, they were greeted by the Royal Marines officer in charge of the garrison. He called out a warning to everyone: 'This area could be mined, so make sure you walk only where I walk.' He then escorted the group around the old whaling station. Cruise director Tim Castle carried his red Cunard umbrella, normally used to identify himself when escorting groups of passengers on shore excursions. Easily noticed was the abandoned Argentinian submarine *Santa Fe*. It had sunk in shallow water alongside the jetty with only the conning tower visible. A sign attached to the conning tower stated that the vessel was out of bounds to all personnel. In February 1985, the submarine was scuttled in deep water on the northern side of the island.

Most of the old timber buildings, factory units, dormitories, storehouses and offices were showing the ravages of harsh South Atlantic winters, but the Norwegian Anglican church was very well preserved. The church, informally known as the Whalers' Church, is a wooden structure with a distinctive pointed spire. It was made in Norway and assembled in Grytviken in 1913.[120] A tradition of the island is that anyone remaining in Grytviken for any period of time should repair and maintain the church.

Second Officer Chris Haughton, who two days earlier had helped navigate the ship through the treacherous ice field, walked ahead to the church. As the rest of the group approached, they were astounded to be greeted by the sound of music floating heavenward from the old organ. Chris, an accomplished musician, had managed to get the organ working and was playing the Toccata and Fugue in D minor, a piece of music credited to German composer Johann Sebastian Bach. The atmosphere of peaceful organ music in such a bleak and isolated setting was unexpected and surreal for other members of the shore party. The whaling station had been abandoned for years, but when entering the church it seemed to engineer officer Martin Harrison as if the last service had been held the day before. Hymn books were lying around and religious robes were hung where they had been left. The church had a well-stocked library in the transept. Tim Castle recalls that one of the first books to catch his eye was a Norwegian translation of D.H. Lawrence's *Lady Chatterley's Lover*.

After visiting the church, the group continued walking around the bay to the old cemetery that lies in view of the whaling station. The cemetery contains the grave of the famous Antarctic explorer Sir Ernest Shackleton (1874–1922). The grave was decorated with the crested shields of visiting ships. Close to Shackleton's final resting place is the grave of Felix Artuso, an Argentine submariner from the *Santa Fe* who was shot on board the vessel in an incident shortly after it was recaptured. He is the only member of the Argentine armed forces buried in South Georgia.

The weather deteriorated as the barometer fell steadily throughout the second day in Grytviken. A north-westerly wind and a growing South Atlantic swell were entering Cumberland East Bay, causing *QE2* to yaw uncomfortably. The worsening conditions made it increasingly difficult for the trawlers to come alongside safely, giving cause for concern. Some damage occurred when the derricks of the trawlers came into contact with the flare of *QE2*'s bow. The port gangway and pontoon were damaged beyond further use by the buffeting they received.

More worryingly, it became apparent that a potential threat to the liner was not far away. That afternoon the ship was notified of an increased risk of air attack. The Argentines had sent a C130 Hercules aircraft into the South Atlantic to search for *QE2* to the north of the Falklands. Unable to find the Cunard flagship, the Hercules had tried to bomb a UK merchant tanker supporting the task force, *British Wye* (Captain D. M. Rundell), which at the time was some 100 miles north-west of South Georgia. Initial press reports indicated that eight bombs were rolled out from the back of the Hercules. However, the ship's officer of the watch reported that the bombs were dropped from racks fitted to the wings of the aircraft.[121] Seven of the bombs missed while the eighth struck the ship but failed to detonate. The tanker escaped serious damage.

The incident was a particular cause for concern as the tanker was a considerable distance from the mainland of Argentina and close to the north-west

Engineer officers John Chillingworth (right) and Eddie Cripps keep a lookout as *QE2*'s launch approaches the quay at Grytviken. (J. Chillingworth)

The conning tower of the sunken Argentine submarine *Santa Fe* lies above the water alongside the quay. In 1985, the submarine was refloated, towed out of the bay and scuttled in deep water. (Wendy Marshall)

Grytviken, South Georgia Island

The trawler *Viola* was one of the other abandoned vessels in the bay. (R.W. Warwick)

QE2 visitors were welcomed ashore to the abandoned whaling station at Grytviken by the Royal Marines garrison. The Argentine flag had flown over Grytviken just over a month earlier. (R.W. Warwick)

The Argentine submarine *Santa Fe* (S-21) shows evidence of the aerial attack that disabled her following an attack from one of HMS *Antrim*'s helicopters. (Wendy Marshall)

The whaling station viewed from the Grytviken cemetery and burial place of Sir Ernest Shackleton. (R.W. Warwick)

Grytviken, South Georgia Island

of South Georgia. By deduction this meant that the ships anchored in Cumberland East Bay were in range and would be at risk should there be any air raids. Another consideration was that the cloudy weather of the first day that had offered some protection from aerial surveillance to the ships in Grytviken was now clearing. There was also a report of high-altitude air activity around South Georgia.[122] If this activity was from Argentine forces, it was almost certainly a Boeing 707 reconnaissance flight.

This news led Captain Jimmy James to exercise his right to issue a new order if a change in the operational environment demanded it. Captain James deemed it necessary for *QE2* to sail as soon as possible to reduce her vulnerability to possible attack. The weather was deteriorating as the remaining military personnel were transferred. The skill and hard work of the tug *Typhoon* and her crew contributed enormously to the final transfers. Unfortunately, however, there was insufficient time to offload all remaining cargo and *QE2* departed from Grytviken with about 60 tons of ammunition still on board. Preparations to put to sea were now in hand. The forward cargo hatch was battened down and the cranes were lowered and secured in their stowage positions. All the shell door openings were closed as well as the watertight doors on all decks. Soon after, *QE2* put to sea.

Captain James later commented, 'I never had any doubt that the Hercules aircraft's task was to find *QE2* and attack her. Our speed of advance and silent tactics I am sure contributed to our safety.' Later it was learned that the Argentinians had used a Boeing 707 with a substantial cruising range to survey the South Atlantic at 18,000ft searching for *QE2*.

Thirty-three years after the conflict, in June 2015, documents were released showing that Prime Minister Margaret Thatcher was unhappy with some of the BBC reporting of the British campaign. By the time *QE2* had left South Georgia, the BBC had reported that some of the bombs deployed by the Argentine Air Force against British warships had failed to detonate because the fuses were incorrectly set. This report drew criticism for providing information that was helpful to the enemy. Mrs Thatcher was also angry at a radio report that announced *QE2* was near South Georgia and transferring troops to other ships. She wrote, 'I knew this was planned but it was devastating to hear the report at about the time it was due to take place. Within eight hours of that broadcast reconnaissance planes were over South Georgia searching.'[123]

The Argentine Air Force was certainly searching for *QE2*. Her departure from Southampton had received global media coverage and the Argentine authorities would have been able to deduce that she was somewhere in the South Atlantic. It is now known that *QE2* was at considerably more risk than was appreciated at the time. In February 2024, an image of a signal was published on the internet from the Argentine Air Force. The signal approved a long-range surveillance flight on 31 May by a Boeing 707 with an attack to be carried out by a C130 Hercules. The text of the signal directs the Air Force to search for 'principal unidades de superficie britanicas en transito al area Malvinas, en especial buque *Queen Elizabeth* escolatado por fragatas y destructores', which translates to: 'main British surface units in transit to the Malvinas area, especially the ship *Queen Elizabeth* escorted by frigates and destroyers.'[124] A map reveals that Argentine forces presumed the probable route of *QE2* would be direct from Ascension to the Falklands. The estimated position of *QE2* on 31 May is shown on the map to be about 1,000 miles to the north-east of the Falklands and the same distance, approximately 1,000 miles, almost due east of Puerto Belgrano. This telegram was, in effect, confirmation of what the Argentine naval attaché in Paris had stated before the ship left the UK: Argentina intended to sink *QE2*.

These documents vindicate the decision of British authorities not to risk *QE2* in the battle zone and to keep her well to the east. This was not, however, anticipated by the Argentines, who believed that the ship would sail direct to the Falklands under armed protection from the Royal Navy. Instead she travelled unprotected to South Georgia, relying on her speed to evade enemy forces. By the time the reconnaissance flight of 31 May took place, *QE2* had departed from Grytviken and was heading north-easterly. However, the air attack on *British Wye* was very likely a mission in search of *QE2*.

The Argentines continued to search the South Atlantic for British ships to attack. On 8 June, a Liberian-registered tanker was attacked by a C130 Hercules 480 miles north-east of the Falklands.[125] The tanker, which somewhat ironically was itself called *Hercules*, was an unarmed merchant ship that had nothing to do with the British war effort. There were no casualties.

11

The Survivors and Their Ships

Four Royal Navy warships were sunk during the Falklands War. HMS *Sheffield* was the first ship to be attacked. *QE2* brought home a total of 632 survivors from the other three ships:

HMS *Ardent*, Commander A.W.J. West: 177
HMS *Antelope*, Commander N. J. Tobin: 202
HMS *Coventry*, Captain D. Hart Dyke: 253

Not all of the survivors returned home on *QE2*. Some were transferred to the hospital ship *Uganda* (Captain J.G. Clark) for urgent medical treatment. One was communications and electronic warfare specialist Chris Howe from HMS *Coventry*, who suffered serious burns when his ship was attacked. Along with other wounded *Coventry* crew, he returned home by sea and air, travelling on board HMS *Hecla* (Captain G. Hope) to Montevideo, Uruguay, before being flown home by the Royal Air Force.

★ ★ ★

HMS *Ardent* was a Type 21 frigate launched in May 1975. The ship's motto was 'Through Fire and Water'. Under the command of Alan West, *Ardent* sailed on 19 April for the Falkland Islands with a crew of 199 officers and ratings.[126] The crew engaged in intensive training on the journey south.[127]

Images of three of the lost ships featured on postal covers for the fortieth anniversary of the conflict. (Buckingham Covers)

On 20 May, *Ardent* entered Falkland Sound from the north. On 21 May, the day of the San Carlos landings, *Ardent*'s orders were to bombard the airstrip at Goose Green, both to divert the attention of Argentine forces from San Carlos and to weaken enemy positions. *Ardent*'s shelling achieved excellent results, including the immobilisation of three Argentine Pucará aircraft on the Goose Green airstrip.[128] However, some Pucará aircraft were able to take off, two of which closed in on *Ardent* before turning back after a Seacat missile was fired from the warship.[129]

Furthermore, *Ardent* was in an exposed position and came under further attacks from Skyhawks. One bomb penetrated the ship's hull but failed to explode, while another exploded in the hangar.[130] *Ardent* continued to defend herself but a further wave of air attacks led to the ship being struck by a further seven bombs.[131] On the helicopter flight deck, a medical assistant, Bob Young, was blasted into the netting surrounding the deck, while Surgeon Lieutenant Simon Ridout was blasted into the sea.[132] He was later rescued by HMS *Broadsword* (Captain W.R. Canning). *Ardent* attempted to make for San Carlos Water, but her steering was damaged and she started listing badly to starboard with her stern on fire. Commander Alan West reluctantly gave the order to abandon ship. Commander West was the last man to leave *Ardent*, stepping off the bow of his ship into the water shortly before 1500 hours.

The frigate HMS *Yarmouth* came alongside *Ardent* to pick up survivors. *Yarmouth* delivered the survivors to *Canberra*, which then departed from San Carlos. That evening in one of *Canberra*'s bars, the survivors were gathered when the ship's master and first lieutenant entered. Commander West addressed the men. He told them he didn't want anyone feeling guilty, saying, 'I was proud to sail with you.'[133] He then read the names of the men who were missing. Commander West then moved around the room talking to his crew individually and doing his best to raise their spirits. *Ardent* sank in the early hours of the following morning. Twenty-two sailors lost their lives during the air raids. At the request of Commander West, a service of remembrance and thanksgiving was held on Sunday, 23 May as *Canberra* headed east.[134]

Shortly after boarding *QE2*, some of the *Ardent* crew could be found in the Pig and Whistle, the crew bar on Three Deck forward, where they were made welcome. *QE2* crew member Steve Jackson discreetly arranged for a supply of beer to Royal Navy survivors for the journey home. Some would return to their cabin to find a crate of beer on their bed.[135] Iain McRobbie, an *Ardent* survivor, remembers being told that they were not allowed to fraternise with the crew and should not drink in crew bars. They went to the Pig and Whistle every night! He also remembers that one night the ship ran into heavy weather and the following morning an announcement over the Tannoy apologised to 'passengers' for the uncomfortable night. 'We just looked at each other and said, "What uncomfortable night?" *QE2* was 67K tons. We were used to 3K ton frigates.'

★ ★ ★

HMS *Antelope* was a Type 21 frigate and a sister ship of *Ardent*. She was launched in March 1972. Her motto was *Audax et Vigilans* ('Daring and Watchful'). Under the command of Commander N.J. Tobin, she sailed from Devonport on 5 April and arrived at Ascension Island on 29 April, the same day as *Ardent*. On 2 May, *Antelope* intercepted an Argentine merchant freight ship, *Rio de la Plata*, which had approached Ascension, and escorted her until she was 100 miles away from the island.[136] *Antelope* arrived off the Falkland Islands on 21 May and entered San Carlos Water the following day to give the shellfire support that *Ardent* had provided prior to her loss.

The same day, four Skyhawks carried out a co-ordinated attack against *Antelope*. The Skyhawks split into two pairs that attacked the ship separately. A bomb from the first pair penetrated the ship's hull but failed to detonate. A Skyhawk from the second raid struck *Antelope*'s main mast.[137] A bomb from this second attack struck *Antelope* amidships and penetrated the hull, again without detonating. Shortly after 1500 hours that day, *Antelope* was anchored near *Argonaut* in San Carlos Water.[138] *Argonaut* had also come under attack earlier and had on board an unexploded bomb. Two Royal Engineers, Warrant Officer John Phillips and Staff Sergeant James Prescott, boarded *Argonaut* where Prescott successfully defused the bomb.

The Royal Engineers then boarded *Antelope*, where they attempted to defuse the bomb that had penetrated amidships. Tragically, the bomb detonated as they worked on it, killing Staff Sergeant Prescott instantly and badly injuring Warrant Officer Phillips.[139] A fire broke out that quickly spread aft. Commander Tobin gave the order to abandon ship. He was the last man to leave HMS *Antelope* shortly after 1800 hours. *Antelope*'s survivors were transferred to the North Sea ferry *Norland*. Two of the crew died on board *Antelope*. The fires burned throughout the night, causing some explosions. Reg Kemp, one of *Norland*'s stewards, recalls that many of *Antelope*'s crew were on *Norland's* outside decks, watching their ship ablaze.[140] By dawn the ship's back was broken. 'She was broken in half with the bow and the stern protruding above the water – what a terrible sight to see,' remembers Reg Kemp. *Antelope* sank later that day in San Carlos Water.

★ ★ ★

HMS *Coventry*, a Type 42 destroyer, was launched in June 1974. After the Argentine invasion, she was ordered to sail south under the command of Captain David Hart Dyke with a crew of 300.[141] At Ascension Island, she took on stores and engaged in further training exercises. *Coventry* sailed south from Ascension Island on 15 April and on arrival at the Falklands was assigned a protection role against Argentine fighter aircraft. This involved using her Sea Dart missiles and directing Sea Harriers towards enemy aircraft.[142] *Coventry* carried out this task to good effect in the early stages of the war, often working with HMS *Broadsword*.

On 25 May, *Coventry* and *Broadsword* were positioned north of West Falkland to guard against enemy aircraft. *Coventry* shot down two Skyhawks that morning with Sea Dart missiles in separate incidents.[143] At about 1400 hours, radar picked up two pairs of Skyhawk aircraft approaching the Falklands. Rather than attack ships at anchor in San Carlos Water, the aircraft moved north to attack *Coventry* and *Broadsword*. The first pair attacked *Broadsword*, releasing four bombs, three of which missed the ship. The fourth ricocheted off the water and penetrated *Broadsword's* hull starboard aft without detonating.[144] The second pair of Skyhawks then appeared, bearing directly towards *Coventry*. They released four bombs, three of which struck *Coventry* on her starboard side. At least two of the three bombs exploded.[145] The ship also sustained cannon fire damage. *Coventry* started shipping sea water immediately after the strikes and could not be saved. Evacuation proceeded in a calm and orderly manner. *Coventry* turned over less than twenty minutes after she was bombed. Captain Hart Dyke waited until everyone was off his ship, then walked down the side of it, jumped into the water and swam to a life raft.[146] HMS *Broadsword* sent rescue boats, and helicopters came from RFA *Fort Austin*. Some of the injured were transferred to a field hospital.[147] Nineteen men lost their lives on board *Coventry*.

In the immediate aftermath of the attack, survivors were accommodated on board *Fort Austin*, *Broadsword* and the hospital ship *Uganda*. The next day, all but the most severely injured survivors were transferred to

The QE2 in the Falklands War

RFA *Stromness*, which departed for Grytviken on 27 May. *Stromness* had accompanied *Coventry* on a tour of the Far East in 1980 and the two ships had exchanged ship crests. *Coventry*'s ship crest was formally presented to Captain David Hart Dyke before he left the ship in Grytviken. He has kept it to this day.[148]

The *Coventry* survivors were the last to embark on *QE2* on 29 May. Many of the survivors were struck by the beauty of South Georgia. Captain David Hart Dyke recalls, 'The sight of those majestic glacial mountains, in hues of blue, green and white, rising out of the translucent pale green sea was extraordinary; I have never seen a more beautiful landscape.'[149]

The survivors from *Ardent* and *Antelope* had boarded *QE2* the previous day. The captains of the three warships were welcomed on board by Captain Jackson and Captain James. Leading writer A.W. Warren of NP1980 headed up a Royal Navy reception committee to welcome the survivors aboard. Upon boarding, a small team of pursers from the three warships moved into the passenger bureau on Two Deck and in liaison with *QE2*'s hotel officers began work to allocate cabins. This job was completed before *QE2* departed at short notice from Grytviken following the news of the attempted bombing of *British Wye*.

12

Homeward Bound
to Southampton

At 1609 hours on 29 May, *QE2*'s engines were put on stand-by. The captain gave orders to weigh anchor at 1710 hours. The anchor was aweigh at 1727 hours. After the liner had manoeuvred clear of the anchorage area, she headed north out of Cumberland East Bay. Thereafter full speed was ordered and an easterly course was set to increase the distance from mainland Argentina and reduce the risk of attack. By 1935 hours, the ice field had been reached and speed was reduced. Second Officer Paul Jowett recalls that shortly before midnight ice could be seen to both sides of the ship. Captain Jackson made the decision to find a suitable gap for the ship to steam through. The last icebergs were sighted at 1100 hours the following day, after which speed was increased to 25 knots.

The hasty departure from Grytviken meant an urgent need to secure the remaining ammunition in No. 1 Hold. All the ship's carpenters were told to report immediately to the hold and shore up the ammunition boxes to prevent sliding should the ship encounter rough weather. Carpenter Bob Farmer recalls that having successfully completed this task, he and his shipmates headed for the Petty Officers' Club for a well-earned drink!

As the ship sailed north, Commander West, captain of HMS *Ardent*, wrote letters to the next of kin of those members of his crew who had died.[150] The officers and crew of *Ardent*, *Antelope* and *Coventry* wished to speak with and reassure their families that they were fine and on their way home. Regretfully, the Radio Room had to decline their requests as radio silence was still being observed. On the evening of departure from

Grytviken, there was a knock on the radio office door. Chief radio officer Allan Holmes recalls:

> An injured survivor from HMS *Coventry* asked if he could call his wife. Sadly, as we were ordered to observe radio silence, I had to refuse his request and I have never forgotten how upset I was in having to do so. He accepted my reason with good grace and quietly left.

With the ship still sailing in dangerous waters, the safety and welfare of all on board remained of paramount importance. Accordingly, early in the morning on the day after departure, Captain James convened a meeting with the three warship commanding officers and Lieutenant Rentell to give a brief on safety routines. This was followed by a boat drill for all hands.

The boat drill created some challenging questions. QE2 is constructed with a combination of steel and aluminium. The part of the hull below Quarter Deck is made of steel and everything above is made of aluminium, a metal that melts at a lower temperature to steel. The boat assembly station for some of the survivors was located on Quarter Deck. One of the assembled naval officers, who had experienced the consequences of burning aluminium, wanted to know why they had to muster in an area where the side of the ship was aluminium rather than steel. Another survivor queried why he was at a muster station with some strangers rather than just his mates from his own ship.

Some of 5 Infantry Brigade had left behind items that they did not wish to take with them. Ship's crew were detailed to clean up cabins and other spaces around the ship. One crew member, who wishes to remain anonymous, remembers:

> After we sailed from Grytviken I was checking the shell door recesses where some of the soldiers had been living on the way south and I came across a piece of pipe lying on the deck. I did not recognise it at first but then it dawned on me – it was the barrel sawn off from a shotgun.

It was never established how the shotgun came to be on the ship, or whether it was in the possession of a crew member or a soldier.

With fewer personnel on board, changes were made to the catering arrangements. On the northbound voyage, the Queens Grill and the Tables of the World were closed. Naval officers dined in the Princess Grill and all other ranks ate in the Columbia Restaurant. Many of the walking wounded took their meals in the Queens Grill. Head waiter Andrew Nelder recalls that despite the ordeal that the sailors had been through, he never once heard anyone complain or feel sorry for themselves. He remembers the sailors were in good spirits.

The on-board complement for the journey north is probably unique in British maritime history. On this civilian ship were the crews of three sunken warships, all with their own commanding officer plus the commanding officer of NP1980 and the master of the ship, Captain Jackson. Five seafaring captains in all!

As the ship sailed north, a system was introduced to allocate duties and work among the crews of the three warships. Every day each ship had to nominate an officer of the day (OOD) and a duty petty officer (DPO). The crews of the three ships took turns as the duty ship. The OOD of the day's duty ship took lead responsibility for allocating tasks to be carried out by the crews of the three ships and for liaising with NP1980 and the ship's officers. The OOD of the duty ship produced a daily orders sheet that detailed work duties and leisure activities.

News emerged later that for three to four days Argentine air power in the South Atlantic had been diverted as far east as possible as the enemy searched for *QE2*. Few sorties were flown to the Falklands, and only when it was clear that *QE2* had escaped did the Argentine Air Force, which by now was badly depleted, turn its attention back to the Falklands. Captain Jackson said after the voyage that an unexpected air strike was his biggest fear, more so than the icebergs. He also said that if it had not been for the extensive cloud cover as the ship steamed southwards, the Argentines could well have found *QE2*.

QE2 had in effect changed its status from the world's largest troopship to its largest hospital ship, albeit without the red crosses that conventionally adorn hospital ships in times of war. The atmosphere on board changed completely. Many of the survivors of the lost Royal Navy vessels had little more than the clothes on their backs and some of those were ragged. Before disembarking, members of 5 Brigade had organised a collection of civilian clothing to donate to the Navy crews. Officers and crew of *QE2* did the same. This helped to make the Royal Navy crews feel welcome on board as they started the process of unwinding from their experiences. Some wore life jackets when walking around the ship. Having lost their ship, they were understandably anxious and prepared for

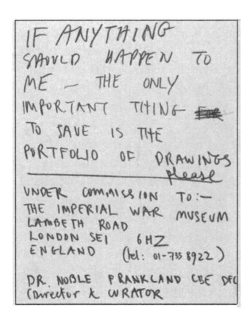

For safekeeping, war artist Linda Kitson left her sketches on board before she disembarked. Several of the crew took the opportunity to look at them before they were parcelled up for onward delivery to the Imperial War Museum in London. (R.W. Warwick)

Executive chef Victor Coward created some new names for the cuisine served at the mess dinner held in the Princess Grill on the journey north. With the exception of watchkeepers, all officers were invited. (Andrew Nelder)

The Cunard Fleet Personnel Office continued to keep in contact with families of the volunteer crew by writing letters and organising coffee mornings. (David Luke) the worst. The ship's finance manager, Gerry Nolan, approved the transfer of £32,000 to the Royal Navy to enable personnel to purchase necessities and other items available in the shop.

Forty of the Navy crew were classified as casualties. Over twenty casualties required hospital care. Some were lucky to be alive. With the hospital full, it was necessary to find alternative berths for the walking wounded. The location of the hospital on *QE2* is Six Deck at the bottom of 'C' Stairway. The location was known as 'C6', an 'address' that was the subject of jokes as it is phonetically similar to 'sea sick'.[151] Patients who could not be accommodated in the hospital were berthed in passenger accommodation on Five Deck near 'C' Stairway, being close to the hospital. *QE2*'s hospital staff worked hard to treat the injured and help them regain their health and peace of mind. Of those requiring hospital care, most had received treatment on board the *Uganda* for bone fractures, shrapnel injuries and smoke inhalation. One sailor still had intracranial shrapnel in his skull, confirmed by the X-ray machine in the hospital.

Some of the survivors bore visible burn injuries. Particularly severe were the injuries of the *Coventry* captain, David Hart Dyke. Coincidentally, Captain Hart Dyke had been in the same school as Dr Alan Kirwin. Dr Kirwin recalls that many of the survivors were suffering the psychological symptoms of survivor guilt, wondering why they had survived and not their friends. In his book *Four Weeks in May*, David Hart Dyke quotes Able Seaman Mick Daniels:

> … the sinking only hit me when we boarded *QE2* in South Georgia … There were some tables with mail and parcels spread out on them. I could not help but stop and stare at the mail for some of our lost shipmates – it was hard not be moved at the sight.[152]

Most of *QE2*'s medical staff had not previously seen many of the injuries they dealt with, such as flash burns from bomb explosions and traumatic amputations from blast injuries. Nursing Sister Wendy Marshall recalls becoming proficient in treating burns with Flamazine, a cream used to treat flash burns and prevent infection.

A heavy saltwater flood had occurred due to a burst pipe on Seven Deck. The water ran into the sauna, darkroom, gymnasium and laundry. The flood was located in an area that was not used during the night and would have been discovered earlier if the watertight doors had not been closed.

The flood water was up to a height of 12in in places. It caused considerable material damage, especially in the laundry where linen was spoiled and some of the wooden decking ruined. Available crew from the deck and hotel departments were deployed on clean-up operations. Stephen Easter, who had been working in the Queens Grill before Grytviken, was one of those drafted in to help remove the water and sort through and dry the stock of linen and other items for relaundering or disposal.

The laundry staff sent a message around the ship inviting crew who were donating clothing items to the survivors to bring them to the laundry room for cleaning before they were made available to the Royal Navy crews. The hardworking laundry 'steam queens' were always happy to rewash clothing for the ship's guests. Crew member Terry Cassidy had volunteered to assist in the laundry when the concessionaire crew were sent home. He vividly remembers that he and other laundry staff did not realise that the sound made by the hydro washing machines might cause panic to the survivors when they started with a bang and went into a high spin. Thereafter, they always gave prior warning to any visitors before turning the machines on.

Clive Dalley managed the gymnasium, which had to be temporarily closed after the flood. When it was reopened a few days later, he reduced the time he spent on duty in the gym and went to work in the hospital. As a trained remedial masseur, he devoted much of his time to giving physiotherapy treatment to some of the wounded. Clive found the crews from *Ardent*, *Antelope* and *Coventry* an inspiration in how they carried on without complaint despite their injuries. He obtained permission from one of the doctors to shut down the chlorine plant to the swimming pool so that it could be used for seawater therapy to aid the healing of wounds. Looking back forty years later, he says the 'hospital staff on board should be very proud of their professionalism'.

A typical day in the hospital involved surgery to extract shrapnel and changing the dressings of inpatients and outpatients. The most common injuries were from shrapnel and bone fractures. Senior Sister Jane Yelland later commented, 'For the first week after leaving South Georgia, it was like working in a very busy accident emergency unit.' *QE2*'s medical team, assisted by the medics from the three warships, was kept busy with doctors Kirwin and Hewetson carrying out most of the general care. Surgeon Lieutenant Simon Ridout, who had been blasted overboard from *Ardent*, was affectionately nicknamed the 'flying doctor'. He helped out during surgical sessions by extracting shrapnel followed by administering delayed primary suturing. This is a technique which involves leaving a wound open for a few days. The wound is not closed until all debris is removed, no infection is present and swelling has subsided. Sister Yelland recalls lots of joking between the patients and hospital staff. Most were still quite traumatised and did not wish to talk about the details of their experience. Some would jump when alarm bells rang, warning that watertight doors were being closed. It is now apparent that many of the men were suffering from what today is called post-traumatic stress disorder.

Some of the SAS men who had embarked in South Georgia also required medical attention. They were berthed in passenger cabins on Five Deck near the 'C' Stairway. Sister Jane Yelland mentioned to their senior officer that the duty nurse would need to check on the SAS patients during the night. He advised the hospital staff not to wake the men by standing close to them or leaning over while they slept. As trained special forces, they might react with defensive measures if awoken suddenly, believing they were under attack. Instead, medical staff were asked to check the men's condition by standing at the end of the bed and gently tapping their toes. Sister Yelland recalls, 'They were very nice guys to look after.'

The medical team helped those who had been burned to recover. Captain David Hart Dyke said that the treatment he received from Dr Patrick Hewetson helped speed his recovery. The ship's doctors and nurses invited some of their patients to social occasions. David Hart Dyke recalls the formal invitation he received to one memorable event: a cocktail party hosted by the QE2 doctors. The invitation read, 'Doctor Alan Kirwin and Doctor Patrick Hewetson invite you to a tincture at 6.30 pm on Monday 7th June on our Helicopter Deck. Wheelchairs at 8.00 pm.'[153] The venue was on the Sports Deck immediately behind the funnel. This area of the Sports Deck was also known as Helicopter Deck. It was used during peacetime for emergency medical evacuations, the occasional arrival of special guests or boarding harbour pilots and port officials. The structure of the deck was not strong enough to take the weight of a Sea King helicopter, so it was not used as a landing pad during the conflict. Instead it was used extensively for physical training exercises.

The shop on Boat Deck remained open. Shop manager Anthony Dance started a tab system so that crew without access to money could purchase items 'on tick'. Crew gave their name, rank and service number, and a running bill was kept of the value of items they purchased. Items that proved popular with members of the Royal Navy looking for gifts for wives and girlfriends included jewellery, watches and perfume. The shop staff were prepared to negotiate with those who were unable to afford the price. One sailor paid £25 for a Seiko La Verne watch priced at £200.

While making a cup of coffee in the Two Deck forward pantry, one of the crew got chatting with a Royal Navy petty officer from HMS *Antelope*. When he asked how he was, the petty officer replied, 'Not too bad now, mate. We were zapped up Bomb Alley.' Bomb Alley was the nickname the Royal Navy had given to San Carlos Water, where the initial landings were made and where the heaviest air raids of the war took place. Some of the Royal Navy crew were willing and relieved to share their stories, while understandably others were not.

On Sunday, 30 May, Captain Jackson held the Sunday church service. Captain James of NP1980 read the lesson and prayers. The service was well attended by the survivors. Once again the final hymn was 'Eternal Father, Strong to Save', as was the case for every Sunday service held during the voyage. However, the hymn now had an immediate poignancy and sadness, given that those attending the service were doing so to honour and remember fallen shipmates. The tradition of singing this hymn every Sunday the liner was at sea began when *QE2* entered service in 1969.

The following day, Captain Jackson gave a lecture in the Theatre on 'The Great Passenger Liners'. This lecture had long been popular with Cunard passengers and was warmly appreciated by the Royal Navy. By now, the weather had deteriorated substantially with a rough head sea and a heavy swell. Even some strong-willed souls were affected. Despite the worsening conditions, however, *QE2* was still able to maintain speed.

QE2's fuel situation was becoming increasingly acute and the ship needed to refuel to make it to Ascension Island. The successful trial of fuel replenishment at sea with *Grey Rover* after leaving Southampton had proved that *QE2*'s refuelling equipment worked perfectly. Taking on fuel would also have the added advantage of improving the stability of the ship. Nowadays a ship's stability is calculated with the aid of a computer, but in 1982 it was necessary for a new set of manual calculations to be made every time weight was added or removed.

Second Officer Chris Haughton, who had carried out the initial calculations on the ship's stability as structural modifications were made in Southampton, was still assigned to this task. Since departure from Southampton, Chris had been carrying out daily recalculations on stability that made allowances for the consumption of fuel from the tanks at the bottom of the ship. To maintain adequate stability, sea water was pumped into available empty ballast tanks to replace the weight of fuel consumed. Chris Haughton's calculations were ongoing during the time in South Georgia as stores, ammunition, fuel, personnel and helicopters were offloaded. His latest calculations showed that the steady consumption of fuel was gradually rendering the ship top heavy, causing *QE2* to roll more than would have been the case had her fuel bunkers been full. Refuelling was necessary not only to power the three boilers but to improve the stability of the liner.

Arrangements were made for a rendezvous with the RFA tanker *Bayleaf* (Captain A. Hunter). When the ships met up on Monday, 31 May, the weather and sea conditions were too bad to attempt a fuel transfer. There was a heavy swell and winds up to gale force 8, about 45mph. The following day, 1 June, similar weather and sea conditions prevailed and continued throughout, but the barometer was beginning to rise. At 1615 hours, speed was reduced to 10 knots and *Bayleaf* kept station on the starboard side. But the conditions remained too severe for a fuel transfer to be conducted safely. By now the fuel situation was severe with the giant liner down to less than 1,000 tons of fuel, enough for just one and a half days' steaming at full power. Despite less-than-ideal conditions it was decided the transfer should take place sooner rather than later. At daybreak on 2 June, the wind had reduced to force 7, about 35mph. There was still a heavy swell but the weather was fine and clear. The decision was made to proceed. Adjustments were made to the speed and course of both ships to reduce the rolling as much as possible.

A party of sailors had been detailed by the day's duty ship, HMS *Antelope*, to muster in Two Deck amidships to stand by for RAS duty. Shortly before 0900 hours, the RAS party was moved to the passageway by the starboard shell door in readiness to haul over the refuelling hose. *Bayleaf* came into position on *QE2*'s starboard side. When the two ships were sailing comfortably side by side, a gunline was fired over to *Bayleaf* from the forward end of Boat Deck. The messenger was secured to the fuel hose, which was then swung out over the sea by the crane on *Bayleaf*. The pipe was then manually hauled aboard by the sailors lined up in the Two Deck starboard alleyway. By 0930 hours, the pipe had been connected on the first attempt. This was an impressive piece of precision work considering the poor weather conditions and a heavy swell. The two ships were rolling 150ft apart with a turbulent sea between them.

The QE2 in the Falklands War

The gunline has been fired from *QE2*. On Two Deck, Royal Navy sailors commence manually hauling in the pipe. (R.W. Warwick)

The fuel pipe has now been hauled on board through the Two Deck starboard midships shell door. (Patrick Hewetson)

The refuelling took place in a heavy swell with strong winds. *Bayleaf* ploughs into the sea with the fuel pipe suspended by her crane. (Patrick Hewetson)

Homeward Bound to Southampton

Some tense moments occurred when the heavy swell caused the two ships to roll in opposite directions. (M. Scanlan)

At times *Bayleaf* had a challenging time keeping station on *QE2*. (J. Chillingworth)

On occasions the two ships came uncomfortably close together. (J. Chillingworth)

The difference in size of the two ships is very noticeable when viewed from RFA *Bayleaf*. (RFA Nostalgia)

Homeward Bound to Southampton

Throughout the transfer of fuel, the two ships continued to roll with *Bayleaf* shipping spray over her decks. At times, the ships rolled in opposite directions, causing the fuel pipe to stretch almost horizontally. Although *QE2* has stabilisers, they were not used due to risk of damage if the ships inadvertently came too close to each other.

As the transfer progressed, the ships kept position with *Bayleaf*'s captain having the additional demanding responsibility of keeping station on *QE2*. On occasion, the two ships strayed closer together than was desirable, but with expert seamanship on both vessels the risk of collision was minimised. At 1835 hours, after twelve and a half hours' refuelling, the decision was made to cease as the steel coupling securing and taking the weight of the pipeline on *QE2* was wearing through. If the coupling had given way, the pipe would have fallen from the ship and oil would have flowed into the sea. *QE2* had taken on board 3,834 tons of fuel before the pipe was disconnected. She now had enough fuel for safe homeward passage.

The event was an impressive demonstration of seamanship by *Bayleaf* and *QE2*, given that the two ships sailed so closely in parallel for such a long time. All involved with the RAS were relieved at the completion of a successful at-sea refuelling under very difficult conditions.

QE2's deck logbook details the following entries for 2 June 1982:

0820 Tanker *Bayleaf* approaching
0832 *Bayleaf* commences final approaching
0842 Rocket line secure on *Bayleaf*
0930 Fuel line connected up
0938 Commenced taking on fuel
1835 Finished bunkers
1848 Pipe disconnected
1850 *Bayleaf* away and clear

As the RAS took place, there was a light-hearted diversion for some of the Royal Navy crew. The daily orders for the day read: 'Teams of six are to muster in the Double Down Room at 13.30. Details of the event will be given at this muster so make sure that your teams are mustered and correct. May the best team win!' The event turned out to be an orienteering challenge. Each team was given a quiz of twenty-five questions about *QE2* and a clue, namely the location where the answer could be found. One of

The QE2 in the Falklands War

the questions was 'Who is the stewardess for cabin 2132? Location: Two Deck.' The answer was Barbara Ward. Another question: 'What aircraft were destroyed on 23 May 1982? Location: notice board on 4 Deck port side.' The answer was five Mirages and seven Skyhawks (all Argentine). A more light-hearted question was 'What three misters have you in the children's room?' The answer, which could be found in the nursery on Sports Deck, was Mr Strong, Mr Happy and Mr Forgetful. There is no record of which team won the event or the winning time.

Tim Castle continued with his evening broadcasts of *Falkland Island Discs* on the ship's radio as *QE2* sailed north. As on the southbound voyage, Tim agreed to requests from members of the armed forces to guest DJ the show. Every evening the broadcast finished with the same song, Rod Stewart's 1970s hit 'Sailing'. The song's lyrics about sailing home across the sea to be with loved ones and to be free resonated perfectly with the mood on board *QE2*.

Tim Castle also helped set up and operate the lighting and audio equipment for an evening crew show hosted by the Royal Navy. The show was called a 'Sods Opera', a form of variety show held by sailors to entertain their shipmates. These shows are often bawdy and raucous, the likes of which had never been seen before on a Cunard liner. The *Coventry* crew organised the event with all four ships' companies participating. Acts were assembled and a programme of comedy and singing was hastily put together. On opening night, the captains and other senior officers occupied front row seats. For those arriving late, it was standing room only. The master of ceremonies was the chief petty officer of *Coventry*, David Kimber, dressed in a borrowed *QE2* cruise staff safari jacket. At the start of the show, he surveyed the audience, including nurses and laundry crew, and said, 'I was not expecting to see so many ladies here tonight. All I can say is, I am so ★★★★ing sorry!' It was the first laugh of the evening and the show was off to a good start.

The first spot was a stand-up comedy routine from another *Coventry* man, cook Leslie Kellett.[154] That evening the Double Down Room rang to the raunchiest jokes and most hilarious non-stop routines ever seen on board *QE2* as everyone unwound to the medicine of laughter. Some of the routines were well rehearsed and very funny, while others were being performed for the first time. Two sailors re-enacted the duet 'Summer Nights' from the film *Grease* with imaginatively reworked lyrics. The John Travolta role was performed by a sailor with an excellent singing voice, while the Olivia Newton-John character wore a *QE2* stewardess's dress.

The Cunard crew also contributed to the evening's sketches. Doctors Patrick Hewetson and Alan Kirwin performed an original comedy script loosely based on The Two Ronnies, a television comedy act popular in the UK in the 1970s and 1980s. Dr Kirwin remembers the fun of rehearsals and performing the sketch before an enthusiastic audience of the four ships' companies. Dr Patrick Hewetson also played clarinet, accompanied by a Royal Navy sailor on guitar. He also sang a cappella in a trio with a naval dental officer and *QE2* Second Officer Chris Haughton. Wearing white religious robes, they performed the popular 1970s song 'Jump' from Derek and Clive. This was memorable for the 'X-rated language and content', recalls Chris, who also sang a solo song with guitar. Hotel officer Rupert Ballantyne performed a phonetic punctuation sketch. Created by the famous comedian Victor Borge, phonetic punctuation involves reading from a script using amusing sound effects in place of full stops, question marks and so on. Victor Borge had entertained passengers during the 1982 world cruise with a performance in the Queens Room.

Waiter Pierre Cornlouer performed a song he had written accompanied by a Navy guitarist. Pierre was an Elvis fan and during that year's world cruise had visited Sam's Tailor in Hong Kong, an outfitter famous among the crew as they produced bespoke, made-to-measure clothes within a few days. During the 'Sods Opera', Pierre wore his new pale-blue Elvis suit while performing his song. He and the Navy guitarist were a hit. Captain's secretary Judy Carpenter remembers that while there had been countless shows before in the Double Down Room, 'never had I witnessed such an atmosphere. It was incredible that after all these men had gone through they could put together such a show. A real credit to the spirit of the British forces.'

The evening wound up with a rousing rendition of the national anthem. Two casualties in wheelchairs made commendable and successful efforts to stand at attention aided by their neighbours. It was a night to remember.

As the ship steamed north, the cold of the South Atlantic slowly gave way to the heat of the tropical latitudes. *QE2* was heading for Ascension Island, but her destination afterwards was unknown. On 3 June, the day before the arrival at Ascension Island, the rumours were finally dispelled. A naval officer made a Tannoy announcement from the Bridge informing everyone that orders had been received from the Ministry of Defence. After Ascension Island, *QE2* was instructed to proceed to Southampton. The ship had succeeded so well in her assignment that she was no longer required in the war zone and could best serve the Crown by bringing the survivors home. By this stage of the conflict, British troops were so well entrenched on the islands that it was a question of when, not if, the war would be concluded in the UK's favour.

The news received mixed reactions. Many crew members had been ready for the ship to go in close to the Falklands and were emotionally prepared to spend more time away. They felt they had not contributed enough towards the campaign and were willing to continue serving the war effort. Such was the *esprit de corps* among the officers and crew of *QE2*, but the decision-makers had different ideas and had never intended to risk the ship by sending her within range of enemy fighter aircraft. The Admiralty did not relax until *QE2* was well out of the danger zone. It was felt that losing *QE2*, world famous and bearing a name almost identical to that of the British monarch, would not be tolerated by British public opinion. The effect on national morale could have cost the UK the war. The hard and unpleasant reality is that the authorities were prepared to risk *Canberra* and *Norland*, both of which twice entered San Carlos to land troops. But *QE2* had accomplished something no other vessel could have done by delivering 5 Infantry Brigade to the war zone in good physical condition along with helicopters, tons of supplies and ammunition – all within two weeks.

The crews of the three warships dealt with the trauma of what had happened to them by showing solidarity to each other. On the morning of 3 June, a private memorial service for the ship's company of HMS *Coventry* was held in the Theatre. Captain Hart Dyke devised and conducted the service. The service included the naval prayer, two verses of the sailors' hymn 'Eternal Father, Strong to Save' and a lesson from *Corinthians*. At the end of the service, the names of the nineteen shipmates lost on 25 May were read, followed by a two-minute silence.[155]

On the evening of 3 June, a naval mess dinner by candlelight was held in the Princess Grill. A total of 105 officers attended from *QE2*, NP 1980 and *Ardent*, *Antelope* and *Coventry*. Three Army officers on board also attended. Before the dinner, a drinks reception was held on Helicopter Deck, the area used for physical training on the journey south.

The dinner was the idea of Captain Jimmy James. It was organised by Lieutenant Philip Rentell, who prepared the seating plan and asked some *QE2* officers to host a table. Second Officer Chris Haughton, a skilled calligrapher, carefully inscribed handwritten name cards for every place, showing name and rank. Public rooms officer Rupert Ballantyne hosted a large table which included Commander Alan West, captain of HMS *Ardent*. Cruise director Tim Castle was on a table with a sub-lieu-tenant who during dinner related how he had stood on deck and watched as Argentine fighter aircraft swooped in to attack his ship. As many offic-ers as possible dressed in formal mess rig, but most of the officers from *Ardent*, *Antelope* and *Coventry* dressed in whatever they could find, bor-rowing shirts, epaulettes, ties and other clothing from the Cunard officers. Those who could not beg or borrow uniform dressed in white T-shirts and black trousers. But while formal mess dining rig was at a premium, high spirits were not. The menu included Melon with Westphalian Ham Ascension, Pommes Frites Goose Green, Bombe Port Stanley, Falkland Cheese Board and UK Biscuits. The menu was signed by Victor Coward, the ship's executive chef. Speeches were made by Captain Peter Jackson and Captain Jimmy James. Hotel officer Terry Foskett recalls that it was 'a very moving event', especially when the national anthem was sung at the end of the dinner.

With the meal over, some of the officers retired to the Queens Grill Bar for naval mess games. Philip Rentell had been approached by some Royal Navy officers and asked to provide various implements for use in the mess games, including empty wine bottles and broom handles. One game involved officers trying to balance on wine bottles while attempting to dismount their opponents, and another was tug of war with both teams sitting in line on the floor, using a broom handle instead of a rope. The occasion served to break some of the strain for all concerned.

On Friday, 4 June, *QE2* approached Ascension Island to rendezvous for the second time with HMS *Dumbarton Castle*. Ten hands from the duty ship, which that day was *Ardent*, mustered on the aft flight deck to assist NP1980 in moving ammunition and stores. About 25 tons of ammunition had been left on board when *QE2* departed hurriedly from Grytviken. Flying stations were called at 1350 hours and shortly after the RAF search and rescue Sea King helicopter, based in Ascension, arrived to commence the transfer to *Dumbarton Castle*.

Some casualties disembarked for repatriation to the UK by the RAF. These included the eight SAS survivors of the crashed helicopter and three sailors from the ships that were lost. One soldier was in the Double Down Room waiting to be carried out to the helicopter when he remembered he had left his gun under his hospital bed. Senior Sister Jane Yelland offered

Some of the more seriously injured military personnel disembarked at Ascension. (Patrick Hewetson)

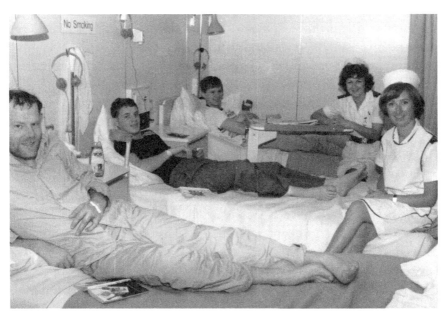

On the way north, Sister Jane Levine (left) and Senior Sister Jane Yelland (right) were kept busy with the injured who had embarked at Grytviken. (Patrick Hewetson)

QE2 nurses made sure that the injured did not miss out on the on-board entertainment, with good seats for the 'Sods Opera' crew show held in the Double Down Room. (Patrick Hewetson)

to fetch it. It was heavy and she half staggered with it back into the Double Down Room, causing the SAS men to burst out laughing. 'So I won't make it into the SAS then?' joked Jane, leading to more laughter.

Once again mail was offloaded and mail received for those on board. Some mail that arrived was for 5 Infantry Brigade, so this was hurriedly sorted, retagged and sent back ashore. The weather had been excellent for the rendezvous and by 1815 hours all the transfers had been completed and *QE2* resumed her course northward.

Unfortunately, mail sent ashore at Ascension Island arrived in the UK only after *QE2* was back in her home port. Now that it was known the ship was going home, there was more work to be done with stores to be ordered for what would be a lengthy lay-up and refit.

The following day, Paul Guest, the ship's photographer, took photographs of *QE2*'s officers and petty officers on the Sports Deck. In the officers' photograph, everyone is lined up formally. In the petty officers' photo, everyone looks relaxed and is smiling in the tropical sun, aware that the risks they had faced were now behind them. Photographs were also taken of the ships' companies of *Ardent*, *Antelope* and *Coventry*.

Back in Southampton, Cunard fleet personnel manager Arnie Williams wrote another letter to next of kin, although he was limited in what he could say:

The QE2 in the Falklands War

> We can only assume that newspaper reports of her having disembarked is [*sic*] correct and that at the present time she is away from the immediate war zone. Snippets of information indicate that morale on board is still good.[156]

The letter, dated 4 June, went on to note that the company was hosting coffee mornings and afternoon tea events for next of kin in areas with a high concentration of crew and their families, namely Southampton, Portsmouth, Bournemouth and Liverpool. Approximately thirty next of kin and close relatives attended a coffee morning at the Suncliff Hotel, Bournemouth, on 9 June. By this time the ship was nearly home. One of those attending with his parents was hotel officer Jamie Luke, whose twin brother David was serving on board the ship. Throughout the conflict the Cunard fleet personnel department worked hard to give assurance to family members that all was well, passing on messages of births and deaths and sending flowers when needed. They were on the quayside when the ship sailed and were there when she returned.

The following day, Saturday, 5 June, a lifeboat drill was held in the morning. Shortly after noon, *QE2* crossed the equator into the northern hemisphere. On this occasion King Neptune and his helpers did not appear, so the line was crossed without the boisterous ceremony that had taken place on the southbound passage. The sea was moderate and the weather fair as a balmy cruise climate prevailed. There was a strong sun and with no Sea King helicopters on board the aft helicopter deck was taken over by crew members and sailors as a sunbathing area.

The crew of HMS *Ardent* formed a Welfare Committee. The daily orders for 5 June showed that this committee met in cabin 1002 at 1030 hours to discuss the support that could be given to survivors as well as to the next of kin of those who had passed away when their ship was attacked. By the time *QE2* reached Southampton, the HMS Ardent Association had been formed. The idea to form such an association was made the day after the ship was sunk 'to foster and promote the name of HMS *Ardent* and provide a focal point to remember our fallen shipmates'.[157]

On Sunday, 6 June, two changes were made that lifted on-board morale. First, the radio silence restriction was lifted and signals could once more be transmitted from *QE2*. The radio officers invited the shipwrecked mariners into the Radio Room to make satellite calls. The calls were routed through Portishead Radio, where the staff worked hard to handle as many calls as possible. The *QE2* crew also had an opportunity to telephone home. The Radio Room had a queue outside throughout the day every day thereafter. A total of 719 calls were made, totalling 3,448 minutes, an average of nearly five minutes per call. In addition, ninety-seven telegrams and thirty-five telexes were sent. Looking back on the voyage over forty years later, chief radio officer Allan Holmes recalls a great team effort throughout the voyage: 'I was very proud of our team and will never forget the experience.'

The second morale booster was that the darken ship routine ceased and permission was given to remove blackouts. The stifling and oppressive atmosphere of life behind a veil of thick black plastic on a darkened ship was lifted, and once more daylight was allowed to flood in. It felt as if *QE2* was finally able to breathe again. As the ship lightened up, so too did the mood of those on board.

The most important role that *QE2* crew played throughout the return journey was one that did not appear in daily orders and was not formally requested. The crew offered companionship, friendship and support to the captains, officers and crew of the three warships, many of whom had seen close friends lost in horrible circumstances. Many were injured. They would return to Southampton as victors. The *QE2* crew had been warned not to question the survivors of the warships about their experiences as most would not want to be reminded of painful memories. The crew were advised that they should concentrate on letting the sailors talk and on listening. All hands did what they could to offer solidarity and friendship to these men, from starting spontaneous conversations in alleyways and pantries to more organised events.

Many of the stewardesses took the time to visit the injured soldiers in the hospital, helping them by washing their hair, repairing their clothing and talking with them. Sue Crozier recalls, 'They were just young lads who had been through a lot.' One evening Sue and some friends smuggled a sailor with a leg injury out of the hospital. They took him to the Hatch, a bar for female crew only on One Deck just forward of the crew's mess. Hotel officer Rupert Ballantyne made a point of calling on officers in their cabins, asking if they were comfortable and if there was anything they would like. The shop staff loaded up cardboard boxes with chocolate, crisps, aftershave and T-shirts, then visited the wounded in the hospital and the makeshift wards on Five Deck.

Captain Hart Dyke noted in his book *Four Weeks in May* the support he received on board:

I began slowly to come to terms with my loss. In this, I was aided greatly by the ship's company, who went out of their way to show sympathy and to help restore my spirits. I was rather far removed from the others in my smart cabin on one of the uppermost decks but this never seemed to stop people coming to see me. It was so good to talk to them …[158]

The Cunard and Royal Navy crews were able to mingle and some friendships were formed that have lasted to this day. The 'two cans a day' rule for the military was widely ignored for much of the homeward journey, with *QE2* crew responding helpfully to any requests from the Navy.

One memorable social evening took place in the Casino Bar on 6 June, the only time the bar was open for the entire voyage. The bar, which on the journey south was a senior ratings' mess area, was stacked high with cases of beer and for one night only the crews of the Royal Navy and *QE2* mixed freely, all of them seemingly intent on drinking the place dry. It was a night of high spirits, animated conversation and exuberance. The bar was full and it was a memorable evening for everyone there. A further example of goodwill came two days later when the *QE2* Social and Athletic Committee donated two cans of beer to every survivor.

The *QE2* Petty Officers' Club set aside a night for Royal Navy petty officers. The club occupied a confined space in the bow area on Two Deck. *QE2*'s petty officers made sure that everyone who walked in the club that evening was well looked after, treated to free drink and, hopefully, good company. Hairdresser Timothy Williams entertained the bar with his original dance routines. He danced theatrically to the song 'Tainted Love' by Soft Cell, a synth-pop duo who were popular in the early 1980s. Timothy made some flamboyant dance moves, at one stage going down on one knee and pretending to pray. His dancing was a real hit with the Navy crew, who laughed and applauded loudly as Timothy entertained them. Navy personnel were also welcomed into other crew bars. Stephen Easter recalls talking to sailors in the Castaways Bar on Three Deck forward. In 1988, after he had left the ship, Stephen was employed at Stanstead Airport when by remarkable coincidence he found himself working alongside one of the sailors he had socialised with years before in the Castaways Bar.

By now the first steps had been taken in forming the South Atlantic Fund, a charity to assist those who had been injured in the war and their families. Efforts were made to raise money for the fund as the ship headed north. *QE2* security petty officer Brian Marshall recalls:

Homeward Bound to Southampton

We had races around the boat deck and wagers were placed. As the crew were paid out, bins were placed near the pay office next to huge notices which read 'It's only money. It could have been your life. Give generously', which they did. On arrival at Southampton we were able to present a cheque to our captain in the sum of £3,000 for the fund.

One evening on the journey north, some of the crew members of *QE2* and HMS *Coventry* were enjoying each other's company in the Theatre Bar on Upper Deck. This had been a senior NCOs' mess on the journey south. It was now an area where any rank could socialise. Accounts petty officer David Humphreys recalls, 'I was sat with Clive Dalley and some of the *Coventry* crew. There was a nice atmosphere to the evening. The *Coventry* lads were great company and it was lovely to talk with them.' But the occasion provided a reminder that some of these men had seen some terrible sights when their ships were attacked. One young sailor suddenly broke down crying. He had seen one of his friends killed when his ship was bombed. His friends rallied around and comforted him, one with an arm around his shoulder, providing solidarity to support a shipmate through a difficult emotional moment. This is the sort of camaraderie that only those who together have a shared difficult experience can offer each other. Commander Tobin related a story about the dobymen (naval parlance for laundrymen) who had lost all their money when *Antelope* sank. His crew had a whip round and soon restored their funds.

On 6 June, Captain Jackson received a signal informing him that requisition of *QE2* would end immediately upon her arrival in Southampton when the liner would be returned to Cunard Line. He was also told that the post-requisition refit would not be completed until 14 August, nine weeks later. The Cunard personnel office at South Western House, Southampton, sent another letter to next of kin notifying them of the ship's return:

You would all I am sure have been delighted to hear the news bulletin on Sunday evening which advised that *Queen Elizabeth 2* is now heading back towards the UK from the South Atlantic and is expected to arrive at 12 noon, Friday, 11th June 1982. We know the ship's company and the military personnel on board, many of whom are survivors from Royal Naval vessels lost during the Falklands crisis will be given a tremendous welcome as *Queen Elizabeth 2* comes up Southampton Water to enter her own home port. It is anticipated that there will be a great number of people assembling at the berth and every effort will be made to give all an opportunity to have a reasonable vantage point.[159]

The letter concluded, 'Finally if you intend being on the dockside for Friday's arrival it may be of assistance to have this letter with you.'

The next day, 7 June, Captain Jackson gave a radio telephone interview to BBC radio in which he noted that:

> In the open sea we were, I felt, very vulnerable. We did not know where the Argentine submarines were and the air force were looking for them. The ship was in danger the whole time we were down there.[160]

The next morning, the ship passed close to the island of Tenerife. Captain Jackson delivered a speech to the crew over the Tannoy:

> Without any doubt it was a successful venture because we were the only ship that could deliver the 5 Infantry Brigade over that great distance in such a short time. You were all volunteers on this voyage to an area of hostilities and I want to thank you all for the manner in which you have carried out your duties, knowing full well that at times the ship was in considerable danger.[161]

Captain Jackson saluted the crews of *Coventry*, *Ardent* and *Antelope*, adding, 'Now we are almost home and I can promise you a reception at Southampton which you will never forget.'[162]

Later that day a competition was held on the Sports Deck for the title of 'Miss QE2'. This 'beauty pageant' had been organised by a petty officer from HMS *Antelope*. At this stage, women were not yet permitted to work at sea with the Royal Navy, so all entrants were male. There were five entries with the title being won by a sailor with a beard! Another form of entertainment was the daily sports competitions held around the ship. The Sports Deck was used for relay runs, five-a-side football, American football and one event which appeared on the daily orders as 'chair moving'. Crew from one of the lost ships acquired materials from the ship's carpenters to build a makeshift pool on the aft deck, and this also provided a sense of achievement and a source of pleasure to those who enjoyed a dip. The ten days at sea on *QE2* helped to restore the physical and mental health of the ship's Royal Navy guests.

The three commanding officers spent time together sharing their experiences of the situations they had endured. They were able to compare notes on the actions they took leading up to the loss of their ships and what happened after. As is the custom in the Navy, all three had to submit a report to their seniors and prepare to face a board of enquiry on their arrival home.

The crews of the warships became adept at creating their own entertainment on board. On one occasion, some of the *Ardent* crew were playing a game of hide and seek. *Ardent* crew member Mark Higgitt recalls this game was 'good fun for big kids on a ship the size of Birmingham'.[163] A sailor recalls rushing out of a lift during one such game and coming face to face with the master of *QE2*, Captain Peter Jackson. Their eyes met; there was a brief silence.

'They went that way,' said Captain Jackson, pointing down an alleyway. 'Cheers,' replied the sailor before turning to chase after his mates.[164]

Three days before *QE2* arrived home, there was a noticeable drop in morale on board as news arrived that the Welsh Guards had suffered dreadful loss of life on board RFA *Sir Galahad* (Captain Philip Roberts) anchored at Fitzroy near Bluff Cove. Anchored nearby was RFA *Sir Tristram* (Captain Robin Green). The two ships came under aerial attack. Three bombs struck *Sir Galahad*, causing a large fireball to tear along the tank deck where Welsh Guards were preparing to disembark.[165] Forty-eight people died on board *Sir Galahad* including thirty-three Welsh Guards.[166] Simon Weston, who later wrote movingly of his time aboard *QE2*, lost three mates in his mortar crew and suffered severe burn injuries.[167] Army MASH Nurse Ian Fletcher, who had assisted in *QE2*'s hospital on the southbound voyage, was thrown by the blast, dislocating his right shoulder and ending up as a patient on the task force hospital ship SS *Uganda*. Lieutenant Commander Hugh Clark RN of 825 Squadron, the first pilot to land a Sea King helicopter on board *QE2*, took part in the search and rescue, later receiving the Distinguished Service Cross for evacuating soldiers from the blazing wreck while hampered by flame bursts and black smoke.[168]

On 10 June, the day before the ship's arrival in Southampton, the news arrived that *QE2* would be welcomed in the Solent by Her Majesty Queen Elizabeth, The Queen Mother on board Her Majesty's yacht, HMY *Britannia*. Many of the Royal Navy crew members who had joined in South Georgia had only the clothes they stood in. They clearly needed to be dressed smartly for the occasion.

Petty Officer (PO) Brian 'Monty' Toms of the Royal Navy Police at HMS *Nelson*, Portsmouth, was tasked with forming a special team to support Navy personnel returning home on board *QE2*. Arrangements were made for PO Toms and his team to join the ship before arrival. Once on board he would give the men advance pay, issue them with new identity papers and give them rail travel warrants so that they could proceed on leave on arrival at Southampton. Late morning on 10 June, a Sea King helicopter took off from Culdrose bound for *QE2*, carrying PO Toms and his team. As the helicopter approached the ship, he remembers spotting *QE2* as 'a lonely dot on a calm, steel grey ocean, [and] as we flew up to her we could see, through the wave battered paint, the beautiful lines of her hull and superstructure'.[169] Once on board, he recalls the dining tables had tablecloths with small vases of flowers and the waiting staff wore neat crimson jackets and dickie bows. He took control of a small area of a restaurant where he set up tables. That afternoon he commenced the task of making the distributions to the survivors. At 1540 hours, the call 'Hands to Flying Stations' sounded again. Another Sea King landed from Culdrose, bringing new navy-blue uniforms for the crews of the three ships.

Meanwhile, around the ship both crew and Navy personnel prepared for arrival. Navy personnel were asked to check their cabins thoroughly for any life jackets and camp beds and to place them outside their cabin door for collection by the ship's crew. The Ocean Trading shop staff prepared to tally up the value of all items signed for by members of the Royal Navy. However, the chits recording the sales had been lost and could not be recovered. The result was that none of the crew from *Ardent*, *Antelope* and *Coventry* who signed for items in the shop between South Georgia and Southampton received a bill. Many *QE2* crew felt the sailors should not have been expected to pay for anything on board. To them the loss of the chits was not a problem!

Some military personnel also arrived on board to give orders about secrecy and how to handle the press. A security debrief was issued to the ship, stating:

> You are leaving an operational area in which you had access to classified operational information ... You are to ensure that the duties you have been undertaking and the operational information which has been available to you are not disclosed to any unauthorised person.[170]

The debrief went on to note 'Under Queen's Regulations, it is your duty to seek permission before talking to the press on any service matter. You also have an absolute right to refuse to talk to the press on any subject.'[171]

At 1715 hours, an announcement was made from the Bridge that at 1740 hours a military press liaison officer would address all personnel, advising what they could and could not say to the press. The announcement duly commenced on time and the officer began by reminding personnel of the old adage that the press will make a story from anything. He went on to talk about the different types of journalists the Royal Navy and *QE2* crews could expect to encounter and how they should deal with them.

He distinguished between three types of journalist in what was an effective and well-prepared announcement. The first type of journalist was from the 'family dailies', who wanted stories on romantic reunions, first meetings of men with newborn children, and so on. Survivors and crew were asked to volunteer these types of stories to the journalists. The second was the more factual journalist who would want to know details of what was happening in the field of operations, including sensationalist stories and scandal. Not far below the surface of the factual journalist was the third type, the 'spy-type' reporter who wished to find out and publish details on military operations, weapons used and their deployment, troop numbers and their positions. This type of journalist, the officer stressed, should be told nothing. It was in the interests of military personnel still engaged in the war zone that nothing was revealed about military strategy or the deployment of forces. He further stressed that thousands of service personnel remained in the Falklands and their safety and morale were extremely important. Finally, the press liaison officer said that Argentine intelligence was likely to be out and about in the pubs of Southampton and that personnel should be careful when striking up casual conversations with strangers.

At 1830 hours, *QE2* passed Mounts Bay near Penzance, and by 2200 hours, the helicopters had departed to return to Culdrose. The liner steamed slowly up the Channel towards a well-earned welcome. Meanwhile, Brian Toms and his team continued working to issue cash, travel warrants, identity cards and uniforms to the naval crews. They had brought sufficient cash to give all the survivors an advance. The last man processed was the Master at Arms of HMS *Coventry*. Petty Officer Toms finally got to bed at 0400 that morning.

QE2's northerly course continued until shortly before 2100 hours, at which time the ship was 3 miles off Lizard Point Lighthouse in Cornwall.

An easterly course was then set and the liner steamed along the south coast of England. About this time, the liner was spotted from the coast by Thomas Stanley, the proprietor of the Lizard Hotel. An ex-Royal Navy man, Thomas used his Aldis lamp to send a signal by Morse code, which read: 'Well done, welcome home, God bless.' He received the reply, 'Message received, thank you'.[172] Good time had been made, so the ship's speed was reduced to fit in with the scheduled dawn arrival at the Southampton pilotage boarding area.

Able Seaman Izzy Isaacs from *Coventry* described that final night of *QE2*'s South Atlantic journey by saying:

> The night before we docked in Southampton we could see the lights on the land. I was up early next morning as was everybody – we could see the cars lining the roads, waiting and flashing their lights both on the mainland and the Isle of Wight.[173]

AB Mark Calter of HMS *Antelope* summed up his time on the voyage home:

> The crew of the *QE2* went out of their way to look after us. Clothing wise, we only had what we arrived in, therefore, jeans, T-shirts were happily supplied by the waiting staff. I will never ever forget their generosity, nor helpfulness at such at stressful time. Thank you.

QE2 had left home in spring, sailed through the heat and humidity of the tropics into the bitter cold of a southern hemisphere winter, then turned around and come all the way back. Around the ship, there was a buoyant mood of expectancy as Royal Navy sailors and *QE2* crew bantered together for the last time. Everyone on board knew this would be no ordinary arrival and tomorrow would be a special day. In the crew bars, it was a channels night like no other.

13

QE2 Arrives Home

11 June 1982. A day to remember. The timetable for *QE2*'s arrival in her home port was carefully choreographed on what turned out to be a glorious sunny day.

Officers breakfasting in the Wardroom that morning found a menu with the following message:

Captain Peter Jackson and his Ship's Company wish you happy landings and smooth sailing in the future. The road to life is hard and long and troubles are not few, but on this very memorable day may all joy be with you.

The final daily orders showed the duty ship as HMS *Antelope*. The last briefings of the crews of the three warships took place at 0755 hours: *Ardent* in the Casino, *Antelope* in the midship's Rotunda and *Coventry* in the Theatre. Later, the crew of each ship were able to collect a bottle of duty-free spirits before being served lunch at the earlier time of 1115 hours.

At 0635 hours, there was an early call for the flight deck crew as the ship steamed slowly past the Isle of Portland. Wessex helicopters landed, bringing the BBC's John Humphrys and several national newspaper reporters, smart men in suits with their notebooks at the ready. Hotel officer Rupert Ballantyne was given the responsibility of greeting the press.

Admiral Sir John Fieldhouse, Commander in Chief of the Royal Navy, landed on board at 0800 hours. He met the commanding officers of *Ardent*, *Antelope* and *Coventry* in Captain Jackson's quarters. He then addressed the three Royal Navy ships' companies, offering generous praise.[174] He was very complimentary about the shipyards that had prepared the ships for the task force. He praised the crews for facing considerable hardship and hazards with courage and fortitude.

Lord Matthews, the chairman of Cunard Line, arrived and made his way around the ship, speaking to personnel. This was followed by a press conference held in the Q4 Room with Captain Jackson, Captain James, Lord Matthews and Admiral Fieldhouse in attendance. Lieutenant Rentell gave an overview of the voyage. Lord Matthews thanked Sir John for his compliments about the Merchant Navy and went on to thank the Royal Navy for protecting the lives of the men aboard *QE2* and the ship herself. The press conference was the last formal event to be held in the Q4 Room, which would vanish in the subsequent refit to re-emerge as the Club Lido.

Captain Peter Driver, Cunard's choice pilot who had guided her down Southampton Water at the start of the voyage, boarded at 0848 hours. The course was adjusted to enter the Solent via the narrow Needles Channel. The liner passed Needles Lighthouse and the impressive tall range of chalk rocks on the starboard side shortly after 0915 hours. While she was steaming along the western Solent, Admiral Fieldhouse departed by helicopter at 0935 hours. As the helicopter disappeared over the horizon, Lieutenant Commander Shaw made his final announcement to the flight deck crew, finishing with the words, 'So for the last time – stand down from flying stations.' As the liner made her way inbound, HMS *Londonderry*, a Type 12 anti-submarine frigate, was on hand to welcome *QE2* home by firing a twenty-one-gun salute.

This was followed by an announcement from the Bridge, asking personnel to muster on deck to greet Her Majesty Queen Elizabeth, The Queen Mother. The crew of *Ardent* stood on the forward helicopter deck and the crews of *Coventry* and *Antelope* stood on the aft helicopter deck. The crew of *QE2* lined up along the Boat Deck. As *QE2* slowly made her way up the Solent, the royal yacht *Britannia* came into view off the coast of Cowes with the Queen Mother, dressed in a light-blue outfit, standing on the aft deck. As *QE2* sailed past *Britannia*, the Queen Mother stood regally, giving her familiar royal wave. The Navy personnel lined up on deck responded with three resounding cheers. Then a Harrier fighter aircraft screamed overhead at no more than 500ft, twisting in a victory roll as it passed over the two ships. The salute from *Britannia* was a particularly poignant moment for the *Coventry* captain David Hart Dyke, who had served as the commander of the royal yacht for two years.[175]

QE2 Arrives Home

As the ships passed, radiogram messages were exchanged between the Queen Mother and Captain Jackson. The Queen Mother sent the first message:

> I am pleased to welcome you back as QE2 returns to home waters after your tour of duty in the South Atlantic. The exploits of your own ship's company and the deeds of valour of those who served in Antelope, Coventry and Ardent have been acclaimed throughout the land and I am glad to add my personal tribute.
> Elizabeth Regina
> Queen Mother

Captain Peter Jackson replied:

> Please convey to Her Majesty Queen Elizabeth our thanks for her kind message. Cunard's Queen Elizabeth 2 is proud to have been of service to Her Majesty's forces.
> Jackson, Master QE2

Later, the messages were immortalised by being engraved on silver plaques and mounted on an Upper Deck bulkhead for all to see.

By now a flotilla of small boats were gathering around the ship. Off Cowes, the ship turned to port and started the familiar journey up Southampton Water towards the passenger berth. Kenneth Littlehales, the son of stewardess Elena, who was working at the Fawley oil refinery, was at hand to wave as his mother's ship passed by. At the same time, the tankers berthed alongside the terminal gave three blasts on their foghorns to salute QE2. To each salute QE2 replied with three blasts in exchange. It was almost as if the ship was bellowing out from sheer relief at coming home. Southampton Water was alive with yachts, cabin cruisers, ribs and a variety of boats, all of which had come out to view the historic occasion of a third Cunard Queen returning from war. The noise from vessels great and small sounding their whistles and horns to salute the liner provided a cacophony of noise normally reserved for a maiden arrival.

As QE2 neared the ocean terminal, tugboats sent up jets of water from their powerful fire hoses. On QE2's previous voyage, she had received a fire hose welcome when arriving in Philadelphia for the city's three hundredth anniversary. But this was different; now QE2 was being honoured and saluted by her home port for a job well done. Some of *QE2*'s officers took the opportunity to walk into the Wardroom and see their ship on air as her arrival was broadcast live on television. On the open decks, music was being broadcast by Tim Castle. He had arranged with the Bridge to let him know when the ship was nearing the berth so that he could avoid piped music competing with the military brass band already assembled on the quay. Tim played a variety of tunes, concluding with 'Men of Harlech', a Welsh military marching song, in tribute to the Welsh Guards who had suffered so badly at Fitzroy three days earlier.

QE2 was assisted to her berth by the tugs *Albert* and *Culver* forward and *Ventnor*, *Chale* and *Calshot* aft. The huge liner carried on a short way past the dock and turned around in a position close to Town Quay, giving thousands of assembled spectators a close view of the ship. Once turned, she approached the berth and those on board started to make out the faces of friends and relatives amidst the enormous throng of people on quayside.

Crowds of people lined the quayside, including families of the crews of the three Navy ships, many with hand-painted 'welcome home' banners and Union Jacks. There were groups of schoolchildren on a guided excursion to witness this unique moment of British maritime history. A military brass band marched up and down the quayside, playing 'Rule Britannia'. It was impossible for those present that day, either on board or quayside, not to get caught up in the sense of occasion. *QE2*'s arrival home was nothing less than triumphant. On-board banners were held aloft. The *Ardent* crew held a handmade White Ensign with the ship's motto 'Through Fire and Water'. Another banner declared 'Falklands First, World Cup Next!'

By 1156 hours, *QE2* was secure port side to the Queen Elizabeth II Terminal. A gangway was put down within minutes. Cunard's flagship had arrived home safe and sound from a mission to the southern hemisphere which had covered a distance of 14,967 nautical miles in just under thirty days.

Marilyn Jackson, the captain's daughter, watched the arrival and remembers:

> … the day of the homecoming was very exciting as we made our way down to the docks to see *QE2* return. We were dockside among the crowds of excited crew and troop family members. We were able to see my father on the bridge as the ship came alongside. Eventually my mother and I were allowed to go on board and were taken to my father's

quarters where he had been meeting various dignitaries. It was with great relief that we later returned to my parents' family home together.

The three Royal Navy commanding officers, Alan West, Nick Tobin and David Hart Dyke, took up position at the bottom of the gangway to bid farewell to their ships' companies. Then, to the strains of 'Hearts of Oak', injured survivors were stretchered off first. They were followed by the youngest naval crew member, a sailor from *Coventry*. The rest of the naval crews then marched down the gangway across a red carpet, many of them carrying kitbags on their shoulders. Despite having arrived on board with nothing, many of the sailors had acquired clothing donated by the ship's crew and other items they had purchased from the ship's shop. As they reached the bottom of the gangway, each was presented with a red rose given by local schoolchildren. They then made their way into the large ground-floor area of the terminal building. This was the area where passengers collected luggage when arriving from a crossing or cruise. If they were unlucky, they might have an enquiring conversation with Her Majesty's Customs. But today there were no formalities and the disembarking passengers were reunited privately with families, sweethearts and children.

QE2's own crew disembarked via the forward gangway where hundreds of family members and friends had gathered to greet them. It was a very emotional day for everyone. Among them was Pat Skelcher, whose husband Robin, a barkeeper, had been employed by Cunard for over thirty years. Their son, Peter, also worked on *QE2* but was on leave during the South Atlantic voyage. Pat said, 'This is the best day of our lives' as they waited for Robin to disembark. Brian Gosney served as a steward on board. While his daughter, Cheryl, waited for him, she said, 'I have mixed emotions today. I am happy to see my dad but there must be many mothers, wives and daughters who must be heartbroken their loved ones will never return.'

Thanks to the care that the wounded received on board, only seven Royal Navy sailors were still in the hospital when the ship arrived home. One casualty who was still suffering from shrapnel wounds was transferred upon arrival to the Royal Naval Hospital Haslar at Gosport near Portsmouth.

The local and national press covered stories of the ship's arrival on their front pages with photographs of Royal Navy personnel and *QE2* crew being welcomed home. There were pictures of Captain David Hart Dyke being welcomed by his wife and two daughters. Fortunately, by the time the ship arrived at Southampton, Captain Hart Dyke's facial burns had healed well. Today, his eldest daughter, who was just 10 years old in 1982, is famous as the comedian Miranda Hart.

Sue Crozier and a shipmate had agreed to travel to London to be interviewed live on television. They had been briefed on what they could and could not say about the voyage. A taxi was waiting to take them to the BBC's studios at Shepherd's Bush, where they were interviewed by BBC journalist Sue Lawley. The taxi then took them back to Southampton, where they joined shipmates at La Margherita, a Southampton pizza restaurant popular with *QE2* crew.

The BBC broadcast the ship's arrival live on television. Among the crew members interviewed were stewardess Lorna Le Peuple, who received media attention during the conflict as the only grandmother in the task force. She was greeted by her family on the quayside. Also interviewed were carpenter Bill Bailey, baker confectioner Alun Davies and waiter Phillip Ward, the latter having served with Cunard during the Second World War. Those interviewed steered clear of discussing where the ship had been. One Royal Navy officer who was interviewed said they were extremely lucky to have come home on *QE2*. He said it was 'the next best thing to coming back in your own ship'.[176]

Commander Alan West, captain of *Ardent*, was interviewed about the air raid that had sunk his ship:

The Skyhawks penetrated our defences. Three bombs hit the ship. You could see them coming, green with red circles, bigger and bigger, then they hit. Two exploded. I had to make the hardest decision of my life. I had to consider the crew.[177]

The front page of the local Southampton newspaper, the *Southern Evening Echo*, described the ship's return with the headline 'Well Done QE2 – Welcome Home'. The *Daily Star* led with 'Back From the War: Joy as the QE2 Sails In'. The *Daily Mirror* showed a picture of the Queen Mother greeting the ship with the headline 'Home Are The Heroes, Home From the Sea'.

Although it was a day of celebration and family reunions, it was impossible to forget those who did not sail into Southampton that day: the forty-three sailors from *Ardent*, *Antelope* and *Coventry* who lost their lives while serving their country. When *QE2* arrived home, it was another difficult day for the families and friends of these men. Petty Officer 'Monty' Toms, who prepared the survivors for arrival, recalls: 'the most poignant thing of all was bringing back mailbags full of unopened letters addressed to those poor souls who were lost during the sinking of their ships.'[178]

Over the next two to three days, the crew who had not sailed with the ship arrived back on board. The ambience of the ship changed once more. There were no longer any military passengers, only ship's crew, Cunard shoreside personnel and contract workers as *QE2* settled into the on-board routine of a lengthy lay-up. The returning crew were eager to hear all the details of the voyage.

QE2's South Atlantic odyssey was in many respects record breaking. When she departed from Southampton on 12 May 1982, she had on board more souls than she had ever carried before. She sailed with her heaviest displacement ever due to the added weight from structural changes, equipment and additional personnel. As a result, *QE2* put to sea below her Plimsoll line for the first and only time in her career.

Arrival day, Southampton. HMY *Britannia* greets *QE2* as she enters the Western Solent. On board *Britannia* was HM The Queen Mother. (Captain P. Jackson)

A variety of small ships and helicopters greeted *QE2* on her triumphant return as HMY *Britannia* escorted the ship up the Solent. (Captain P. Jackson)

As *QE2* sailed past HMY *Britannia*, the naval sailors gave three cheers. (Stephen Hallam)

QE2 Arrives Home

A collage of newspaper headlines after *QE2* arrived home. Media around the world provided coverage of the liner's safe return. (R.W. Warwick)

Captain N.C.H. James RN (left), of Naval Party 1980, greets the senior management of the Cunard Line, who had joined the liner by helicopter as she steamed up Southampton Water, Lord Victor Matthews (centre) and Eric Parker (right). (Malcolm Scanlan)

The survivors from the three sunken Royal Navy warships were the first to disembark to the sounds of a military brass band. (Patrick Hewetson)

A gangway was rigged for the crew on Five Deck forward. (Patrick Hewetson)

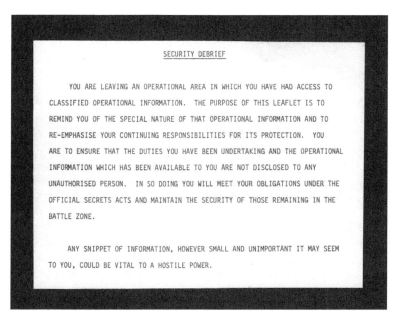

Before arrival at Southampton, all hands received a security debrief and were given advice about what not to say to the media. (David Luke)

The liner delivered 5 Infantry Brigade to South Georgia physically fit and in good morale. She then cared for and brought home the crews of the three warships. The return voyage from Grytviken to Southampton was the longest passage *QE2* ever made without stopping at a port or anchoring.

In her service life of nearly forty years with Cunard Line, *QE2* sailed more than 5 million miles, visiting over 300 ports around the world. She had many memorable voyages, but her most epic journey was to the South Atlantic in 1982. *QE2* played a vital role in the success of Britain's campaign and much of the credit for that goes to Captain Peter Jackson, whose experience, judgement and calm authority were an inspiration to those he led under very testing circumstances. Captain Jackson remained convinced his ship shortened the war: 'She was the only ship in the world that could have done the job. If *QE2* hadn't been used, the war would definitely have been much longer.'[179] *QE2* takes her rightful place in the pantheon of proud merchant ships to have provided outstanding service to Crown and country in time of need.

14

Military Units Embarked on *QE2*

5 Infantry Brigade was made up of the following units that embarked on *QE2* and sailed from Southampton on 12 May 1982 bound for South Georgia:

1st Battalion the Welsh Guards
1st Battalion the 7th Duke of Edinburgh's Own Gurkha Rifles
2nd Battalion the Scots Guards
4th Field Regiment Royal Artillery (97 Field Battery)
5 Infantry Brigade HQ and Signals Squadron
5 Infantry Brigade Platoon of 160 Provost Company Royal Military Police
8 Field Cash Office Royal Army Pay Corps
9 Parachute Squadron Royal Engineers
10 Field Workshop Royal Electrical and Mechanical Engineers
16 Field Ambulance Royal Army Medical Corps
32 Guided Weapons Regiment Royal Artillery
36 Engineer Regiment Royal Engineers
55 Field Surgical Team
63 Squadron RAF Regiment
81 Intelligence Section
81 Ordnance Company Royal Army Ordnance Corps
91 Ordnance Company Royal Army Ordnance Corps
407 Troop Royal Corps of Transport
601 Tactical Air Control Party

602 Tactical Air Control Party
656 Squadron Army Air Corps
825 Naval Air Squadron – Fleet Air Arm with 2 Sea Kings
Blowpipe Troop 43 Air Defence Battery

On Departure from Southampton, 12 May 1982

QE2 crew:	660
5 Infantry Brigade:	2,988
Naval Party 1980:	51
Total:	**3,699**

Joined at Ascension, 20 May 1982

132 Field Battery Royal Artillery:	17
Major General Jeremy Moore and staff:	Not known

Disembarked to HMS *Antrim*, 27 May 1982:	88

On Departure from Grytviken, 29 May 1982

QE2 crew:	654
Survivors from HMS *Ardent*:	177
Survivors from HMS *Antelope*:	202
Survivors from HMS *Coventry*:	253
5 Infantry Brigade:	2
Special Air Service:	8
RAF Movement Control:	3
Naval Party 1980:	51
Total:	**1,350**

Northbound
Medical disembarks at Ascension, 4 June 1982: 10 estimated. Exact number not known.

15

QE2 Logbook Extract

Date	Latitude at Noon	Longitude at Noon	Distance Nautical Miles	Average Speed Knots	Total Distance	Fuel Used Tons	Fuel Remaining Tons	Remarks
04 May 1982	In port							Arrived Southampton. Moored starboard side to Queen Elizabeth II terminal.
05 May 1982	In port							Conversion in progress.
06 May 1982	In port							Conversion in progress.
07 May 1982	In port							Conversion in progress.
08 May 1982	In port							Conversion in progress.
09 May 1982	In port							1015: Commenced loading ammunition into No. 1 hold.
10 May 1982	In port							2330: Ceased loading ammunition.
11 May 1982	In port							0715: No. 1 hold ready to continue loading ammunition – awaiting Ministry of Defence representative and fire department. 0756: Commenced loading ammunitior. 2010–2155: Bunkering. Fuel oil received 3455 tons.
12 May 1982	In port & At sea & At anchor						5969	0545: Commenced embarkation of troops. 0645–0850: Bunkering. No. 10 & 12 lifeboats lowered & exercised. 1500: Pilot Peter Driver on board. 1547: Tugs Albert, Brockenhurst, Calshot, Clausentum & Romsey made fast 1603: Let go lines. 1626: Vessel swung and proceeding to sea. Tugs except Albert let go. 1732: Commenced rounding West Brambles Bank. 1749: Tug Albert let go. 1927: Nab East buoy abeam to stbd. 2001: Pilot departs at Nab Tower. 2031: At anchor. Nab Tower bearing 018° × 2.8m. Finished with engines.
13 May 1982	50° 13'N	002° 04'W	50	20.83	50	36	5933	0120: Tug Bustler alongside delivering stores. 0130: Tug departs. 0911: Standby engines. 0928: Anchor aweigh. 0936: Departure. (Two boilers in use) 1030: Boat Drill. Lifeboats lowered to embarkation level. 1200: Course 248°. 1717: Manoeuvring for helicopter operations. 1745: Helicopter departs. 1836: RFA Grey Rover approaching. 1847: Lines exchanged. 1900: Bunkering hose connected. 1920: Hose and lines disconnected. 1929: Resumed passage. 2035: Helicopters landed & secured.
14 May 1982	43° 37'N	009° 54'W	532	22.17	582	354	5579	Heading towards Freetown. 1030: Embarked forces assembled at Boat Stations and instructed. 1C50: Watertight doors tested from Bridge control. 1200: Course 207°.
15 May 1982	34° 22'N	014° 36'W	599	24.96	1181	407	5172	0000: Third boiler on line – engine revs 140. 0930–1030: Firearms practice. 1045: Crew Emergency & Boat Drill. 1200: Course 200°. 1400–1603: Flying operations.

QE2 Logbook Extract

Date	Latitude at Noon	Longitude at Noon	Distance Nautical Miles	Average Speed Knots	Total Distance	Fuel Used Tons	Fuel Remaining Tons	Remarks
16 May 1982	25° 04'N	018° 46'W	631	25.24	1812	396	4776	0400: Clocks retarded 1 hour. 0915: Hand steering tested. 1200: Course 177°. 1358–1625: Flying operations. Church service conducted by Captain Jackson.
17 May 1982	15° 10'N	018° 14'W	593	24.71	2405	367	4409	0150: Settings on degaussing coils adjusted. 1000–1200: Flying operations. 1050: Watertight doors tested. 1200: Course 179°. 1845–2030: Flying stations.
18 May 1982	At sea & In port		551	25.05	2956	359	4050	0930: Standby Engines. 1000: Arrival. 1025: Pilots Kenokai & Jones on board. Tugs Sena & Intermani in attendance. 1110: Swung & approaching berth. 1145: All fast port side to. 1320: Commenced fuelling from barge. 1450: Commenced fuelling from quay. 1930: Stopped fuelling from barge. 2130: Stopped fuelling from quay. 2200: Pilots on board. 2253: All gone fore & aft. 2311: Pilots away. 2400: Departure – set course south towards Ascension. Fuel received: 1867 tons.
19 May 1982	03° 51'N	014° 07'W	301	25.03	301	195	5722	0000: Blackout in force. 1050: Watertight doors tested. 1200: Course 182°. 2117: Crossed Equator.
20 May 1982	05° 57'S	015° 10'W	594	24.75	895	442	5280	1200: Course 182°. 1330–1609: Flying stations. 1445: Dumbarton Castle approaching. Two helicopters being used for transfers. 1453: RAF Sea King lands. 1840: Blackout in force.
21 May 1982	08° 18'S	014° 33'W	482	20.08	1377	349	4931	0000: Vessel off Ascension Island. 0800: Flying stations. Personnel, stores & mail taken on board.
22 May 1982	08° 53'S	015° 06'W	548	22.83	1925	408	4523	0040: Contact made with Atlantic Causeway. 0656: Flying stations – helicopter transfers with Atlantic Causeway. 1030: Crew emergency and boat drill. 1040: Completed helicopter operations. 1200: Course 335°. 1250: Flying stations. 1300: Helicopter transfer from Atlantic Causeway. 1310: Flying operations completed. 1600: Emergency drill for troops.
23 May 1982	19° 03'S	18° 42'W	643	25.72	2568	462	4061	0200: Radars off. Blackout enforced. 0400: Clocks retarded 1 hour. 1100: Watertight doors tested from Bridge control. 1200: Course 199°. 1745: Watertight doors on 6, 7 & 8 decks closed.
24 May 1982	28° 41'S	20° 46'W	620	25.83	3188	424	3637	0000: Radars shut down. 1200: Course 153°. 1745: Watertight doors on all decks closed. Average engine revs: 143 per minute.

Date	Latitude at Noon	Longitude at Noon	Distance Nautical Miles	Average Speed Knots	Total Distance	Fuel Used Tons	Fuel Remaining Tons	Remarks
25 May 1982	38°39'S	20°18'W	610	25.42	3798	444	3193	0000: Radars shut down. 1200: Course 202°. 1430–1635: Flying operations.
26 May 1982	47°59'S	25°20'W	602	25.08	4400	416	2777	0000: Radars shut down. 1200: Course 205°. 1534–2000: Reduced visibility. Engines on standby. 2024: Commenced evasive steering – courses various.
27 May 1982	52°43'S & At anchor	35°51'W	540 Noon to arrival: 95	21.60	4940 5035	365	2412	0000: Evasive steering in force. Vessel on ice routine. Restricted visibility – extra lookouts posted. 0400: Clocks retarded 1 hour. 1130: Rendezvous with HMS *Antrim*. 1337: Transfer of personnel completed. 1804: Right Whale Rock bearing 182° × 4.5m. 1812: End of Passage. 1907: Starboard anchor let go in Cumberland East Bay. 2120: Trawler *Cordellia* alongside. 2145: Commenced disembarkation of troops. 2310: Stores from No. 1 hold being transferred to deck. 2340: Tug *Typhoon* alongside. 2350: HMS *Leeds Castle* manoeuvring alongside.
28 May 1982	At Anchor					252*	2160	0000: Disembarkation of troops continues by trawlers *Cordella, Pict, Farnella* & *Northella*. 0630–0732: Luggage being discharged onto tug *Typhoon*. 0805: Launch from HMS *Endurance* alongside. Helicopters transferring stores & ammunition. 1645: Completed flying operations. Helicopters transferred to *Canberra*.
29 May 1982	At anchor & At sea					120*	2040	0000: Transfer of stores into trawlers continues. 0840: Nos. 8 & 10 lifeboats launched. 1609: Standby engines. 1710: Commenced weighing anchor. 1727: Anchor aweigh. 1742: Departure. Courses various through ice fields. 2200: Clear of ice – increased speed.
30 May 1982	50°38'S	026°15'W	441	24.10	441	313	1727	0000: Blackout observed. 0730: Radars off. 1020: Emergency & boat drill. 1055: Watertight doors tested. 1200: Course 060°.
31 May 1982	–	–	578		1019	417	1310	0000: Blackout enforced. Radars off. 0400: Clocks advanced 1 hour. 0615: Chemical spillage on 2 Deck Aft. 1115: Lat 43°05'S Long 017°56'W. 1200: Course 000°.
01 Jun 1982	33°34'S	017°59'W	592	24.67	1611	424	886	0000: Radars off. 1050: Watertight doors tested. 1200: Course 000°. 1645: Standby for rendezvous with RFA *Bayleaf*. (Weather too bad to transfer fuel)
02 Jun 1982	27°56'S	017°43'W	357	15.52	1968	213	673	0400: Clocks advanced 1 hour. 0804: Reduced speed. 0820: RFA *Bayleaf* approaching. 0840: Rocket line secured. 0853: Distance line secured. 0903: Pipe line connected. 0938: Commenced taking fuel. 1200: Course 300°. 1945: Bunkering completed. 1850: *Bayleaf* away & clear. 1851: Resumed passage. Bunkers received 3834 tons.

QE2 Logbook Extract

Date	Latitude at Noon	Longitude at Noon	Distance Nautical Miles	Average Speed Knots	Total Distance	Fuel Used Tons	Fuel Remaining Tons	Remarks
03 Jun 1982	20°13'S	017°27'W	497	20.71	2465	315	4192	0000: Radars off. Blackout enforced. 1200: Course 012°. 1830: Watertight doors closed.
04 Jun 1982	10°09'S	015°21'W	614	25.58	3079	435	3757	0000: Radars off. Blackout enforced. 1200: Course 012°. 1350: Flying stations. 1500: HMS *Dumbarton Castle* on station. Transfers in progress. 1815: Helicopter operations completed.
05 Jun 1982	00°47'S	016°51'W	573	23.89	3652	394	3363	0000: Radars off. Blackout enforced. 1030: Emergency & Boat Drill exercised. 1200: Course 355°. 1323: Crossed Equator.
06 Jun 1982	09°21'N	017°42'W	610	25.42	4262	440	2923	0100: Hand steering tested. 1100: Church Service. 1200: Course 355°. Average engine revs: 140 per minute.
07 Jun 1982	19°29'N	018°12'W	607	25.29	4869	437	2486	0200: Hand steering tested. 1200: Course 000°. Average engine revs: 143 per minute.
08 Jun 1982	29°10'N	015°48'W	606	25.25	5475	426	2060	0200: Hand steering tested. 1050: Watertight doors tested from Bridge control. 1200: Course 019°.
09 Jun 1982	37°51'N	012°13'W	550	22.92	6025	343	1717	0300: Hand steering tested. 1200: Course 019°.
10 Jun 1982	47°27'N	007°00'W	620	26.96	6645	461	1256	0300: Hand steering tested. 0400: Clocks advanced 1 hour. 1200: Course 023°. 1540–1945: Flying stations.
11 Jun 1982	At sea & In port		331	15.76	6976	180	1076	0200: Eddystone Lighthouse bearing 318° × 10'. 0635: Flying stations. 0800: End of passage. 0845: Pilot Peter Driver on board. 0945: Passing HMY *Britannia*. 1051: Tugs *Albert, Calshot, Chale, Culver & Ventnor* in attendance. 1130: Approaching berth. 1145: Lines ashore. 1156: All fast port side to. Ammunition being discharged. 2300: Ceased discharge of ammunition.

The fuel remaining figures for the voyage have been calculated by the authors based on the daily logbook entries of fuel consumed, taking into account fuel bunkered in Freetown and from RFA *Bayleaf*.

* Fuel consumption at Grytviken calculated from logbook entries.

VOYAGE SUMMARY

Distances

Southampton to Freetown:	2,956m
Freetown to Grytviken:	5,035m
Grytviken to Southampton:	6,976m
TOTAL DISTANCE:	14,967 nautical miles

Fuel

On Departure Southampton:	5,969t
Taken at Freetown:	1,867t
Taken from RFA *Bayleaf*:	3,834t
Total:	11,670t
On arrival Southampton:	1,076t
FUEL CONSUMED:	10,594 tons

Passage Time

Southampton–Freetown:	5d 01h 24m	Av Spd: 24.35 k
Freetown–Grytviken:	8d 20h 12m	Av Spd: 23.90 k
Grytviken–Southampton:	12d 12h 18m	Av Spd: 23.30 k

16

The Cost of
the Requisition

When *QE2* was requisitioned by the Department of Trade on behalf of Her Majesty's Government, the majority of the costs associated with the operation of the ship became the ministry's responsibility. As a result, a dialogue was soon established between the Department of Trade and Eric W. Parker, Group Managing Director of Trafalgar House, the owners of *QE2*. The managing of the costs as they accrued were handled by the accounts department of Trafalgar House. They received day to day input from the Cunard office in Southampton and the accounts department on *QE2*, known on board as the Control Office. All financial activities on board were very strictly managed. During the charter period, the department was led by senior hotel officer Gerry Nolan with the assistance of David Luke, David Humphreys and five other staff.

In addition to *QE2*, three other Cunard ships were requisitioned by the government for the campaign. These were *Atlantic Conveyor*, *Atlantic Causeway* and *Saxonia*. The cost associated with the hiring of the three ships was dealt with separately from *QE2* and is not included in the summary of expenditure below.

Shortly after the requisition, the Department of Transport agreed to make an advance payment to Cunard to cover costs incurred during the first thirty days of the charter. Many of the costs that were agreed upon included the daily hire rate of the vessel, crew wages and wages of crew left ashore. The agreed rate was £100,000 per day. It was further agreed that 'running costs' would be refunded at the middle of each month against invoices submitted. This arrangement enabled Cunard's cash flow to operate on a reasonably orderly basis, given that the company had to make a considerable number of refunds on both sides of the Atlantic to those who had paid for voyages that had to be cancelled as a result of the requisition.

Cunard was required to estimate the value of the liner in case she was lost due to enemy action. To do this trading figures were submitted to the Department of Trade. On receipt of the figures, the ministry questioned the daily charter fee and arbitrarily concluded that the rate was too high. Having reached this conclusion, it stopped making further payments on receipt of invoices. The last payment for running costs was made on 21 June. Mr Parker was obviously concerned about this development, so he wrote a letter to Mr Michael Franklin (later Sir Michael), who at that time was the Permanent Secretary of the Department of Trade. In his letter he pointed out that the situation could cause serious financial problems for Cunard with money flowing out and very little income being received. By the end of June, Cunard had submitted invoices to the value of over £3.5 million but it was not until 12 July that payments recommenced.

Compensation for consequential losses incurred as a result of the requisition often led to protracted and lengthy negotiations with the government. The London-based Concorde Travel Club Ltd specialised in holidays for passengers travelling between London and New York on the supersonic airliner Concorde. Passengers would travel one way on *QE2* and the other way by Concorde. Solicitors acting for the Club wrote to the government, pointing out that two cancelled tours arranged for May and June had resulted in losses in the region of £100,000. Ocean Trading Ltd, the company that operated the shops on *QE2*, estimated its loss of profit between the requisition dates to be £272,300.

At the other end of the financial spectrum was a loss incurred by Walport Ingram Ltd. This firm provided Cunard with films to be shown to passengers on board. It submitted a claim to the government for compensation to the tune of £1,838.40.

One of the more forceful claims submitted by Cunard was for the consequential losses suffered by the company on its cruise ships operating in the Caribbean and, in particular, MV *Cunard Countess*. Cunard argued that losses had arisen due to substantial number of cancellations made by South American passengers sympathetic to Argentina. Negotiations on this claim continued for quite some time after the end of the conflict. It was not until late March 1983 that Cunard was informed by the government that it would not accept any claims of this nature. This decision was rather unfortunate for the company, which estimated the loss of business to be over £600,000.

An interesting claim was submitted by a Scottish hotel owner in Southampton, who said his business was £5,000–6,000 out of pocket because of the requisition. This was because coach-loads of Americans would normally stop at the hotel, having travelled across the Atlantic on *QE2*. Cunard declined to comment on the claim. The claim, however, does highlight the financial impact the liner had on the city of Southampton and the UK economy in general.

The authors have not been able to find the value that *QE2* was insured for. However, the *Guardian* newspaper reported on 1 May 1982 that the liner was insured for £30 million and that sources at Lloyd's said Cunard had inquired about raising this to £50 million. The newspaper also said that Cunard had refused to disclose the amount of insurance cover it had taken out but the premium was believed to be substantial. The risk was being shared by a marine syndicate at Lloyd's.

An unconfirmed report suggested that the government paid out more than £54 million for the hire of all the merchant ships used in the task force.

When *QE2* returned to the UK, Cunard decided to take the opportunity to refurbish parts of the ship and make some structural changes. This decision inevitably led to lengthy negotiations on which refurbishment costs were incurred as a direct result of the requisitioning and which were unrelated and should be borne by Cunard.

The government paid in the region of £2 million towards repairs and Cunard spent an estimated additional £5 million for remodelling and improvements. The following figures are from invoices submitted to the government by Cunard Line:

Hire of ship for 107 days: £7,378,405

Port charges: £158,286
Hire of river and docking pilots, tugs, linesmen, berths, gangways and conveyors, security, water, cranes, garbage disposal.

Fuel and lubricating oil: £718,702
Heavy fuel for main engines, diesel for auxiliary machinery and lubricating oil.

Crew wages: £3,400,943
Wages for all crew members embarked for the voyage, those not required to sail and those on paid leave.

Food and liquor: £1,413,410
Supplies for crew, troops and survivors. Revenue from the sale of liquor has been deducted.

Insurance: £216,390
Extra danger premiums. Insurance for valuables landed ashore.

Management costs: £3,338,646
In 1982, Cunard had a fleet of three passenger ships managed from offices in Southampton and New York, so a proportion of the costs were applied to *QE2*. Among other things, staff on both sides of the Atlantic were engaged in dealing with cancelled bookings direct with passengers or with the numerous travel agents worldwide.

Cunard did not know until *QE2* passed Ascension northbound that she was soon to be released from requisition. This gave little time for the company to change *QE2* from a troopship back to a luxury liner and to promote future Atlantic crossings and cruises.

Forward exchange and interest losses: £811,753
As the company dealt mainly in the pound sterling and US dollar, considerable losses were incurred with the existing forward exchange contracts.

Overhaul and repairs: £315,554
Although the Ministry of Defence paid for the removal of the helicopter decks and the reinstatement of superstructure, there were numerous areas of the vessel that had to be repaired. This included inadvertent damage to cabins, carpets, furniture and open wood decks.

Consequential losses and advertising: £3,204,884
There was no precedent for the government to make restitution for losses attributed to consequential losses, so compensation in this area was more difficult to quantify and was the subject of lengthy discussions with the Ministry of Defence. Factors included the cancellation of bookings and the inability to guarantee future bookings due to the uncertainty of how

The Cost of the Requisition

long the liner would be out of service. In 1982, Cunard had budgeted for one of its biggest advertising campaigns for *QE2*, the benefit of which was now lost.

Miscellaneous: £58,120
Payments for third-party claims, legal charges, additional computer equipment and air fares to repatriate laundrymen to Singapore.

Total: £21,015,093

17

The Volunteer Crew of *QE2*

In 1982, on a normal voyage *QE2* was, on average, manned with a crew of 1,015. Approximately 35 per cent of these were not required when the ship was requisitioned.

All Merchant Navy crew are required to sign Ship's Articles. This procedure is known as 'signing on'. The articles are a legal employment contract between the master of a vessel and the individual members of the crew. A contract would be for twelve months, with the employee having the option of ending it if he or she gave reasonable notice. Invariably, the time spent on board was much shorter to fit in with a regular leave rota organised by the employer.

A set of articles might span two or three months. This means that a set could have commenced a few months prior to the requisitioned voyage. During an individual's time signed on articles, he or she may be promoted to a higher position but any such changes are not reflected in the list that follows.

A total of 660 seafarers were selected to sail, although many more than that had volunteered. Alongside the names in the following list is the job the crew member initially signed on to do. Employment on a Cunard liner was highly sought after, and often one had to accept a lower position on board in order to get one's foot in the door before being promoted to a higher rank.

All of the names of those remaining on board at the time of sailing, plus the names of those who joined before the voyage commenced, were extracted from the articles into a list. A copy of the list was landed ashore before the ship sailed. Copies of the list were issued to a few select senior officers on board. The list, held in the Cunard archives at the University of Liverpool, is dated 12 May 1982. The names have been reproduced in their original format without correcting any typing errors. On the original list some of the seafarers' ranks were abbreviated and these are now shown in full.

Some of the crew members listed were known on board by a different first name than their legal name given on the list. Accordingly, anyone researching an individual who is named earlier in this book should also check the list that follows here. A number of those named went on to serve many more years with the Cunard Line, some rising to the most senior position in their department.

On departure from Southampton, the crew was made up of:

Captains:	2
Officers:	84
Deck ratings:	51
Engine ratings:	67
Medical ratings:	3
Hotel service ratings:	9
Hotel catering ratings:	289
Kitchen ratings:	115
Financial control ratings:	5
Contractors:	25
Ocean Trading shops:	6
Photographers:	1
Steiners hairdressers:	2
Union representative:	1

Total: **660**

THE QE2 *VOLUNTEERS*
Names or ranks in italics are known to the authors to be different from those written in the main text of the book.

Abbott, George – 1st Pantryman
Adamou, George – Wine Steward

The Volunteer Crew of QE2

Adams, Walter – Assistant Storekeeper
Agnew, Kevin – Carpenter
Ah-Tow, Eileen – Laundress
Alford, Basil – Mechanic
Alford, Mark – Officers' Steward
Allen, Julian – Waiter
Allen, Stephen – Waiter
Amess, Brian – Assistant Steward
Amos, William – 3rd Baker Confectioner
Anderson, John – Hotel Services Engineer
Anderson, Robert – Specialist Cook
Anscombe, Arthur – Assistant Mechanic
Armstrong, Neal – Assistant Butcher
Arnold, John – Assistant Engineer's Writer
Arnold, Stephen – 8th Electrical Officer
Ashfield, Peter – 1st Fish Cook
Ashman, Paul – Assistant Steward
Ashton, John – Coxswain
Atkinson, Brian – Senior Mechanic
Austin, Colin – Contractor
Avery, Phillip – 5th Engineer Officer
Ayloff, Simon – Assistant Cook
Aylward, Kevin – Assistant Steward
Ayres, Derek – Carpenter
Bailey, Malcolm[†] – NUS Representative
Bailey, William – Senior Carpenter
Baker, George – Bedroom Steward
Ball, John – Utilityman
Ballantyne, *John R* – 2nd Hotel Officer
Bantock, Robert – 3rd Baker Confectioner
Barber, Robert – Waiter
Barnett, John – Waiter
Batinica, Mirko – Assistant Mechanic
Bayley, Ronald – Cafe Steward
Beattie, William – Bedroom Steward
Beauchamp, David – Assistant Mechanic
Beer, Frank – 1st Officer
Bellenie, Alan – Waiter

269

Bellows, John – Senior Mechanic
Beswick, Phillip – Waiter
Bick, Terence – Waiter
Biggs, Mark – Kitchen Porter
Blackmore, Brian – Senior Mechanic
Boatwright, Martin – *Waiter*
Bond, Allan – Senior Assistant Barkeeper
Boston, Graham – Kitchen Porter
Boulton, David – Assistant Steward
Boyes, Paul – Waiter
Boyle, Thomas – Glory Hole Steward
Boyle, William – Roast Cook
Bracey, Gareth – Assistant Mechanic
Bradford, Stephen – Assistant Cook
Brady, John – Contractor
Brewer, Rupert – Waiter
Broadbent, Norman – Chef de Rang
Brocks, Geoffrey – Officers' Steward
Bromby, Clive – Senior Mechanic
Brookshaw, Peter – Night Steward
Broomfield, Jane – Assistant Stewardess
Broughton, Martin – Ocean Trading Shops
Brown, Frederick – Senior Mechanic
Brown, Ian – Chef Tournant
Brown, Mark – Kitchen Porter
Brown, Robert – 2nd Cook
Bryceland, Michael – Wine Steward
Budd, David – 3rd Hotel Officer
Budd, Paul – Waiter
Bunn, Laurent – Assistant Cook
Burden, Raymond – Bedroom Steward
Burge, George – 2nd Hotel Officer
Burge, Paul – Utilityman
Burgess, Michael – Senior Mechanic
Burrell, Ian – Senior 1st Hotel Officer
Burton, Harold[†] – Senior Mechanic
Butler, Michael – Kitchen Porter
Butler, Stephen – Specialist Cook

The Volunteer Crew of QE2

Butts, Anthony – Ocean Trading Shops
Bygrave, Jane – Stewardess
Cable, Michael – Vegetable Cook
Cadet, Terence – Able Seaman
Cain, John – Wine Steward
Callaghan, Maria – Assistant Stewardess
Cameron, Hugh – 2nd Electrical Officer
Caplan, Lionel – Waiter
Carless, Peter – Junior 5th Engineer Officer
Carpenter, Judith – Captain's Secretary
Carroll, Peter – Public Room Steward
Carson, Leonard – Wine Steward
Carter, Leonard – Waiter
Carver, John – Waiter
Cassel, Wayne – Waiter
Cassford, David – Assistant Mechanic
Cassidy, Terence – Linen Delivery Man
Castle, Timothy – Senior 1st Hotel Officer
Chadwick, Michael – Assistant Waiter
Chapman, Reginald – Bedroom Steward
Child, Stanley – Deputy Chief Engineer
Chillingworth, John – Junior 2nd Engineer Officer
Cifuentes, Joaquin – Waiter
Cilia, John – Specialist Cook
Clark, Barbara – Assistant Stewardess
Clark, Michael – Assistant Steward
Clark, Norman – Assistant Steward
Clark, Stephen – Kitchen Porter
Clarot, Italo – Waiter
Clements, William – Assistant Steward
Clover, Adrain – Specialist Cook
Clow, Dennis – Public Room Steward
Clyde, Paul – Assistant Steward
Cobain, Robert – Junior 5th Engineer Officer
Cockram, Derek – Senior Mechanic
Coles, George – Bedroom Steward
Collins, David – 3rd Butcher
Collins, John – 1st Pantryman

Connolly, Martin – Waiter
Coopey, Mark – Waiter
Coppin, Alan – Waiter
Cornlouer, Pierre – Waiter
Cosgrove, David – Assistant Mechanic
Cotter, Andrew – Assistant Cook
Cotton, Stephen – Able Seaman
Coward, Victor – *1st Chef*
Crabtree, William – Contractor
Craddock, Cambell – Assistant Steward
Cripps, Edwin – Senior 3rd Engineer Officer
Crocker, Adrian – Assistant Baker Confectioner
Cross, William – Chief Security Petty Officer
Crowe, Ian – Specialist Cook
Crozier, Susan – Stewardess
Cueto, Richard – Able Seaman
Cunningham, Stewart – Assistant Mechanic
Curtis, Mark – Efficient Deck Hand
Dale, Alan – Senior 5th Engineer Officer
Dalley, Clive – *Assistant Steward*
Dallyn, Tessa – Assistant Stewardess
Dance, Anthony – *Ocean Trading Shops*
Dart, Frederick – 1st Chef
Davidson, Ronald – Able Seaman
Davies, Alun – Assistant Baker Confectioner
Davies, John – Waiter
Davies, Ronald – Carpenter
Davies, Thomas – Assistant Steward
Davis, James – Senior Mechanic
Dawes, Brian – Waiter
Dawkins, Colin – 5th Electrical Officer
Dawson, Dennis – Public Room Steward
Dawson, Michael – Contractor
Day, George – Chief Baker
Day, Stephen – Able Seaman
Day, Victor – 1st Baker Confectioner
De Vaal, Eric – Officers' Steward
Deane, Derek – Mechanic

The Volunteer Crew of QE2

Denton, Brian – Bosun's Mate
Dickinson, Paul – Waiter
Dix, Richard – Public Room Steward
Dixon, James – Waiter
Dixon, Malcolm – Printer
Dolley, Robert – Hotel Services Engineer
Donovan, Graham – Printer
Door, Peter – Kitchen Porter
Doughty, Samuel – Waiter
Dove, Graham – Hospital Attendant
Duffin, Colin – 2nd Cook
Duffy, Michael – Mechanic
Dunec, Pauline – Laundress
Dunford, Ralph – Able Seaman
Dunger, Neil – Specialist Cook
Dunn, Charles – *Specialist Cook*
Dunn, Kevin – Waiter
Duvall, Leon – Waiter
Duzelman, Paul – Utilityman
Dyke, Gary – Utilityman
Earley, Rodney – Assistant Mechanic
Easter, Stephen – *Commis*
Edmonds, Steven – Senior Assistant Barkeeper
Edwards, Constance – Laundress
Edwards, David – Utilityman
Edwards, Kenneth – Senior Assistant Barkeeper
Edwards, Ronald – Waiter
Eker, Eric – Assistant Mechanic
Elliot, Lee – Officers' Steward
Ellis, Eric – Wine Steward
Ellis, Graham – Waiter
Elrick, Michael – Waiter
Emery, Peter – Senior Assistant Barkeeper
Etheridge, Nicholas – Waiter
Evans, Anthony – Waiter
Evans, Geoffrey – Contractor
Evans, Martyn – Assistant Mechanic
Evans, Steven – Officers' Steward

Evans, Terence – Contractor
Evans, William – Night Steward
Ewer, Peter – Accounts Petty Officer
Eyres, John – Bedroom Steward
Fair, Roderick – Junior 4th Engineer Officer
Falzon, Paul – Kitchen Porter
Farmer, Robert – Carpenter
Fergus, Leonard – Security Petty Officer
Ferris, John – Assistant Cook
Fisher, Paul – Senior Mechanic
Fitt, Stewart – Chief Crew Cook
Fitton, Robert – Officers' Steward
Fleet, Peter – Assistant Mechanic
Fleming, Cornelius – Contractor
Flewers, Alan – Assistant Steward
Flint, Andrew – Engineer Cadet
Flute, Marc – Waiter
Flute, Stephen – Commis Waiter
Ford, Kenneth – Bedroom Steward
Fosbery, Robert – Chief Confectioner
Foskett, Terence – Junior 1st Hotel Officer
Fowler, Robert – Carpenter
Franks, Valda – Assistant Stewardess
Fraser, George – Senior Mechanic
Fraser [sic], Kent – Ocean Trading Shops
French, Elizabeth – Assistant Stewardess
Frolish, Thomas – 1st Baker Confectioner
Furmage, Ronald – Waiter
Gadsby, Ralph – Waiter
Gahegen, Frederick – 3rd Electrical Officer
Galbraith, Neil – Specialist Cook
Gallagher, Bernard – Assistant Steward
Gardner, Daniel – Waiter
Gatrell, Gerald – Bedroom Steward
Gibbons, Ronald – Waiter
Gibson, Thomas – Senior Assistant Barkeeper
Giles, Peter – Security Petty Officer
Gilligan, Wayne – Assistant Cook

The Volunteer Crew of QE2

Goff, Kenneth – Night Steward
Goldsworthy, Wayne – Senior Mechanic
Goodwin, Alan – Senior Mechanic
Gore, Stuart – Kitchen Porter
Gosney, Brian – Leading Glory Hole Steward
Goulding, Noel – Specialist Cook
Grant, Austin – Bedroom Steward
Grant, John – Chief Engineer
Grant, Michael – Carpenter
Gray, William – Junior 3rd Engineer Officer
Graydon, Richard – Deck Boy
Green, Richard – 8th Electrical Officer
Greenhouse, Terence – 1st Sauce Cook
Gregory, Bryan – 2nd Engineer Officer
Grice, Douglas – Hairdresser
Griffin, John – 2nd Electrical Officer
Griffin, Reginald – Able Seaman
Griffin, Tony – Utilityman
Griffiths, Christopher – Kitchen Porter
Griffiths, Glyn – Contractor
Guest, Paul – Photographer
Hallam, Stephen – 2nd Baker Confectioner
Hallett, Mark – Assistant Mechanic
Hammond, Andrew – Assistant Cook
Hampton, Peter – Efficient Deck Hand
Hancock, Lynda – Stewardess
Hanlon, David – Assistant Mechanic
Harding, Dennis – Head Waiter
Hardy, Dennis – Public Room Steward
Harfield, Margaret – Assistant Stewardess
Harkett, Donald – Specialist Cook
Harper, Thomas – Public Room Steward
Harrison, Edward – Waiter
Harrison, Martin – Bedroom Steward
Harrison, Martin – Junior 2nd Engineer Officer
Harrison, Robert – Waiter
Harvey, Clive – Assistant Steward
Harvey, Harold – 1st Soup Cook

Hastings-Prosser, William – Waiter
Haughton, Christopher – 2nd Officer
Hawgood, Edwin – Public Room Pantryman
Hawker, John – Assistant Mechanic
Hay, Leslie – Bedroom Steward
Hayes, Anthony – Efficient Deck Hand
Hayward, Robert – 1st Officer
Hayward, Spencer – Night Steward
Hayward, Trevor – Efficient Deck Hand
Hazell, David – Waiter
Head, Michael – Bedroom Steward
Hearn, Terence – Bedroom Steward
Hennessey, Edmund – Assistant Steward
Henry, Denis – Assistant Cook
Henshaw, Robert – Mechanic
Herdman, Kim – Public Room Pantryman
Hession, Patrick – 3rd Baker Confectioner
Hewetson, Patrick – Medical Officer
Hewett, Gary – Night Assistant Steward
Hewett, John – Night Assistant Steward
Hewison, John – Senior 1st Hotel Officer
Higgins, George – Utilityman
Highmore, Frederick – 2nd Hotel Officer
Hinkley, Philip – Assistant Waiter
Hoctor, John – Specialist Cook
Hodges, Raymond – Wine Steward
Hogg, Susan – Bureau Assistant
Holmes, Allan – Chief Radio Officer
Holmes, Michael – 2nd Hotel Officer
Holter, Christopher – Bosun's Mate
Hopson, John – Ocean Trading Shops
Hotchkin, Timothy – Leading Assistant Steward
House, Ian – Waiter
Howes, Michael – Assistant Cook
Hughes, David – Able Seaman
Hughes, Peter – 2nd Radio Officer
Humphreys, David – Senior Accounts Petty Officer
Hunter, Robert – 4th Engineer Officer

Hutcheson, Alexander – Staff Captain
Hutchinson, John – Assistant Mechanic
Ireland, Richard – Assistant Steward
Irvine, Angus – Utilityman
Jackson, Clive – Deputy Chief Barkeeper
Jackson, Peter – Master
Jackson, Stephen – Utilityman
James, Derek – Contractor
James, John – Senior Mechanic
Jenkinson, Adrian – 3rd Engineer Officer
Jewitt, Clive – Specialist Cook
Jobson, Kirk – Utilityman
Johnson, George – Waiter
Jones, Andrew – Assistant Steward
Jones, Buller – Officers' Steward
Jones, Christopher – Assistant Cook
Jones, John – Carpenter
Jones, John – Waiter
Jones, John D. – Baggage Master
Jones, John S. – Baggage Master
Jones, Mark – Utilityman
Jones, Philip – Utilityman
Jones, Selwyn – Contractor
Jordan, Paul – Head Waiter
Jowett, Paul – 2nd Officer
Kato, Tadashi – Oriental Chef
Kehoe, Joseph – Bedroom Steward
Kelly, James – 5th Engineer Officer
Kelly, Ronald – Hotel Manager
Kenny, Stephen – Assistant Mechanic
Keyzor, Adrian – Accounts Petty Officer
Kirwin, *Patrick A.* – Medical Officer
Knight, Vincent – Efficient Deck Hand
Koudellas, Peter – 1st Larder Cook
Lacy, Peter – Assistant Waiter
Lamb, Ernest – Chief Barkeeper
Langley, Peter – Waiter
Law, Peter – Waiter

Lawrence, Michael – Waiter
Lawton, Alistair – Specialist Cook
Le Peuple, Lorna – Assistant Stewardess
Leach, George – Assistant Storekeeper
Leatherbarrow [*sic*], Clifford – Head Waiter
Leigh, Daniel – Assistant Cook
Leigh, Derrick – 2nd Chef
Leigh, Sylvia – Stewardess
Leighfield, Barry – Waiter
Lenehan, Pat – Public Room Steward
Leonard, Steven – Senior Officers' Steward
Leroy, Louis* – Kitchen Porter
Letherbarrow, Jeremy – Waiter
Levine, Jane – Nursing Sister
Lewis, Edward – Able Seaman
Light, William – 1st Larder Cook
Lineham, David – Assistant Mechanic
Littlehales, Elena – Stewardess
Longman, Paul – Assistant Butcher
Lovell, Wayne – Contractor
Low, Douglas – Carpenter
Lowles, David – Waiter
Lugg, James – Kitchen Porter
Luke, David – Senior 1st Accounts Officer
Lyhane, Douglas – Assistant Mechanic
Lyon, Gary – Mechanic
Mac Donald [*sic*], Michael – 1st Crew Cook
Macey, Mark – Assistant Cook
Mac Kenzie [*sic*], David – Extra Radio Officer
Magee, Charles – Bedroom Steward
Maguire, Simon – Assistant Cook
Mahoney, Anthony – Contractor
Mamo, Emmanuel – Kitchen Porter
Manning, Patrick – Assistant Cook
Manwaring, Jeffrey – 5th Engineer Officer
Marriott, Phillip – 1st Radio Officer
Marshall, Brian – Security Petty Officer
Marshall, Royston – Assistant Steward

The Volunteer Crew of QE2

Marshall, Wendy – Nursing Sister
Marston, John – Officers' Steward
Martin, Brian – 2nd Radio Officer
Martin, Herbert – Senior Mechanic
Mason, *Anthony* – Waiter
Masters, Andrew – Assistant Mechanic
Masters, Dale – Senior Mechanic
Masterson, Timothy – Specialist Cook
Mathews, Ian – Assistant Mechanic
Matthews, Anthony – Kitchen Porter
May, Thomas – 2nd Radio Officer
Mayhew, Malcolm – Senior 1st Hotel Officer
Mc Art [*sic*], Augustine – Bedroom Steward
Mc Caskey [*sic*], Scott – Crew Lounge Steward
Mc Clure [*sic*], Ronald – Senior Mechanic
Mc Dermott [*sic*], Robert – Waiter
Mc Donald [*sic*], Robert – Utilityman
Mc Donnell [*sic*], Michael – Waiter
Mc Donnell [*sic*], Thomas – Waiter
Mc Ghee [*sic*], Alexander – Senior Mechanic
Mc Greechan [*sic*], Hugh – Security Petty Officer
McKay, Gordon – Bedroom Steward
Mc Kenna [*sic*], John – Contractor
Mc Lean [*sic*], Diane – Nursing Sister
Mc Mahon [*sic*], Patrick – Waiter
Mc Mullan [*sic*], John[†] – Contractor
Mc Phearson [*sic*], Peter – Chief Crew Cook
Mellor, Thomas – 1st Baker Confectioner
Melnyczuk, Slawku – Assistant Cook
Merewood, Roy – Bedroom Steward
Merrylees, Andrew – Officers' Steward
Mew, Raymond – Wine Steward
Middleton, Roger – Assistant Cook
Millar, Victor – Bedroom Steward
Millen, Michael – 3rd Electrical Officer
Miller, James – Specialist Cook
Miller, Julian – Waiter
Miller, Michael – Waiter

Miller, Paul – Assistant Steward
Miller, Stanley – Kitchen Porter
Milroy, *Dorothy F.* – Senior 1st Hotel Officer
Mingay, Graham – Waiter
Molley, John – Waiter
Moore, Clifford – Coxswain
Moore, Kevin – Assistant Cook
Morant, Bernard – Senior Assistant Barkeeper
Morris, Richard – Assistant Mechanic
Mosley, Brian – Assistant Cook
Mullett, Paul – Utilityman
Murray, James – Waiter
Musslewhite, Stuart – Efficient Deck Hand
Nel, Calvin – Waiter
Nelder, Andrew – Head Waiter
Newborn, Gary – Assistant Steward
Nicholas, Francis – Kitchen Porter
Nicholson, Frank – Equipment Supervisor
Nilsen, Kathleen J – Senior Telephonist
Nolan, Gerald – Controller
Norman, John – Bedroom Steward
Norton, *John* – Head Waiter
O'Brien, James – Assistant Mechanic
O'Connor, Thomas – Assistant Steward
O'Keefe, John – Coxswain
O'Neill, Hugh – Contractor
O'Neill, Terence – Waiter
Orwin, Brian – 4th Engineer Officer
Osborne, Kevan – Assistant Steward
Owen, Arthur – Senior Public Room Steward
Owen, Glyn – Junior 5th Engineer Officer
Owen, Merfyn – Engineer Cadet
Owen, Myra – Laundress
Owen, Steven – Assistant Butcher
Owens, John – Senior Assistant Barkeeper
Oxford, Nigel – Senior Mechanic
Oxley, Paul – Deck Cadet
Padden, Graham – Waiter

The Volunteer Crew of QE2

Page, Albert – Assistant Mechanic
Paisley, Peter – Junior 5th Engineer Officer
Palmer, Stephen – Kitchen Porter
Parker, Geoffrey – Security Petty Officer
Parker, Iris – Assistant Stewardess
Parkinson, Frank – Bosun's Mate
Partington, James – Specialist Cook
Peacock, Christopher – Kitchen Porter
Pearce, Peter – Night Steward
Pearce, Robert – Waiter
Pearson, Martin – Fish Cook
Perry, Derek – Specialist Cook
Petley, Andrew – Ocean Trading Shops
Phillips, Paul – Assistant Cook
Pickering, Gary – Public Room Steward
Pine, Peter – Contractor
Pollard, Frank[†] – Assistant Mechanic
Pope, Christopher – Waiter
Pope, David – 1st Officer
Porter, Alan – Contractor
Porter, Joseph – Contractor
Povey, Stephen – Waiter
Powell, Winston – Night Steward
Power, James – Gloryhole Steward
Pratt, Sinclair – Contractor
Prentice, Leslie – Waiter
Print, Stephen – Able Seaman
Pullinger, John – Senior 1st Hotel Officer
Purcell, Gerald – Wine Steward
Purchase, Christopher – Utilityman
Purves, Frederick – Mechanic
Purvis, Allen – Kitchen Porter
Rath, Patrick – Able Seaman
Rawles, Kenneth – Waiter
Read, Donald – Waiter
Reid, Alan – Assistant Steward
Reid, Walter – Bedroom Steward
Rendell, Robert – Chef de Rang

Rentell, Philip – *1st Officer*
Reynolds, Roy – Public Room Pantryman
Rich, George – Security Petty Officer
Richards, Roy – Accounts Petty Officer
Riddell, Mark – Senior Assistant Barkeeper
Risdon, Christopher – Specialist Cook
Roache, Loulick – Specialist Cook
Robert-de-Vere [*sic*], Jon – Kitchen Porter
Robertson, Robert – Bedroom Steward
Robins, David – Assistant Steward
Robins, Jack – Contractor
Robinson, Peter – Kitchen Porter
Rolfe, Christopher – Public Room Pantryman
Rolle, Garry – Waiter
Rolle, Glenn – Waiter
Rolt, Dennis – Waiter
Romain, Dale – Able Seaman
Roscoe, John – Assistant Pantryman
Rowe, Victor – Assistant Mechanic
Russell, Frank – Waiter
Ryan, Janet – Telephonist
Salter, Andrew – Specialist Cook
Sanders, Colum – Leading Bedroom Steward
Sant, Carmel – Waiter
Saunders, Leslie – Assistant Steward
Scanlon, Malcolm – 1st Officer
Scourfield, Barry – Senior Mechanic
Serafin, Gerald – Waiter
Shakspeare, James – 2nd Chef
Sharpe, David – Night Telephonist
Shaw, Brian – Bedroom Steward
Sherwood, Peter – Assistant Mechanic
Sibbald, Robert – Deck Storekeeper
Siggery, William – Soup Cook
Simmons, Clive – Specialist Cook
Simmons, Peter – Assistant Mechanic
Simpson, Mexaxoulla – Public Room Stewardette
Simpson, Peter – Assistant Cook

The Volunteer Crew of QE2

Sinclair, Fraser – Assistant Mechanic
Sinclair, Islay – Printer
Singer, Rooney – Assistant Steward
Skelcher, Robin – Senior Assistant Barkeeper
Skelton, Graham – Senior Mechanic
Slee, Roger – Specialist Cook
Smart, Norman – Hotel Services Engineer
Smith, Arthur – Utilityman
Smith, Claude – Assistant Steward
Smith, David – Waiter
Smith, Francis – Efficient Deck Hand
Smith, Harry – Assistant Hotel Manager
Smith, John – Night Steward
Smith, Malcolm – 1st Accounts Officer
Smith, Martin – Assistant Steward
Snell, Andrew – Assistant Steward
Soutter, William – 2nd Chef
Spake, Richard – Assistant Waiter
Spicer, Robert – 6th Electrical Officer
Staff, Andrew – Wine Steward
Stafford, Mark – Waiter
Stainer, Gerald – Chief Engineer's Writer
Stainton, Raymond – Chief Pantryman
Stamp, Paul – Assistant Cook
Stevenson, David – Assistant Steward
Stewart, William – Utilityman
Storrow, Alan – 2nd Chef
Strickland, Derrick – Hospital Attendant
Stroud-Drinkwater, John – Assistant Mechanic
Stubbs, Kevin – Assistant Cook
Summers, Stephen – Senior Mechanic
Sutherland, John – Specialist Cook
Sutton, Robert – Mechanic
Swain, Mark – Assistant Waiter
Sweetman, Michael – Commis Waiter
Taylor, Kenneth – Public Room Pantryman
Taylor, Martin – Public Room Pantryman
Taylor, Michael – Deck Cadet

Taylor, Steven – Waiter
Tazzyman, Barbara – Stewardess
Thomas, Albert – Kitchen Porter
Thomas, Charles – Bosun
Thomas, Keith – Assistant Steward
Thomas, Nigel – Able Seaman
Thomas, Paul – Waiter
Thompson, Alan – Efficient Deck Hand
Thornton, Herbert – Bedroom Steward
Tissington, Colin – Public Room Pantryman
Tomlins, John – 2nd Engineer Officer
Tomlinson, Lesley-Ann – Public Room Stewardette
Townsend, Michael – Medical Petty Officer
Treacher, John – Able Seaman
Trew, Michael – Senior Mechanic
Tubb, Harry – Bedroom Steward
Turnell, Charles – Senior 1st Hotel Officer
Twigg, Cecil – Bedroom Steward
Uglow, Paul – Assistant Waiter
Vamplew, Edmund – Larder Cook
Vickers, *George B.* – Purser
Vickers, Gordon – Senior Mechanic
Vickers, Ian – 1st Sauce Cook
Vince, Alan – Senior Mechanic
Voice, John – Fruitman
Voisey, Rita – Assistant Stewardess
Volney, John – Public Room Steward
Wabich, Bruno – Night Steward
Walker, John – Assistant Steward
Walker, Melvyn – Gloryhole Steward
Wall, Dennis – 4th Engineer Officer
Wall, Raymond – 1st Larder Cook
Walton, John – Assistant Writer
Ward, Phillip – Waiter
Ward, Ronald – Gloryhole Steward
Ward, Stephen – Accounts Officer
Ware, Graham – Mechanic
Warne, Herbert – Public Room Steward

The Volunteer Crew of QE2

Warry, Joan – Laundress
Warwick, Ronald – Chief Officer
Watters, Ronald – Wine Steward
Weatherstone, Peter – Specialist Cook
Webber, Paul – Assistant Cook
Weigh, Peter – Contractor
Wemyss, Gordon – Contractor
West, David – Assistant Steward
Whatley, Hugh – Assistant Steward
Wheat, James – 3rd Engineer Officer
Whelan, Gary – Assistant Steward
White, Jacqueline – *Assistant Stewardess*
White, Michael – Able Seaman
Whitefield, David – Assistant Cook
Whitehead, Leslie – Assistant Mechanic
Whitehead, Wilfred – Public Room Steward
Whittaker, Stephen – Accounts Petty Officer
Whyte, Brian – Waiter
Whyte, John – Senior Mechanic
Wildridge, Thomas – Specialist Cook
Wilkinson, Lee – Assistant Steward
Willey, Keith – Commis Waiter
Williams, David – Assistant Steward
Williams, John – Mechanic
Williams, Paul – Assistant Baker Confectioner
Williams, Timothy – Hairdresser
Wilson, Jack – Security Officer
Wilson, Mark – Assistant Steward
Wingrove, Mark – Student Cook
Winter, Alec – Grill Cook
Wood, George – Assistant Cook
Wood, Harold – Laundry Staff
Wood, Janice – Telephonist
Wood, Leonard – Gloryhole Steward
Wood, Michael – Waiter
Woodhouse, Paul – 2nd Baker Confectioner
Woodley, Michael – Senior Assistant Barkeeper
Woods, Robert – Utilityman

Wooller, Paul – Waiter
Wordley, Peter – Waiter
Workman, Brian – Senior Assistant Barkeeper
Worsley, Edward – Bedroom Steward
Wright, Geoffrey – Contractor
Yeardley, David* – Lloyd's Surveyor
Yeates, Colin – 3rd Baker Confectioner
Yelland, *Victoria J. – Nursing Sister*
Yorke, Jonathan – Waiter
Young, Robert – Waiter
Young, Sidney – Contractor
Young, Thomas – Efficient Deck Hand

* Left the ship at Freetown, Sierra Leone, 18 May.
† Left the ship at Ascension Island, southbound voyage, 20–21 May.

Names are shown as they appear in the crew list typed on board before the ship sailed for the South Atlantic in 1982. Names identified with typographical errors are accompanied by [*sic*]. In the course of their research, the authors have identified three incorrect spellings of surnames. The correct spellings are Kent Frazer, Clifford Letherbarrow and Jon Robert de Vere. Many surnames with the patronymics Mc and Mac included a space before the main surname in the list. For example, the correct spelling for Mac Donald should be MacDonald, Mc Art should be McArt, and so on.

18

Afterword

Three days after *QE2* arrived home, Argentina surrendered on 14 June. It would be a while before the full story emerged of the contributions to the British campaign made by those whom *QE2* took to the South Atlantic.

Major General Moore sailed on HMS *Antrim* to the war zone and transferred to HMS *Fearless*, where he set up his command headquarters.[180] Moore and his staff had prepared for this role through conducting exercises in a mock-up of *Fearless*'s operations room on board *QE2*. Unfortunately, however, these exercises were hindered due to the SCOT satellite communications system not working, which prevented communications with other ships and units in the field.

From South Georgia, 5 Infantry Brigade sailed west towards the Falkland Islands with the Welsh and Scots Guards on board *Canberra* and the 7th Gurkha Rifles on board *Norland*. Some other units of the Brigade sailed on board RFA *Stromness*. *Canberra* and *Norland* entered San Carlos, where the troops they were carrying were landed ashore on 2 and 3 June. Moving 5 Infantry Brigade forward from San Carlos was complicated following the loss of *Atlantic Conveyor*, which resulted in the destruction of several helicopters. With insufficient helicopters to transport the Brigade to the front, alternative transport was needed. Most of the Brigade was ferried by sea from San Carlos along the southern coast of East Falkland. After arriving at the front line, all three battalions of the Brigade were involved in engagements and suffered casualties.

This is not the place to provide a comprehensive overview of the order of battle of the Falklands War. To attempt to do so would run the risk of omitting key events and causing inadvertent offence to the military personnel who successfully prosecuted the British land campaign. For readers who wish to know more about the role of the troops that *QE2* delivered to the South Atlantic, we have provided suggestions for further reading in the Bibliography. The study by military historians Nicholas van der Bijl and David Aldea, *5th Infantry Brigade in the Falklands 1982* (published in 2003), details in depth the roles played by the Brigade in the war.

Linda Kitson and Paul Haley remained embedded within 5 Infantry Brigade after leaving *QE2*. They followed British forces across East Falkland to Stanley just behind the front line, enduring harsh conditions in often freezing temperatures. Linda made over 400 drawings, many of which featured in her book *The Falklands War: A Visual Diary*.[181] Paul Haley took one of the most iconic images of the war: a group of Scots Guards celebrating on Mount Tumbledown at the news of Argentina's surrender. Back in Southampton there was considerable pride among *QE2*'s crew at the important contribution that 5 Infantry Brigade had made to winning the Falklands War.

With the cessation of hostilities, much of 5 Infantry Brigade remained to garrison the islands. The Scots Guards, Welsh Guards and 7th Gurkha Rifles were reunited with their musical instruments at war's end. The Gurkhas' instruments had been transferred to another ship in Grytviken, possibly *Canberra*, and were eventually delivered to Port Stanley, where they were found in a shed. They were then transported by helicopter to Goose Green, where the Gurkhas were based after the war. Major David Willis recalls that when the Gurkhas pipers and drummers were reunited with their musical instruments, they played for the local community which was 'a great boost for morale'.

After arriving home, *QE2* stayed alongside the passenger terminal in Southampton for a few days while the remaining military stores and equipment were unloaded. She was then moved up Southampton Water to dry dock, where her helicopter pads were dismantled and those parts of the superstructure that had been cut off were replaced. Cunard took advantage of the lay-up to refurbish the interior décor and furnishings.

On the voyage south, there was close cooperation between Cunard crew and the Army personnel, with excellent working relations between ship's officers and Naval Party 1980. Captain James reserved special praise for Captain Peter Jackson and Captain Alexander Hutcheson as 'men of the highest calibre with whom it has been a privilege to serve'. There is no doubt that morale on the journey south was enhanced through military

Afterword

personnel and *QE2* crew interacting and showing support to each other. A balance was struck between the need to respect each other's important roles and the human need to connect with comrades committed to a shared endeavour. For many of the *QE2* crew interviewed for this book, meeting and interacting with the soldiers of the Brigade helped make the voyage memorable and meaningful. The troops arrived at Grytviken physically fit and in good spirits. They disembarked to words of encouragement and cries of support from the crew.

Similarly, on the journey north, the crew did their best to take care of the Royal Navy survivors. The twelve-day voyage home provided a period of adjustment that was beneficial to all survivors, who had time to talk among themselves about what had happened. The welcoming reception from the *QE2* crew and the comradeship that was extended were important in enabling the men of the Royal Navy to come to terms with their experiences among friends old and new. Many crew visited the survivors in hospital, providing them with clothing and companionship. The most important way that the crew helped the survivors was in listening to them share their stories. Those who choose to work afloat will always empathise with fellow seafarers who have lost their ship at sea.

Canberra arrived back in Southampton on 12 July, one month after *QE2*. She sailed up Southampton Water surrounded by small boats and displaying dozens of flags and banners. Southampton gave the ship a rapturous welcome. *Canberra* deserved it. Her war had been more eventful than *QE2*'s, but both ships had done everything that had been asked of them. Crew on board *QE2* could witness her arrival, the two liners together again for the first time since the icy chills of Grytviken. Other *QE2* crew stood among the crowds on the quayside to welcome home the P&O liner, some with their families. Clive Dalley was among them with his daughters Elizabeth (aged 6) and Helen (3) waving Union Jacks.

Two weeks later on 26 July, the Falklands Islands Service was held at St Paul's Cathedral, London. The service was a major state occasion, both a commemoration of the lives lost and a thanksgiving for the cessation of hostilities. Representing *QE2* in uniform was Captain Peter Jackson, attending with his wife Pamela. Hotel officer Terry Foskett also attended. The congregation included Her Majesty The Queen, senior members of the royal family, the prime minister and her cabinet, along with the commanding officers of the armed forces. Terry remembers the service as 'a solemn occasion with a defining feeling of pride in the British nation'.

Shortly after the end of the conflict, waiter Jeremy Letherbarrow was unexpectedly visited at his New Forest home by one of the three Royal Artillery officers whose uniforms he had brought home from the South Atlantic. The officer told Jeremy that when they arrived on the Falkland Islands, they found a deserted barn, where they drank the bottle of red wine Jeremy had given them. All three officers survived the war. Tragically, that was not the case for the two Welsh Guardsmen whom Jeremy and his cabin mate Kevin Dunn had befriended. Neither returned home. Kevin took the time to write messages of condolence to the parents of the soldiers.

The camaraderie between ship's crew and military personnel survived long after the war. Sharing risks together forges friendships. Carpenter Bill Bailey and NP1980 petty officer Jim Ahern still exchange Christmas cards every year. There are many other examples of friendships formed which have stood the passage of time.

With the exception of those crew who left the ship at Freetown or Ascension Island, all crew members received the South Atlantic Medal with rosette. The obverse of the medal bears the head of Her Majesty Queen Elizabeth the Second and the reverse bears the Falklands Islands' crest and the islands' motto: 'Desire the Right'. Each medal has the name of the recipient inscribed on the rim. In 1997, the South Atlantic Medal Association (SAMA) was formed. Many *QE2* crew have joined SAMA, which holds annual reunion events.

At the end of the 1982 season, Her Royal Highness Queen Elizabeth, The Queen Mother, paid a personal tribute to the liner when she visited the ship at Southampton on 2 December 1982. The Queen Mother toured the ship with Lord Matthews and Captain Peter Jackson, and spoke to many members of the ship's company who had sailed to South Georgia. She presented a handsomely embossed silver plaque to the ship to commemorate the vessel's service in the Falkland campaign. The plaque records the messages exchanged between the Queen Mother and Captain Jackson as *QE2* steamed past the royal yacht in the Solent on her return voyage. The plaque was displayed between the Royal Standards situated between the Casino and the Theatre Bar on Upper Deck. At lunch, Lord Matthews made a speech welcoming the Queen Mother who responded by saying:

I thank you, Lord Matthews, for your words of welcome aboard this ship which bears the name of my daughter Queen Elizabeth the Second.

Afterword

The war ended three days after *QE2* arrived back in Southampton. On 14 June, Imperial War Museum photographer Paul Haley took this photograph of the Scots Guards celebrating the news of the Argentine surrender on Mount Tumbledown. (Paul Haley, Imperial War Museum)

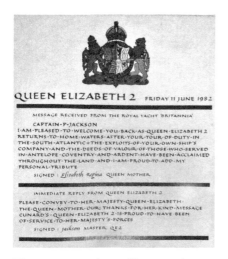

The messages exchanged between the Queen Mother and Captain Jackson were engraved on a silver plaque and mounted for passengers to view. (David Luke)

Falkland Islands battle honours were presented to *QE2* by the First Sea Lord, Admiral Sir John Fieldhouse. The battle honours were displayed at the forward end of Two Deck. (R.W. Warwick)

The QE2 in the Falklands War

All *QE2* crew who sailed on the requisitioned voyage south of Ascension Island received the South Atlantic Medal with rosette. The name of the recipient is engraved on the rim. They also earned the right to wear the Armed Forces Veterans badge. (R.W. Warwick)

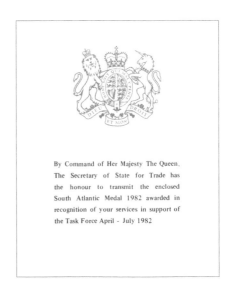

Small certificate given to those who were awarded the South Atlantic Medal. It was folded in four and included in the medal box. (R.W. Warwick)

The Petty Officers' Club produced a commemorative plaque for its members. This plaque was issued to carpenter Michael Grant. (R.W. Warwick)

Her Majesty The Queen Mother personally signed a luncheon menu for Captain Jackson when she visited *QE2* on 2 December 1982. (Captain P. Jackson)

Afterword

The citizens of Southampton recognised the contribution made by the Merchant Navy to the campaign by mounting a plaque in the Second World War bomb-damaged shell of Holyrood Church on Southampton High Street. (R.W. Warwick)

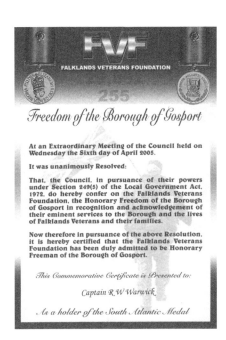

On 6 April 2005, the Falklands Veterans Foundation was admitted as an Honorary Freeman of the Borough of Gosport in Hampshire. (R.W. Warwick)

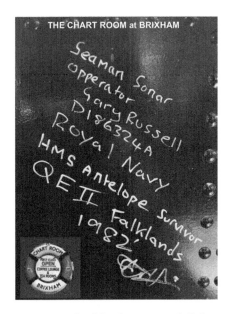

Reunions of Falkland veterans of all the armed forces and Merchant Navy are held around the country and abroad. The Bristol Steam Packet Company in Brixham has dedicated a wall for visiting veterans to sign. (Bob Higginson)

The QE2 in the Falklands War

The Rt Hon. The Baroness Thatcher commemorated *QE2*'s role in the campaign by unveiling this plaque on the occasion of the twentieth anniversary on 14 June 2002. (R.W. Warwick)

Over the years, *QE2* has featured in dozens of newspaper cartoons. This one appeared shortly after the liner returned to passenger service. (News Licensing)

An iconic illustration of *QE2* in Grytviken featured on a postage stamp of South Georgia and the South Sandwich Islands, issued in 2015. (R.W. Warwick)

Afterword

When I launched her predecessor, the great liner *Queen Elizabeth*, I was confident that the Cunard tradition symbolised the spirit and strength of the British merchant marine. That my belief was justified was clearly shown by the record of the *Queen Elizabeth* in World War II and her achievements in the years which followed.

Once again, some nine months ago, in the time of our country's need, the Merchant Navy was called upon to support Her Majesty's Armed Forces. The record of 5 Brigade, who travelled south in *Queen Elizabeth 2*, is now part of history, and I am delighted that it is represented here today.

When this ship, her mission completed, was nearing Southampton, I was proud to be able to welcome her and all those on board to a homecoming so richly deserved.

It is right that these splendid exploits should be recorded. And today it is my great pleasure to unveil this plaque to mark the voyage of *QE2* to the Falkland Islands and her service in the South Atlantic.[182]

In October 1983, the government announced that all ships that had served in the campaign in the Atlantic Ocean area between latitudes 35° and 60° south during the period from 2 April to 14 June 1982 would receive battle honours.[183] To mark this, *QE2* received a large wooden plaque presented by the First Sea Lord, Sir John Fieldhouse. The plaque was displayed on the starboard side at the forward end of Two Deck.

Following the untimely passing of Captain Hutcheson in 1984, Pierre Cornlouer organised a sponsored walk in his memory, with funds going to leukaemia research. After Pierre left the sea, he became an Anglican priest. Every year since 2013, he has conducted a memorial service at the Falklands National Monument, Alexandra Gardens, Cardiff.

One of the men who sailed south with *QE2* was Dean Regan, a member of 91 Ordnance Company who transferred in Grytviken to RFA *Stromness*. After leaving the armed forces, he became an artist specialising in paintings of the Falklands War. He produced a beautiful painting of the scene in Grytviken, showing a Sea King helicopter transferring stores from *QE2* to *Canberra*. Dean called the painting *Corporate Cruise* after Operation Corporate, the name of the military operation to retake the Falklands. He donated a copy to *QE2*.

For many of the crew, *QE2*'s South Atlantic adventure is one of the most significant events in their lives. Some have developed a lifelong interest in the Falklands. Many have visited the islands when serving with the

Merchant Navy. Others have travelled by air from Brize Norton to RAF Mount Pleasant. Many of these visits have been organised by SAMA.

After the conflict, carpenter Bob Farmer was transferred to *Cunard Countess*. In April 1983, *Cunard Countess* sailed to the Falklands with the next of kin and families of British servicemen who had fallen during the conflict. She sailed over the positions where the four Navy warships had sunk. Over each, a service was conducted on deck and wreaths were cast into the sea. Services were also held for those who had died on other ships, including *Atlantic Conveyor* and *Sir Galahad*. A service was held at the British Military Cemetery at San Carlos attended by 600 family members of those who had fallen. After the service Bob was one of the crew members who visited the cemetery to pay his respects to the servicemen who had served their country but never came home. A slate panel honours those interred in the cemetery and 'the abiding memory of the sailors, soldiers and airmen who gave their lives and who have no grave but the sea'.

In 1992, *QE2* hosted a celebration to commemorate the tenth anniversary of the conflict. The guest of honour was the Right Honourable Margaret Thatcher MP. Sir Nigel Broackes, chairman of Trafalgar House, welcomed Mrs Thatcher and guests, including Captain Peter Jackson, Captain Jimmy James RN, Sir Rex Hunt and other dignitaries. Jacqui White, Jane Yelland and Wendy Marshall were among the officers who hosted tables.

On 22 January 1993, Jacqui White and Andrew Nelder were on board *QE2* when she made her maiden visit to Port Stanley. Passenger tender boats ran from the ship to the public jetty, where those disembarking were greeted by islanders waving Union Jacks. Jacqui attended an invitation-only cocktail reception at Government House.

Her Majesty The Queen opened the Falkland Islands Memorial Chapel, located in the grounds of Pangbourne College, near Reading, in March 2000. The chapel is dedicated to those who died in the war. An extensive collection of published books along with personal accounts and press reports are held in the Chapel Library.

In April 2005, all South Atlantic Medal holders were admitted as Honorary Freemen of the Borough of Gosport in Hampshire. On 14 June 2022, the fortieth anniversary of the war, the Falkland Islands Legislative Assembly voted unanimously to confer the Freedom of the Falkland Islands upon 'all South Atlantic Medal Holders who served in the Falkland Islands and in the waters surrounding the Falkland Islands for the preservation of the liberty and right to self-determination of the people of the Falklands Islands'.[184]

Afterword

On the thirtieth anniversary in 2012, bureau assistant Susan Hogg visited the islands with her son Aidan and daughter Emilie on a tour arranged by SAMA. They stayed at Liberty Lodge, accommodation that was built for veterans of the war and their families. Susan attended a service at Christ Church Cathedral and visited military graveyards around the islands.

Clive Dalley visited the islands in 2017 to mark the thirty-fifth anniversary. He laid a wreath at the stone memorial at Bluff Cove. The memorial's inscription reads, 'In Memory of those Welsh Guards killed in action, Falkland Islands 1982, 1st Battalion Welsh Guards'. The names of the Welsh Guards who lost their lives during the war are inscribed with the words, 'We will remember them'. Clive looked through some of the wreaths that had been laid and was surprised to find a well-preserved message from November 2010. It had been attached to a wreath laid by a seaman from RFA *Black Rover*, Pierre Cornlouer, who was a *QE2* waiter in 1982. Pierre had written a heartfelt message:

I have come to say my final goodbyes. Memories of sadness and pride as I remember those who never came back. We still hear the laughs and the fun and the banter we all had between the Welsh and Scots Guards and others on the *QE2*. Friends were made. You will always be remembered.[185]

In 2022, the South Atlantic Medal Association and the Royal British Legion offered 100 flights to the islands for veterans and the families of those who fell during the conflict. This was the year that all medal holders were granted the Freedom of the Falkland Islands, so demand for places was high. *QE2* stewardess Tessa Dallyn was one of the lucky ones selected. She spent a week travelling the islands by Land Cruiser and boat, meeting islanders and ex-service personnel who have settled in the islands.

Captain Jackson retired from sea service in 1983 but continued to give his popular lecture about ocean liners to groups around the country. He passed away in 2008 aged 86. Many of those who served on *QE2* during the Falklands voyage remained with the Cunard Line and rose through the ranks, attaining the highest positions in their departments. John Chillingworth became chief engineer. Frances Milroy became the first female hotel manager of *QE2*. Jacqui White followed in her footsteps and served as hotel manager on *Queen Mary 2*. Waiter Kevin Dunn became Cunard's fleet training manager and later hotel manager of the *Sea Goddess*. After leaving *QE2*, Jane Yelland worked in Cunard's shoreside medical department, rising to become the manager of medical operations for Carnival UK. Martin Harrison remained with *QE2* and was a member of the crew that took the ship to Dubai in 2008, where she is now retired as a floating hotel.

Others left the Cunard Line and went to new pastures. Philip Rentell, who served as an RNR lieutenant during the South Atlantic voyage, was appointed captain of the cruise ships *Saga Rose* and *Saga Ruby*, and visited Port Stanley with both these ships. He wrote his memoirs and received the Merchant Navy Medal in 2016. Second Officer Chris Haughton, the navigator who first detected icebergs on the radar as *QE2* approached South Georgia, came ashore to indulge his long-held passion for education in the maritime sector before setting up his own consultancy, Haughton Martime, in 2004. After leaving *QE2*, David Luke worked in Cunard's shoreside offices in Southampton before relocating to Florida, where he worked in condominium property management. Jeremy Letherbarrow worked for a variety of shipping companies after leaving Cunard. His most memorable appointment was as chief steward on board *Star Flyer*, a four-masted sailing ship built for cruise passengers. Stephen Hallam, who spent much of *QE2*'s voyage south making slab cake for the troops, went on to become an award-winning pie maker and was awarded the MBE in the 2023 King's Birthday Honours. Timothy Williams moved to London, where he now runs his own hairdressers' business. Rupert Ballantyne joined the English Tourist Board as a hotel inspector. Stephen Ward left Cunard after twenty years but couldn't resist the temptation to return to seafaring four years later with Regent Seven Seas Cruises, visiting the Falklands as an officer on board *Seven Seas Voyager* in 2007. Second Officer Paul Jowett left the sea to become operations manager at Heathrow Airport but not before passing the lure of the ocean to his son, Alex Jowett, who is now a deputy captain in the Cunard Line. After leaving *QE2*, Terry Foskett worked on board Royal Caribbean ships as chief purser. Like Paul Jowett, Terry passed on to his family an enthusiasm for a life at sea. His daughter Jennifer followed in Terry's footsteps and became a *QE2* purser.

When *QE2* made her final voyage in 2008, she became the longest-serving ship in the history of the Cunard Line. This book tells the story of a very brief time in the life of a great liner and shares the memories of those who sailed with her to the South Atlantic, both the crew and the military forces with whom the authors of this book were privileged to sail. We have tried our best to do their stories justice and to create a written tribute to all who served on board *QE2* during her wartime adventure. This book is our salute to them.

Notes

Where a quotation has been cited from a published source, a reference number has been provided in the text. Where no reference number has been provided, the quotation has been provided direct to the authors either in written form or verbally. We thank all those who agreed to be interviewed and who provided written quotations.

1. Sunday Times Insight Team, *The Falklands War: The Full Story*, Sphere, 1982, p. 33.
2. Graham Pascoe, *Falklands Facts and Fallacies: The Falkland Islands in History and International Law*, Grosvenor House, 2022.
3. Sunday Times Insight Team, 1982, p. 34.
4. Britannica, 'History of the Falkland Islands', the editors of *Encyclopaedia Britannica*, www.britannica.com/place/Falkland-Islands/History.
5. Max Hastings and Simon Jenkins, *The Battle for the Falklands*, Michael Joseph, 1983, pp. 3–4.
6. Sunday Times Insight Team, 1982, p. 38.
7. Britannica, 'Falkland Islands'.
8. Sunday Times Insight Team, 1982, p. 38.
9. Sunday Times Insight Team, 1982, p. 39.
10. BBC, 'UK planned to give Falklands to Argentina', 8 January 1999, news.bbc.co.uk/1/hi/special_report/1999/01/99/1968_secret_history/244319.stm.
11. John Simpson and Jana Bennett, *The Disappeared: Voices from a Secret War*, Robson Books, 1985, p. 306.
12. Lord Shackleton, with R.J. Storey and R. Johnson, 'Prospect of the Falkland Islands', *Geographical Journal*, vol. 143, part I, March 1977, pp. 1–13.
13. Sir Lawrence Freedman, *The Official History of the Falklands Campaign*, Routledge, 2007; 'UK held secret talks to cede sovereignty', *The Guardian*, 2 October 2023, www.theguardian.com/uk/2005/jun/28/falklands.past.
14. Robert Fox, *Antarctica and the South Atlantic: Discovery, Development and Dispute*, BBC, 1985, p. 212.
15. Fox, 1985, p. 15.
16. Julian Manyon, *Kidnapped by the Junta: Inside Argentina's Wars with Britain and Itself*, Icon, 2022, p. 42.

17. Simpson and Bennett, 1985, p. 324.
18. Fox, 1985, p. 27.
19. Jimmy Burns, *The Land that Lost Its Heroes: Argentina, the Falklands and Alfonsín*, Bloomsbury, 1987, pp. 41–5; Hastings and Jenkins, 1983, pp. 68–9.
20. Simpson and Bennett, 1985, p. 315.
21. Sunday Times Insight Team, 1982, pp. 82–3.
22. Sunday Times Insight Team, 1982, p. 22.
23. Hansard, vol. 21, cc. 633–68, 3 April 1982, api.parliament.uk/historic-hansard/commons/1982/apr/03/falkland-islands.
24. Hansard, vol. 21, cc. 633–68, 3 April 1982.
25. United Nations Security Council Resolution 502, Falkland Islands (Malvinas), unscr.com/en/resolutions/502
26. Chris Frame and Rachelle Cross, *180 Years of Cunard*, The History Press, 2020, p. 17.
27. The Maritime Executive, 'Cunard Pays Tribute to War Service', 2015, maritime-executive.com/features/cunard-pays-tribute-to-war-service.
28. Stephen Harding, *Great Liners at War*, Tempus, 2007, p. 9.
29. Frame and Cross, 2020, pp. 44–9.
30. John Maxtone-Graham, *The Only Way to Cross*, Macmillan, 1972, p. 125; Harding, 2007, pp. 74–7.
31. Maxtone-Graham, 1972, pp. 125–9; Sam Warwick and Mike Roussel, *Shipwrecks of the Cunard Line*, The History Press, 2018, p. 70.
32. Warwick and Roussel, 2018, p. 70.
33. Warwick and Roussel, 2018, pp. 92–3.
34. Terry Coleman, *The Liners: A History of the North Atlantic Crossing*, Allen Lane, 1976, p. 160.
35. William H. Miller and David F. Hutchings, *Transatlantic Liners at War: The Story of the Queens*, David & Charles, 1985, pp. 21, 51; Harding, 2007, p. 264.
36. Frame and Cross, 2020, p. 64; Warwick and Roussel, 2018, pp. 104–5.
37. Chris Frame, *Franconia*, www.chriscunard.com/history-fleet/cunard-fleet/1900-1930/franconia/.
38. Frame and Cross, 2020, p. 66.
39. Harding, 2007, pp. 158–61.
40. Dwight D. Eisenhower, cited in 'The unsung heroes of our fourth service', www.rivieramm.com/news-content-hub/news-content-hub/the-unsung-heroes-of-our-fourth-service-59299.
41. Winston Churchill, cited in 'The unsung heroes of our fourth service', www.rivieramm.com/news-content-hub/news-content-hub/the-unsung-heroes-of-our-fourth-service-59299.
42. Margaret Thatcher Foundation, 'Remarks on the recapture of South Georgia' ('Rejoice'), 25 April 1982, margaretthatcher.org/document/104923.
43. Press conference by Ian McDonald, Ministry of Defence spokesman, 3 May 1982, www.gettyimages.co.uk/detail/video/requisitioned-england-london-mod-cms-ian-mcdonald-sof-news-footage/815429226.
44. Telegram from Department of Trade to Captain Peter Jackson, 3 May 1982, 1110 hours, ref. 24730SEAMOV. Captain Peter Jackson, personal archive.
45. Margaret Thatcher, *The Downing Street Years*, HarperCollins, 1993, p. 215.
46. *Lloyd's List*, 4 May 1982.

Notes

47. *Daily Express*, 5 May 1982.
48. *Daily Express*, 5 May 1982.
49. Robert Harry Arnott, *Captain of the Queen*, Ulverscroft, 1982, pp. 60–1.
50. Martin Middlebrook, *The Falklands War*, Pen and Sword Military, 1985, pp. 79–80.
51. Jennifer Davies, *Saying It with Flowers*, Headline, 2000, p. 163.
52. Secretary of State for Trade notification to The Master, 11 May 1982. Captain Peter Jackson, personal archive.
53. Department of Trade notification, 'Merchant Shipping Exemption Dangerous Goods, 10 May 1982'. Captain Peter Jackson, personal archive.
54. N.M.B. Agreements, *Queen Elizabeth 2* at Southampton, 12 May 1982. Captain Peter Jackson, personal archive.
55. *The Times*, 11 May 1982.
56. Telegram to Captain of *QE2*. The name of the sender has been deleted by the authors. Captain Peter Jackson, personal archive.
57. United Nations, *Geneva Convention Relative to the Treatment of Prisoners of War*, 1949, www.ohchr.org/en/instruments-mechanisms/instruments/geneva-convention-relative-treatment-prisoners-war.
58. British Forces Identity Card F/Ident/189. Capital letters in original.
59. International Committee of the Red Cross, *Convention (VIII) Relating to the Conversion of Merchant Ships into Warships*, 1907, ihl-databases.icrc.org/assets/treaties/210-IHL-22-EN.pdf.
60. Nicholas van der Bijl and David Aldea, *5th Infantry Brigade in the Falklands*, Leo Cooper, 2003, p. 6.
61. 5 Infantry Brigade newsletter, *QE2*, Edition 9, 23 May 1982.
62. Van der Bijl and Aldea, 2003, pp. 10–11.
63. *Daily Mail*, 4 May 1982.
64. Hastings and Jenkins, 1983, p. 336.
65. Van der Bijl and Aldea, 2003, pp. 40, 73.
66. Gregory Fremont-Barnes, 'An A to Z of the Falklands War', *A Companion to the Falklands War*, The History Press, 2017, www.thehistorypress.co.uk/articles/an-a-z-of-the-falklands-war/.
67. Hastings and Jenkins, 1983, pp. 336–7.
68. Simon Weston, *Walking Tall*, Bloomsbury, 1989, p. 75.
69. Cited in *Daily Mail*, www.dailymail.co.uk/news/article-9872495/Falklands-War-hero-Simon-Weston-calls-luckiest-guy-alive-60th-birthday.html.
70. Weston, 1989, p. 77.
71. Cited in E.D. Smith, *Valour: A History of the Gurkhas*, Spellmount, 1997, p. 155.
72. Jonathan Chadwick, cited in *Daily Express*, 12 May 1982.
73. Claire Carolin, 'The "Inevitable Suggestion of Latin America": Linda Kitson and Leon Golub Report to London in the Aftermath of the Falklands/Malvinas War of 1982', *Revista de Estudios Globales y Arte Contemporáneo*, vol. 5, no. 1, 2018, pp. 341–84.
74. Linda Kitson, cited in *Daily Express*, 12 May 1982.
75. Captain Peter Jackson, cited in *Daily Express*, 13 May 1982.
76. Telemessage to *QE2* from St James School, Grimsby, 11 May 1982, ref. WOK4147. Captain Peter Jackson, personal archive.
77. Telex message received in *QE2* Radio Room. The name of the sender is not given. Captain Peter Jackson, personal archive.

78. Telegram to *QE2*, 12 May 1982, ref. ICB198. The names of the senders are not given. Captain Peter Jackson, personal archive.
79. 825 Squadron Fleet Air Arm, www.helis.com/database/sqd/825-Squadron/.
80. John Smith, *74 Days: An Islander's Diary of the Falklands Occupation*, Century, 1984, p.145.
81. Middlebrook, 1985, p. 176.
82. David Brown, *The Royal Navy and the Falklands*, Leo Cooper, 1987, p. 190.
83. Mike Seear, *With the Gurkhas in the Falklands: A War Memorial*, Pen and Sword Books, 2018.
84. Miller and Hutchings, 1985, p. 138.
85. Telegram routed through Ministry of Defence, 17 May 1982, MODUK ref. ICB225. Captain Peter Jackson, personal archive.
86. Message from Reverend Peter Brooke to Captain Peter Jackson, 17 May 1982, from cabin 3021. Captain Peter Jackson, personal archive.
87. Linda Kitson, cited on SSAFA the Armed Forces Charity website: www.ssafa.org.uk/support-us/our-national-campaigns/falklands-40/falklands-40-linda-kitson.
88. Brown, 1987, p. 201.
89. The difficulty that Major General Moore had in communicating securely due to problems with the on-board SCOT satellite communications equipment is noted in several published sources on the Falklands War. See, for example, Hastings and Jenkins, 1983, p. 338; High Bicheno, *Razor's Edge: The Unofficial History of the Falklands War*, Phoenix, 2006, p. 199; Cedric Delves, *Across an Angry Sea: The SAS in the Falklands War*, Hurst and Company, 2020, p. 243. It should be noted that the problematic equipment was installed by the Ministry of Defence shortly before *QE2* sailed. *QE2*'s own communications equipment continued to function well.
90. Linda Kitson, cited on SSAFA the Armed Forces Charity website: www.ssafa.org.uk/support-us/our-national-campaigns/falklands-40/falklands-40-linda-kitson.
91. Fremont-Barnes, 2017, 'An A to Z of the Falklands War', www.thehistorypress.co.uk/articles/an-a-z-of-the-falklands-war/.
92. Freedom of Information request, email to David Humphreys from Ministry of Defence DBS CIO-KI Records FOI, ref. FOI2023/11361, 29 September 2023.
93. Van der Bijl and Aldea, 2003, p. 95.
94. 'A Message To Next of Kin Of Kin Of Our Staff Sailing In Queen Elizabeth 2', Fleet Personnel Manager, Cunard, 26 May 1982.
95. 'A Message To Next of Kin Of Kin Of Our Staff Sailing In Queen Elizabeth 2', Fleet Personnel Manager, Cunard, 26 May 1982.
96. Card offering assistance to *QE2* families mailed by the Missions to Seamen, Royal College Hill, London (undated).
97. *The Leek* (on-board magazine), Issue 2, 27 May 1982.
98. Philip Rentell, *Not Yet! Ruminations from a Passenger Ship Captain*, Blue Water Publications, 1998, p. 70.
99. Weston, 1989, p. 86.
100. 'A Message from the Commander, M.J.A. Wilson, Brigadier', *5 Infantry Brigade* (on-board newsletter), Edition 12, 26 May 1982, p. 1.
101. Message on Cunard notepaper from Charles F. Dunn, kitchen clerk, to Brigadier M.J.A. Wilson, 26 May 1982. Captain Peter Jackson, personal archive.
102. David Yates, *Bomb Alley: Falkland Islands 1982*, Pen and Sword Maritime, 2006, p. 165.
103. Chris Parry, *Down South: A Falklands War Diary*, Penguin, 2012, p. 228.

Notes

104. Yates, 2006, p. 156.
105. Parry, 2012, pp. 230–1.
106. Miller and Hutchings, 1985, p. 141.
107. Van der Bijl and Aldea, 2003, p. 55.
108. Brown, 1987, p. 243.
109. Weston, 1989, p. 89.
110. Miller and Hutchings, 1985, pp. 145–6.
111. Cited in Van der Bijl and Aldea, 2003, p. 54.
112. Reg Kemp and Michael Wood, *MV Norland: Secret Weapon of the Falklands War*, The History Press, 2021, p. 98.
113. Kemp and Wood, 2021, p. 99.
114. Andrew Vine, *A Very Strange Way to Go to War: The Canberra in the Falklands*, Aurum Press, 2012, pp. 227–8.
115. Mark Higgitt, *Through Fire and Water: HMS Ardent – The Forgotten Frigate of the Falklands*, Lume Books, 2021, p. 414.
116. Higgitt, 2021, p. 407.
117. Vine, 2012, p. 225.
118. Vine, 2012, p. 225.
119. Cited in *Torbay Express*, 28 June 1982.
120. Fox, 1985, p. 51.
121. Middlebrook, 1985, p. 287.
122. Tom Rowley, 'Margaret Thatcher papers: BBC "assisted the enemy during the Falklands War"', *Daily Telegraph*, 18 June 2015, www.telegraph.co.uk/news/politics/margaret-thatcher/11684868/Margaret-Thatcher-papers-BBC-assisted-the-enemy-during-the-Falklands-War.html.
123. Rowley, 2015.
124. Document published on the internet by an Argentine historian.
125. 'Tanker attacked in South Atlantic', *New York Times*, 9 June 1982, www.nytimes.com/1982/06/09/world/tanker-attacked-in-south-atlantic.html#:~:text=The%20Hercules%20was%20carrying%20an,British%20around%20the%20Falkland%20Islands.
126. Paul Brown, *Abandon Ship: The Real Story of the Sinkings in the Falklands War*, Osprey, 2021, p. 80.
127. Brown, 1987, pp. 92, 95.
128. Brown, 2021, p. 88.
129. Brown, 2021, pp. 88–9.
130. Middlebrook, 1985, p. 224.
131. Sandy Woodward, with Patrick Robinson, *One Hundred Days: The Memoirs of the Falklands Battle Group Commander*, Harper, 2012, pp. 370–1.
132. Brown, 2021, p. 98.
133. Cited in Higgitt, 2021, p. 364.
134. Vine, 2012, pp. 207, 211–14.
135. Higgitt, 2021, p. 422.
136. Brown, 1987, p. 82.
137. Middlebrook, 1985, p. 233.
138. Brown, 2021, p. 131.
139. Brown, 2021, p. 133; Woodward, 2012, p. 390.

140. Kemp and Wood, 2021, p. 91.
141. David Hart Dyke, *Four Weeks in May: The Loss of the HMS Coventry*, Atlantic Books, 2007, p. 15.
142. Brown, 2021, p. 153.
143. Hart Dyke, 2007, p. 163.
144. Woodward, 2012, p. 406.
145. Woodward, 2012, p. 408; Brown, 2021, p. 170.
146. Hart Dyke, 2007, p. 165.
147. Brown, 2021, p. 177.
148. Hart Dyke, 2007, p. 195.
149. Hart Dyke, 2007, p. 198.
150. Lord Alan West, www.legasee.org.uk/veteran/lord-alan-west/.
151. *C-Six* was the title of a book written by a *QE2* doctor who did not sail on the South Atlantic voyage. Nigel Roberts, *C-Six: Ten Years as the Doctor of the QE2*, Sidgwick and Jackson, 1988.
152. Hart Dyke, 2007, p. 199.
153. Hart Dyke, 2007, p. 208.
154. Hart Dyke, 2007, p. 208.
155. Hart Dyke, 2007, p. 209.
156. 'A Further Message To Next Of Kin Of Our Staff Sailing in Queen Elizabeth 2', Fleet Personnel Manager, Cunard, 4 June 1982.
157. HMS Ardent Association website: hmsardent.org/.
158. Hart Dyke, 2007, p. 205.
159. 'A Further Message To Next Of Kin Of Our Staff Sailing in Queen Elizabeth 2', Fleet Personnel Manager, Cunard, 7 June 1982.
160. Cited in *Daily Express*, 8 June 1982.
161. Quotations from Captain Peter Jackson's handwritten notes of his speech to the ship's company, 8 June 1982. Captain Peter Jackson, personal archive.
162. Quotations from Captain Peter Jackson's handwritten notes of his speech to the ship's company, 8 June 1982. Captain Peter Jackson, personal archive.
163. Higgitt, 2021, p. 439.
164. Higgitt, 2021, p. 439.
165. Brown, 1987, p. 302.
166. National Army Museum, 'The British Army and the Falklands War', www.nam.ac.uk/explore/british-army-and-falklands-war.
167. Weston, 1989.
168. Brown, 2021, p. 247; Van der Bijl and Aldea, 2003, p. 139.
169. Brian 'Monty' Toms, unpublished manuscript.
170. Ministry of Defence, 'Security Debrief' issued to *QE2*, 10 June 1982.
171. Ministry of Defence, 'Security Debrief' issued to *QE2*, 10 June 1982.
172. *Daily Mail*, 11 June 1982.
173. Cited in Hart Dyke, 2007, p. 213.
174. Hart Dyke, 2007, p. 213.
175. Hart Dyke, 2007, p. 214.
176. Cited in *Navy News*, July 1982.
177. Cited in *Daily Mail*, 12 June 1982.
178. Brian 'Monty' Toms, unpublished manuscript.

Notes

179. Captain Jackson, cited in Sunday Express Magazine Team, *War in the Falklands: The Campaign in Pictures*, Weidenfeld and Nicolson, 1982, p.95.
180. Royal Navy, 2001, www.axforsabode.org.uk/pdf-docs/fearles7.pdf; 'HMS *Fearless* arrives home', BBC, 18 March 2002.
181. Linda Kitson, *The Falklands War: A Visual Diary*, Mitchell Beazley, 1982.
182. Queen Mother response circulated as a Cunard Line internal memorandum.
183. Hansard, 'The Falklands Campaign Battle Honours', 25 October 1983, api.parliament.uk/historic-hansard/written-answers/1983/oct/25/the-falklands-campaign-battle-honours.
184. Text from the certificate granting 'The Freedom Of The Falkland Islands On the Occasion of the Fortieth Anniversary on 14th June 2022 of the Liberation of the Falkland Islands from Argentine Occupation'.
185. Handwritten tribute left by former *QE2* crew member Pierre Cornlouer, Welsh Guards memorial, Bluff Cove, November 2010. Cited with the kind permission of Pierre Cornlouer.

Bibliography and Sources

Adams, Thomas A., and Smith, James R., *The Royal Fleet Auxiliary: A Century of Service*, Chatham Publishing, 2005.

Arnott, Robert Harry, *Captain of the Queen*, Ulverscroft, 1982.

Bicheno, Hugh, *Razor's Edge: The Unofficial History of the Falklands War*, Phoenix, 2006.

Boyce, D.G., *The Falklands War: Twentieth-Century Wars*, Bloomsbury, 2005.

Brown, David, *The Royal Navy and the Falklands*, Leo Cooper, 1987.

Brown, Paul, *Abandon Ship: The Real Story of the Sinkings in the Falklands War*, Osprey, 2021.

Burns, Jimmy, *The Land that Lost Its Heroes: Argentina, the Falklands and Alfonsín*, Bloomsbury, 1987.

Butler, Daniel Allen, *The Age of Cunard*, Lighthouse Press, 2003.

Calvert, Peter, *The Falklands Crisis*, Frances Pinter, 1982.

Carr, Jean, *Another Story: Women and the Falklands*, Hamish Hamilton, 1984.

Clapp, Michael, and Southby-Tailyour, Ewen, *Amphibious Assault Falklands: The Battle of San Carlos Water*, Pen & Sword Military, 1996.

Coleman, Terry, *The Liners: A History of the North Atlantic Crossing*, Allen Lane, 1976.

Cunard, *Sailing in a Great Tradition: A Souvenir of Queen Elizabeth 2 1982 World Cruise*, Joint Marketing and Publishing Services, 1982.

Davies, Jennifer, *Saying It with Flowers*, Headline, 2000.

Delves, Cedric, *Across an Angry Sea: The SAS in the Falklands War*, Hurst and Company, 2020.

Dillon, G.M., *The Falklands, Politics and War*, St Martin's Press Inc., 1989.

Fletcher-Rodgers, D.G., *Conways and the Falklands*, Conway Club, 1983.

Flouders, Eric, and Gallagher, Michael, *The Story of Cunard's 175 Years*, Ferry Publications, 2015.

Fox, Robert, *Antarctica and the South Atlantic: Discovery, Development and Dispute*, BBC, 1985.

Frame, Chris, and Cross, Rachelle, *180 Years of Cunard*, The History Press, 2020.

Freedman, Sir Lawrence, *The Official History of the Falklands Campaign*, Routledge, 2007.

Fremont-Barnes, Gregory, *A Companion to the Falklands War*, The History Press, 2017.

Gamba, Virginia, *The Falklands/Malvinas War: A Model for North–South Crisis Prevention*, Allen & Unwin, 1987.

Harding, Stephen, *Great Liners at War*, Tempus, 2007.

Hart Dyke, David, *Four Weeks in May: The Loss of HMS Coventry*, Atlantic Books, 2007.

Hastings, Max, and Jenkins, Simon, *The Battle for the Falklands*, Michael Joseph, 1983.

Higgitt, Mark, *Through Fire and Water: HMS Ardent – The Forgotten Frigate of the Falklands*, Lume Books, 2021.

Johnson-Allen, John, *They Couldn't Have Done It Without Us*, Seafarers Books, 2011.

Kemp, Reg, and Wood, Michael, *MV Norland: Secret Weapon of the Falklands War*, The History Press, 2021.

Kitson, Linda, *The Falklands War: A Visual Diary*, Mitchell Beazley, 1982.

Manyon, Julian, *Kidnapped by the Junta: Inside Argentina's Wars with Britain and Itself*, Icon, 2022.

Maxtone-Graham, John, *The Only Way to Cross*, Macmillan, 1972.

Maxtone-Graham, John, *Cunard: 150 Glorious Years*, David & Charles, 1989.

Middlebrook, Martin, *The Falklands War*, Pen and Sword Military, 1985.

Middlebrook, Martin, *Argentine Fight for the Falklands*, Pen and Sword Military, 2003.

Miller, William H., and Hutchings, David F., *Transatlantic Liners at War: The Story of the Queens*, David & Charles, 1985.

Parry, Chris, *Down South: A Falklands War Diary*, Penguin, 2012.

Pascoe, Graham, *Falklands Facts and Fallacies: The Falkland Islands in History and International Law*, Grosvenor House, 2022.

Puddefoot, Geoff, *No Sea Too Rough: The Royal Fleet Auxiliary in the Falklands War*, Chatham Publishing, 2007.

Reginald, Robert, and Elliott, Jeffrey M., *Tempest in a Teapot: The Falkland Islands War*, Borgo Press, 1983.

Rentell, Philip, *Not Yet! Ruminations from a Passenger Ship Captain*, Blue Water Publications, 1998.

Roberts, Nigel, *C-Six: Ten Years as the Doctor of the QE2*, Sidgwick & Jackson, 1988.

Seear, Mike, *With the Gurkhas in the Falklands: A War Memorial*, Pen and Sword Books, 2018.

Simpson, John, and Bennett, Jana, *The Disappeared: Voices from a Secret War*, Robson Books, 1985.

Smith, E.D., *Valour: A History of the Gurkhas*, Spellmount, 1997.

Smith, John, *74 Days: An Islander's Diary of the Falklands Occupation*, Century, 1984.

Sunday Express Magazine Team, *War in the Falklands: The Campaign in Pictures*, Weidenfeld and Nicolson, 1982.

Sunday Times Insight Team, *The Falklands War: The Full Story*, Sphere, 1982.

Thatcher, Carol, *QE2: Forty Years Famous*, Simon & Schuster, 2007.

Thatcher, Margaret, *The Downing Street Years*, HarperCollins, 1993.

Van der Bijl, Nicholas, and Aldea, David, *5th Infantry Brigade in the Falklands*, Leo Cooper, 2003.

Villar, Roger, *Merchant Ships at War*, Conway Maritime Press, 1984.

Vine, Andrew, *A Very Strange Way to Go to War: The Canberra in the Falklands*, Aurum Press, 2012.

Bibliography and Sources

Warwick, Ronald W., *QE2: The Cunard Line Flagship*, W.W. Norton, 1983.

Warwick, Ronald W., and Warwick, Sam, *QE2: The Cunard Line Flagship, Queen Elizabeth 2*, The History Press, 2019.

Warwick, Sam, and Roussel, Mike, *Shipwrecks of the Cunard Line*, The History Press, 2018.

Weston, Simon, *Walking Tall*, Bloomsbury, 1989.

Woodward, Sandy, with Robinson, Patrick. *One Hundred Days: The Memoirs of the Falklands Battle Group Commander*, Harper, 2012.

Yates, David, *Bomb Alley: Falkland Islands 1982*, Pen and Sword Maritime, 2006.

OTHER SOURCES

Cunard Archives at Liverpool Maritime Museum.

Cunard Archives at University of Liverpool.

Imperial War Museum Archives.

Interviews with members of 5 Infantry Brigade, Royal Navy survivors and *QE2* crew.

Press reports and magazine articles.

Television reports.

'The Media and the Military in the Falkland War', dissertation by Richard Huley.

The National Archives at Kew.

Various editions of the South Atlantic Medal Association 1982 Newsletter.

Written responses to questionnaires sent to *QE2* crew.

WEBSITES

www.falklandsveterans.org.uk

www.qe2abstractlog.com

www.theqe2story.com

www.uk.forceswarrecords.com

FACEBOOK GROUPS

736 Club

Falkland Islands – News & History

Falklands 82 War Heritage Centre

Glimpses of the Falklands War

QE2 Crew – The Online Wardie

The Falklands War of 1982

The Merchant Navy Association

The QE2 Appreciation Society

The South Atlantic Medal Association 1982 [SAMA(82)]

The Ultimate Falklands1982 War Diary – start to finish

X-QE2 CREW banter

Acknowledgements

The authors thank Admiral The Rt Hon. the Lord West of Spithead for writing the foreword to this book and for his years of support to the Merchant Navy.

We extend our heartfelt thanks to all our shipmates and to the embarked military personnel who so generously shared their memories of *QE2*'s South Atlantic voyage. So many people shared their stories with us that we will not attempt to name them all here. But if you find your name in the preceding pages and in the index to this book, please rest assured we greatly appreciated your written contributions and thoroughly enjoyed the meetings, telephone conversations, emails and text chats when you entrusted your memories and reminiscences with us. Conversing with you was our pleasure and privilege. This book would not have been written without you.

Over the years we have collected a wealth of books, manuscripts, documents and photographs on *QE2* and the Falklands. But we have not collected everything. We are very grateful to Judy Carpenter, Chris Haughton, David Luke and Jacqui White, who between them helped fill in the gaps by sending us a range of documents, logbook pages, newsletters, images and artwork from the voyage. Some of you even kindly shared with us personal diaries from the voyage. A very special thank you, Mrs Pamela Jackson, widow of the late Captain Peter Jackson, and his daughter, Dr Marilyn Monkhouse, for your recollections and memories. Please know Ron will always be grateful for the mentoring and friendship of Captain Peter Jackson, and for his gift of photographs and documents.

Thank you to everyone who shared their photographs and illustrations. They came from a variety of sources but particular mention goes to: the late Captain Peter Jackson, Rupert Ballantyne, John Chillingworth, Anthony Dance, Mike Di Fiore, Stephen Hallam, Martin Harrison, Paul Haley, Patrick Hewetson, Jamie Luke, Wendy Marshall, Andrew Nelder, Malcolm Scanlan, Robin Smith, Simon Weston and Jane Yelland. All the images from 1982 were pre-digital. Many of those were taken on small instamatic-type cameras, so special thanks goes to David Golby whose skill made them suitable for publication.

We are particularly grateful to Major Mike Seear of the 7th Gurkha Rifles, who read this manuscript and provided many helpful comments and suggestions.

Tara Doel and Janice Jeffery, thank you for organising the memorable 2024 reunion in Southampton that brought together hundreds of former *QE2* crew, including

Acknowledgements

twenty-seven volunteers from the South Atlantic voyage. Thank you also to Dr Leda Blackwood, Lynda Bradford, Roger Bryant, Clive Dalley, Denise de Martini, Tracy Evans, Paul Fisher, Ian Fletcher, Terry Foskett, Michael Gallagher, Jane Haughton, Ken Henderson, Andy Holloway, Richard Hulley, Susan Hogg, Marie Hurcum, Rob Lightbody, Cheryl Littlehales, Ken Littlehales, Kiara Millard, Shindi Poonia, Paddy Redding, Martin Scott, David Willis and Stephen Ward.

Thank you to the staff of The National Archives at Kew, the South Atlantic Medal Association (SAMA), SSAFA The Armed Forces Charity, the Imperial War Museum, University of Liverpool Archives and The QE2 Story. Many thanks to Amy Rigg, Chrissy McMorris and to all at The History Press for commissioning the book and for their invaluable advice and help in guiding us to completion.

Finally, we thank our families for their understanding while we absented ourselves from family life for long periods to write this book. So a very special thank you to Kim, Rebecca, Sam and Hilary Warwick, and to Colette, Timothy and Anna Humphreys, for their patience, encouragement and tireless support as we worked on this book. For our grandchildren, Beth and Theodore, it may be years before you read this, but we hope it will give a sense of how proud we were to be present on board *QE2*, representing the Cunard Line and our country, during a time unique to our family histories.

Fair winds and following seas.

The Authors

Commodore Ronald W. Warwick OBE served as chief officer on board *QE2* during the South Atlantic voyage. He commenced his sea-going career at the age of 15 as a cadet on the pre-sea training ship HMS *Conway* in North Wales. After spending twelve years serving on a variety of ships, he joined the Cunard Line in 1970. In 1986, he was appointed command of the *Cunard Princess*, and was given his first command of *QE2* in July 1990. He was appointed master designate of *Queen Mary 2*, while under construction, and promoted to commodore when *QM2* arrived in Southampton for the first time in December 2003. In 2004, he was presented with the Ship Master of the Year award by The Princess Royal. Commodore Warwick retired from active sea service in 2006. He was one of the first recipients of the Merchant Navy Medal and was awarded an LLD by the University of Liverpool. He is a Fellow of the Nautical Institute and a Younger Brother of Trinity House. Warwick has authored four editions of his book, *QE2*. The most recent edition of *QE2: The Cunard Line Flagship, Queen Elizabeth 2*, co-authored with his son, Sam Warwick, was published by The History Press in 2019. He also co-authored, with Gary Chambers, *Captains of the RMS Queen Mary* in 2022.

David Humphreys served as senior accounts petty officer on board *QE2* during her South Atlantic voyage. He later served as a supply officer with the Royal Fleet Auxiliary. In 1995 he joined the Open University, where he served twenty-eight years. He dedicated his academic career to research, teaching and publishing on environmental degradation. He has served on five UK delegations to the United Nations Forum on Forests. His book *Logjam: Deforestation and the Crisis of Global Governance* won the International Studies Association's Harold and Margaret Sprout Award for the best book of the year on international environmental problems. David Humphreys retired in 2022 as Professor of Environmental Policy.

The Authors

Also by Ronald W. Warwick

Captains of the RMS Queen Mary (independently published, 2022), with Gary Chambers

QE2: The Cunard Line Flagship, Queen Elizabeth 2 (The History Press, 2019), with Sam Warwick

Also by David Humphreys

Forest Politics: The Evolution of International Cooperation (Earthscan, 1996)

Logjam: Deforestation and the Crisis of Global Governance (Earthscan, 2006)

Subject Index

The forenames of people in this index are those used in the main narrative of the book. Some *QE2* crew were known on board by a diminutive while others preferred to be known by their middle name. Hence the names below are not necessarily the forenames as they appear in the crew list in chapter 17.

Ackerman, Paul 116
Admiralty 228
Affleck-Graves, Major H.E. 28, 91, 137
Ahern, Jim 290
Aldea, David 288
Ardiles, Osvaldo 172
Argentina 9, 12, 75, 93, 214, 262; foundation of 12; invasion of Falklands 16–17, 69; junta 14–6; National Day 152; negotiations with Britain on Falkland Islands 12–4; submarines 146–7, 154, 168, 176, 178–9, 200–4, 236; surrender 288, 291
Argentine Air Force 15, 108, 117–8, 169, 175–6, 215; searches for *QE2* 201, 205–6
Army units embarked onboard *QE2;* 1st Welsh Guards 65–8, 87, 100, 103, 105, 108–10, 116–7, 119, 161, 166, 171, 180, 187–9, 196, 237, 244, 288, 290, 297; 132 Field Battery 149–50; 2nd Scots Guards 65–7, 75, 94, 100, 102–3, 112–3, 118–9, 138–9, 154, 162, 166, 196–7, 287–8,

291, 297; 5 Infantry Brigade 8, 49, 58, 66–71, 74, 76, 103–4, 108, 115, 137, 139, 145, 152–3, 166, 170–1, 178–82, 198, 214, 228, 231, 236, 252, 287–9; 7th Gurkha Rifles 65–8, 70, 86–7, 99–100, 102–3, 110–1, 115, 119, 131, 138, 141, 145, 161, 187, 196, 198, 287–8; 55 Field Surgical Team 196; 81 Intelligence Section 111, 125; 81 Ordnance Company 117, 147; Blues and Royals 196; Royal Army Medical Corp (RAMC) 167; Royal Army Pay Corp 117; Royal Military Police 63, 103, 112, 120
Arnott, Captain Robert H. 29
Artuso, Felix 201
Ascension Island 106, 123, 125–6, 139, 144, 146–8, 150–4, 167–8, 170, 180, 186, 197–8, 206, 210–1, 220, 227, 229, 290; repatriation of crew and military personnel from 147, 229–31

Bahna, Ralph 28, 73
Bailey, Bill 112, 115, 124, 126, 167, 172, 246, 290
Bailey, Malcolm 57, 147
Baliprasad Rai 68
Ballantyne, Rupert 25, 86, 101, 111, 153, 227, 229, 233, 242, 298
Barker, Captain Nicholas 16, 186
BBC (British Broadcasting Corporation) 24–5, 85, 87, 106, 115–6, 153–6, 169, 205, 236, 241, 246
Bicain, Captain Horacio 178
Bishop, Lt R.J. 186
Black, Captain J.J. 18
Black, Lt 171
Blue Funnel Line 29
Blue Riband 20
Boatwright, Martin 59
Bonzo, Captain Hector 32
Bougainville, Louis-Antoine de 11
Bramble Bank 85
Bramwell, Sir John E. 73
Brinkworth, Lance Corporal 171
British Antarctic Survey 12, 14–5, 118
British Forces Post Office (BFPO) 151

Subject Index

British United Trawlers 186
Broackes, Sir Nigel 296
Brooks, Reverand Peter 109, 117
Broughton, Martin 60
Burne, Captain Christopher 186
Burton, Harold 147
Butterworth, Andy 152
Butts, Anthony 60, 188
Byron, Captain John 11

Calshot Spit 85
Calter, Mark 240
Canning, Captain W.R. 211
Cape Sierra Leone light 120
Carpenter, Judy 109, 168, 176, 188, 196, 227
Carty, Charles 110
Cassidy, Terry 218
Castle, Tim 24, 59, 101, 116, 138, 144, 169, 200–1, 226, 229, 244
Chillingworth, John 159, 202, 297
Churchill, Winston 7, 21–2
Clark, Lt Cdr Hugh 85, 237
Clark, Captain J.G. 207
Clark, Major Ronald 199
Cocking, Major R.G. 70
Commando Brigade, Three (3 Commando Brigade) 66, 152, 177
Concorde Travel Club 262
Cook, Captain James 12
Cordy, Lance Corporal 171
Cornlouer, Pierre 25, 111, 118, 188, 227, 295, 297
Crimean War 19
Cripps, Eddie 110, 202
Crozier, Sue 56, 174, 187, 233, 246
Cuéllar, Javier Pérez de 106
Culdrose 85, 92, 238–9
Cunard 9, 18–22, 25–9, 32, 49, 52–3, 55–60, 73–4, 76–7, 84, 87, 93, 97, 103–4, 154, 166, 169–70, 177, 188, 194, 197–201, 226–7, 231–2, 235, 242–7, 252, 261–5, 268–8, 288, 295–8

Dalley, Clive 24, 59, 114, 139, 188, 218, 235, 289
Dalley, Elizabeth 289

Dalley, Helen 289
Dallyn, Tessa 297
Dance, Anthony 25, 31, 60, 86, 113, 188–9, 198, 219
Daniels, Mick 217
Dare, Christine 60
Davidoff, Constantine 15
Davies, Alun 246
Davies, John 56, 112
Davis, Captain John 11
Davison, Steve 113
Day, Vic 110
Defence Review 1981 13–14
Denton, Brian 195
Department of Trade 26, 52, 261–2
Desert Island Discs 116
Dickinson, Captain J.D. 197
Dobson, Keith 70
Driver, Captain Peter 75, 242
Dunn, Charles 177–8
Dunn, Kevin 56–7, 116, 290, 298

Easter, Stephen 58, 175, 218, 234
Eisenhower, General Dwight D. 21
Elizabeth, The Queen Mother, Queen 237, 242–3, 246–7, 290–1
Ellerby, Captain M. 186
equator 123, 138, 144–5, 155, 232
'Eternal Father, Strong to Save' (naval hymn) 109, 220, 228
Evans, Captain H. 18, 194
Evans, Tracy 67, 110, 189
Everall, Lt Cdr R.H.S. 85
Evita (musical) 73
Exercise Welsh Falcon 66–7

FA Cup final 1982 172
Fair, Rod 112
Falkland Islands 11–4, 16–8, 66, 295–8; Argentine invasion 12, 15–6, 19, 59, 65, 69, 211; Bluff Cove Welsh Guards memorial 297; British Military Cemetery, San Carlos 296; discovery of 11; Legislative Assembly 296; Liberty Lodge 297; Port Stanley 8,

11, 13, 87, 118, 167, 288, 296, 298; RAF Mount Pleasant 296
Falkland Islands Defence Force 16
Falkland Islands Memorial Chapel, Pangbourne College 296
Falklands National Monument, Cardiff 295
Falklands War; Bluff Cove 237, 297; Fitzroy 237, 244; Goose Green 209, 229, 288; Mount Tumbledown 288, 291; San Carlos 68, 152, 169, 178, 194, 198, 209–11, 220, 228, 289, 296
Fallon, Major Mike 150
Farmer, Bob 172, 213, 296
Fawley oil refinery 243
Fieldhouse, Sir John 18, 147, 241–2, 295
First World War 19; Cunard ships service in 19–20
Fisher, Paul 85, 112, 167, 179
Fleet Air Arm 69, 85, 125; 825 Naval Air Squadron 85, 105, 107, 180, 199, 237; Sea King helicopters 34, 85, 92, 115, 125–6, 139, 146, 150–1, 170, 189, 194–5, 199, 237
Fletcher, Ian 145, 237
Flewers, Alan 58
Foot, Michael 17
foreign object damage (FOD) 88, 92, 195
Foskett, Jennifer 298
Foskett, Terry 24, 32, 59, 70, 108, 118, 153, 166, 229, 289, 298
Franklin, Michael 262
Frazer, Kent 60, 113, 188
Freedman, Lawrence 13
Freedom of The Falkland Islands 296–7
Freetown 20, 87, 93, 97, 117, 120–1, 123, 139, 185

Galtieri, Leopoldo 16, 114
Garwood, Lt Cdr D.G. 186
Geneva Convention Relative to the Treatment of Prisoners of War, 1949 61, 106
Godden, Sandra 59

315

Goodrick, Sandra 74
Gosney, Brian 59, 245
Gosney, Cheryl 59, 245
Gosport, Borough of 170, 245, 296
Grant, John 85, 103, 116
Green, Captain Robin 237
Greenop, Lt J.P.S. 186
Griffin, John 123, 125
Grytviken 12, 14, 15–6, 171, 174–5, 178, 186–213, 229, 288–9, 295; Cemetery 201; Norwegian Anglican Church 200; QE2 arrival 185–6; QE2 departure 205–6
Guest, Paul 138, 231

Hagman, Larry 32
Hague Convention VII Conversion of Merchant Ships into War-Ships 1907 62
Haig, Alexander 18
Haley, Paul 69–70, 138–9, 145, 198, 288, 291
Hallam, Stephen 110, 298
Hamilton, Lt Cdr C.F.B. 186
Harrison, Captain E. 66, 145
Harrison, Martin 105, 201
Hart, Miranda 246
Hart Dyke, Captain David 169, 197, 207, 211–2, 217, 219, 228, 233–4, 242, 245–6
Hastings, Max 67
Haughton, Chris 91–2, 175, 200, 227–9, 298; and calculation of ship's stability 34–5, 220–1
Haughton Maritime 298
Hayes, Alfred 106
Hayward, Robert 91, 175
Hearn, Lance Corporal Garry 68
Henderson, Ken 150
Hewetson, Dr Patrick 101, 218–9, 227
Hewison, John 198
Higgitt, Mark 237
Hogg, Susan 58, 106, 297
Holloway, Lt M.C.G. 186
Holmes, Allan 61, 153, 200, 214, 233
Holt, Ian 68

Holter, Chris 195
Hong Kong 24, 115, 193, 227
House of Commons 16–17
Howe, Chris 207
Humphreys, David 52, 60, 75, 174, 180, 235, 261
Humphrys, John 242
Hunt, Regimental Sergeant Major 91
Hunt, Sir Rex 15–6, 296
Hunter, Captain A. 221
Hunter, Guardsman 171
Hutcheson, Captain Alexander J. 24–5, 28–9, 60–1, 103–4, 117, 151, 195, 288,
Hydrographic Office, Taunton 52

Imperial War Museum 69
Isaacs, Izzy 240

Jackson, Andrew 147
Jackson, J. 150
Jackson, Marilyn 76, 155, 244
Jackson, Pamela 76, 289
Jackson, Captain Peter 22, 28–9, 56, 59, 70, 74–7, 99, 109, 112, 115, 117, 119–20, 126, 146, 196, 212, 215, 220, 229, 235–7, 241–2, 289–90, 296–7; navigation of QE2 through icefield 175–6, 214; on QE2's contribution to Falklands War 252; radiogram message to HM The Queen Mother 243, 291; Second World War service of 29; working relationship with Captain James RN 13, 62, 103–4, 288
Jackson, Captain Robert 117
Jackson, Steve 209
James, Captain N.C.H. 'Jimmy' 27–8, 103, 117–8, 123, 176, 178, 186, 198, 212, 214, 220, 228–9, 242, 288, 296; decision to depart Grytviken 205; strategic command of QE2 28, 62
Jenkins, Captain R. 66, 146
Jenkins, Simon 67
Jones, Harbour Pilot 120

Jowett, Alex 298
Jowett, Paul 24, 147, 169, 213, 298

Kellett, Leslie 226
Kelly, Ron 101, 103, 198
Kemp, Reg 196, 210–1
Kenokai, Harbour Pilot 120
Kimber, David 226
King's Own Yorkshire Light Infantry 65
Kirwin, Dr Alan 101, 125, 217–9, 227
Kitson, Sir Frank 73
Kitson, Linda 62, 69, 138, 142–3, 154, 198–9, 288
kukri knifes 100, 196

Lamb, Ernie 198
Lambe, Major Brendon 65, 91, 103, 174
Langley, Major General H.D.A. 73
Lawley, Sue 246
Lawrence, D.H. 201
Le Peuple, Lorna 63, 246
Letherbarrow, Clifford 116
Letherbarrow, Jeremy 116, 174, 290, 298
Leyard, Captain Michael G. 169
Leyman, Dawn 74
Littlehales, Elena 25, 102, 187, 243
Littlehales, Kenneth 243
Lizard Point Lighthouse 239
Ludgershall military depot 52
Luke, David 56, 126, 166, 232, 261, 298
Luke, Jamie 56, 232
Lloyd's 121, 263

MacKenzie, David 61, 153, 200
Madeira 108
Marconi 51, 147, 153
Marriott, Phillip 153
Marshall, Brian 234–5
Marshall, Wendy 84, 111, 144–5, 217
Martin, Brian 153
Mason, Paul 108
Matthews, Lord Victor 73, 242, 290
May, Thomas 153

Subject Index

McCowen, Norman 73
McDermid, Danny 67
McDonald, Ian 25
McLean, Diane 53
McMullan, John 147
McQuarrie, Rab 178
McRobbie, Iain 209–10
Mecca Sportsman 26, 60
Meherman Tamang 68
Merchant Navy 18, 21, 25,
 28–9, 59, 69, 103–4, 155,
 169, 186, 242, 267, 295–6,
 298; Liverpool 'pool' 58
Merchant Navy Discipline
 Organisation 62
Merchant Shipping (Life
 Saving Appliances)
 Regulations 1980 51
Méndez, Nicanor Costa 14
Middleton, Captain L.E. 18
Mill Hill Barracks 151
Milroy, Frances 104, 297
Ministry of Defence 25, 28,
 32, 50, 61, 67, 69, 121, 123,
 154, 166, 179, 198, 227,
 264
Ministry of Transport 35
Missions to Seamen 170
Mobile Army Surgical
 Hospital (MASH) units 100
Moore, Major General Jeremy
 147, 150, 152–3, 175,
 178–9, 198, 287
Morgan, Lt Colonel David 66
Morris, Captain J.N. 186
Mos, Enrique 14

NAAFI (Navy, Army and Air
 Force Institutes) 113
National Maritime Board
 (NMB) 57; Warlike
 Operations Agreement 57
National Union of Seamen
 (NUS) 57–8, 147
Naval Discipline Act 1957 62
Naval Party 1710 (NP1710)
 (*Canberra*) 186, 197
Naval Party 1840 (NP1840)
 (*Atlantic Conveyor*) 169
Naval Party 1980 (NP1980)
 (QE2) 27–8, 55, 61–2, 65,
 85–6, 91, 99, 103–5, 108,
 112, 115, 150, 153, 197, 212,
 215, 220, 228–9, 288
NAVSAT 139, 144

Needles Lighthouse 242
Nelder, Andrew 100, 175,
 215, 296
Nilsen, Kathleen 61
Nimrod anti-submarine
 aircraft 146, 154
Nolan, Gerry 29, 217, 261
Norman, Major Mike 16
North, Captain Ian H. 18,
 29, 87
Nott, John 73, 115

Ocean Pictures 60
Ocean Trading 26, 60, 113,
 189, 198, 238, 262
O'Connell, Maggie 26
O'Keefe, Nigel 110
Official Secrets Act 61
Oliver, Dr Peter 56
Onslow, Captain James 12
Operation Corporate 18, 147,
 154, 175, 295
Operation Rosario 16

P&O 18, 60, 186, 197, 289
Parker, Eric W. 261–2
Parkinson, Frank 97–9, 167,
 179, 195
Parr, Gary 120
Parry, Lt Christopher J.
 179–80
Penn, William 23
Perón, Eva 73
Perón, Isabel 13, 15
Philadelphia 23, 27, 56, 243
Phillips, John 210
Pickfords 50
Pollard, Frank 147
Poole, Cdr David A. C. 28,
 33, 91
Pope, Captain Alexander 29
Pope, David 120
Port Everglades Pilots
 Association 117
Pratt, Captain J.W. 93
Prescott, James 210
Primor'ye spy ship (Soviet
 Union) 146

Queen Elizabeth 2 (QE2);
 accommodation for troops
 28, 68, 70, 91, 110, 150;
 advance party of military
 officers 27, 31; alcohol use
 policy on board 101, 111–2,

174, 234; ammunition
 stowage 51–2, 70, 99, 117,
 168, 194–5, 213; blackout
 123–6, 233; Boat Deck 52,
 70, 74–5, 86, 94, 98, 105,
 111–2, 116–7, 120, 126,
 166, 168, 179, 187–9, 219,
 221, 235, 242; boilers 76,
 86, 221; Bridge 24–5, 28,
 51, 70, 73, 75–6, 91, 98–9,
 106–8, 120, 138, 145, 147,
 150–1, 155–6, 166, 172,
 175, 227, 239, 242, 244;
 Brigade Headquarters
 111; carpenters 50, 105,
 112, 115, 124–6, 144,
 172, 212; Cashiers' Office
 151; Casino 26, 50, 60,
 234, 241; Castaways
 (crew bar) 234; 'channels
 night' 24, 240; Children's
 Playroom 110, 226;
 Classified Area behind
 Bridge (Royal Navy) 108;
 Columbia Restaurant
 25, 108–9, 119, 155, 215;
 command structure 27–9,
 62, 205; commander's
 conference 106, 115;
 conversion to troopship
 31–53; crew briefing
 on southbound voyage
 117–8; crew-brigade social
 events 104–5, 114–5;
 crew-military relations
 on board 61, 103–4, 113,
 288–9; crossing the line
 ceremony 144–5, 171;
 daily newsletter 106, 177;
 damage control team
 99; defensive weapons
 155–6; departure from
 Southampton 73–6,
 85–7; discipline 62;
 disembarkation of troops
 187; Double Room 99,
 101, 110, 118, 155, 225–7;
 duty ship system 215, 221,
 229, 241; embarkation of
 5 Infantry Brigade 66–8,
 70–1; embarkation of
 crews of *Ardent*, *Antelope*
 and *Coventry* 196–7,
 199–200; Engine Room 76,
 85–6, 116; entertainment

317

events 101–3, 116, 119, 226–7; evacuation drills 99–100; 'Falkland Island Discs' 116, 226; financial costs of requisition 261–5; flood 217–8; flying operations 85, 106–7, 125, 139, 150–1, 194, 199, 229–30; fuel consumption 256–60; gymnasium 114, 218; hardboard covering of carpets 49–50, 109, 118–9, 126; Harding launches 172, 179; Hatch (crew bar) 233; homecoming 241–7; Hospital 50, 52–3, 100, 180, 215, 217–9, 233, 237, 245, 289; iceberg field, navigation through 167, 174–7, 185, 194, 199, 213, 215; kitchens 102, 111, 177; laundry 58, 217–8; liaison meetings 87–8; lifeboat drills 91–2, 98, 109, 232; live firing practice 66–7, 91, 107–8, 117, 146, 156, 167–8; medical department, cooperation with military medical personnel 100–1, 218–9; menus 50, 166, 229, 241; mess games 229; Midships Bar 111, 153; morale during voyage 74, 99, 126, 154, 171, 232–3, 237, 252; noon announcement 92; number 1 hold 51–2, 194, 213; officers' dress code 104; officers' mess dinner 228–9; penthouse suites 25, 28, 70, 74, 126, 145, 150; Petty Officers' Club 25–6, 112, 115, 213, 234; physical training for military personnel 86, 105, 114, 116, 166, 168, 219, 228; Pig and Whistle (crew bar, aka Three Deck Pig) 112, 209–10; Princess Grill 110, 228; public rooms, change in use of 87, 101, 110, 126, 139, 150; Q4 Room 33, 91, 103, 110, 242; Queens Grill 110, 112, 174–5, 180,

214–5, 218, 229; Queens Room 110, 119, 154–5, 187, 227; radar 156, 175–6, 185, 298; Radio Room 74, 91, 106, 153, 232–3; refuelling by RFA *Bayleaf* 221, 225; refuelling by RFA *Grey Rover* 93–4, 97; religious services 101, 109, 115, 156, 220; rendezvous with HMS *Antrim* 178–80; rendezvous with *Atlantic Causeway* 147, 150; rendezvouses with HMS *Dumbarton Castle* 146–7, 229; requisitioning of 23–7; Safety Control Room 94; shops 26, 31, 60, 86, 113–4, 188–9, 198, 217, 219–20, 238, 262; 'Sods Opera' 226–7; Sound and Reproduction Equipment (SRE) Room 116; Sports Deck 52, 110, 194, 219, 226, 231, 236; stability calculations 34–5, 220–1; Tables of the World restaurant 102, 110, 155, 214; Theatre 57, 101, 106, 109, 115, 117, 156, 166, 187, 220, 241; troop training 86–7, 98–101, 106, 108, 139, 153, 166; volunteer crew 55–63, 267–86; watertight doors 109, 156, 166, 205, 217; weapons training 139; world cruise 1982 22, 193

Rasch, Kapitän Hermann 28
Reagan, Ronald 16
Red Cross 167
Redding, Lt Paddy 70, 102
Regan, Dean 295
Regent Seven Seas Cruises 298
Rentell, Philip 24–5, 33, 123, 125, 150, 176, 185, 214, 228–9, 242, 298; as Lieutenant RNR 55, 91
replenishment at sea (RAS) 35, 49, 93, 220
Requisitioning of Ships Order in Council 1982 26–7
Rickett, Lt Colonel John 171
Ridley, Nicholas 13

Ridley, Captain T.D. 28
Ridout, Lt Simon 209, 218
Roberts, Captain Philip 237
Roosevelt, Franklin 21
Royal Air Force (RAF) 67, 146, 154, 207, 229; RAF Regiment 155
Royal British Legion 297
Royal College of Art 69
Royal Fleet Auxiliary (RFA) 7, 18, 35, 61, 93–4, 97, 153, 194, 199–200, 211, 221, 237
Royal Marines 16, 28, 147, 198, 200
Royal Naval Air Station (RNAS), Culdrose 85, 92, 238–9
Royal Naval College, Greenwich 65
Royal Naval Hospital, Haslar 245
Royal Naval Reserve (RNR) 28, 55, 91
Royal Navy 7–8, 13, 16, 18, 28, 31, 35, 49, 62, 73–4, 101, 104–5, 107–8, 146–7, 153–4, 178, 186, 196–7, 207–12, 225, 234, 237–8, 240, 241–2, 245–6, 289; 11th Mine Countermeasures Squadron 186; see also entries above under Naval Party
Rundell, Captain D.M. 201
Ryan, Major James 145, 196
Ryan, Janet 61, 111

Salt, Captain James 32
Schweiger, Kapitän Walther 20
SCOT (Satellite Communications Terminal) 51, 147, 152–3, 287
Scott, Captain A. 66
Scott-Masson, Captain W. 87
Second World War 7, 17; Cunard ships service in 20–22; QE2 crew service in 29
Seear, Major Mike 99
Sennybridge 66–7, 69
Shackleton, Lord Edward 13; survey of Falkland Islands 13–4
Shackleton, Sir Ernest 13, 201

Subject Index

Sharp, Captain Rudolph 21
Sharpe, David 61
Shaw, Lt Cdr N.B. 28, 150, 242
Shepherd, Dennis 170
Ships Taken Up from Trade (STUFT) 18, 27, 62, 121, 186
Sholing, Eddie 33
shuttle diplomacy 18
Sierra Leone 20, 87, 120–1
Sinclair, Islay 167
Skelcher, Peter 245
Skelcher, Robin 245
Smith, John 87
Soft Cell 234
Soldier Magazine 69–70, 139
Southampton 23–7, 31–3, 35, 51–2, 55–60, 68, 73–6, 86–7, 93, 154, 166, 170, 194, 205, 220, 231–3, 235–47, 252, 261, 263, 288–90; Queen Elizabeth II Terminal 27, 68, 75, 244
Southampton County Court 74
South Atlantic Fund 234
South Atlantic Medal 111, 290, 296
South Atlantic Medal Association 290, 297
Southern Evening Echo 246
South Georgia 8, 12–3, 15, 118, 154, 171, 174, 177–8, 185–206, 212, 217, 287; Argentine invasion of 16; British recapture of 23, 178; Cumberland East Bay 185–6, 189, 201, 205, 213; Right Whale Rocks 185; Stromness 12, 15; see also Grytviken
South Sandwich Islands 12
Special Air Service (SAS) 197, 219, 229, 231

Stanley, Thomas 240
Steiners 24, 60, 111, 118–9
Stevens, John 111
St James School, Grimsby 74
St Paul's Cathedral Falkland Islands Service 289
Strong, Captain John 11
Suncliff Hotel, Bournemouth 232
Swaine, Lt Robin 61
Sweeny, Des 58

Territorial Army 53
Thatcher, Margaret 13, 17, 27, 205, 296
Thomas, Charlie 98, 172, 195
Thompson, Brigadier Julian 66
Thornton, Herbert 29
Tippet, Admiral Anthony S. 73
Tobin, Cdr N. J. 169, 196, 207, 210, 235, 245
Toms, Brian 238–9
Trant, Lt R.B. 73
Treliske Hospital, Truro 92
Turner, Captain William 20

Uglow, Paul 58
United Nations; Secretary General 106; Security Council resolution 502 17

van der Bijl, Nicholas 288
Vespucci, Amerigo 11
Vickers, Brian 29, 56, 102
Vosper Thornycroft 33, 49

Walker, Captain William 29
Ward, Barbara 226
Ward, Phillip 29, 246
Ward, Stephen 32, 56, 174, 194, 298
Warlow, Lt Cdr B 28
Warren, A.W. 212

Warwick, Ronald W. 28, 32–3, 87, 123–4, 126, 172, 186, 189
Warwick, Cdre William E. 60
Werner, Commander Wilhelm 20
West, Cdr A.W.J. 169, 197, 207, 209, 213, 229, 245–6
Weston, Simon 67, 161, 176–7, 188–9, 237
White, Jacqui 58, 75, 85, 94, 115, 144, 296–7
Whitehead, Wilfred 100
Wideawake Airfield 146
Williams, Arnie 56, 231
Williams, Timothy 24, 59, 119, 170, 188, 234, 298
Willis, Major David 100, 187, 288
Wilson, Brigadier M.J.A. 'Tony' 58, 65–6, 69–70, 103, 106, 117–8, 145, 153, 175, 177–9, 181
Withal, Major General N.J. 73
Wood, Cdr N.D. 146
Wood, Janice 61
Woodward, Admiral Sandy 179
Worsley, Edward 29
Wreford-Brown, Cdr Christopher 32
Wright, Geoffrey 59
Wright, Nicola 59

Yates, David 179–80
Yeardley, David 121
Yelland, Jane 53, 56, 92, 104, 112, 139, 144–5, 218–9, 231, 296, 297–8
Young, Bob 209
Young, Captain Brian G. 23, 178
Young, Jimmy 25
Young, Thomas 33, 112, 188

Zumwalt, Admiral Elmo 93

Vessel Index

Alaunia 20
Albert (tug) 75, 244, 256, 259
Almirante Storni 13
Andania 20, 60
Antelope, HMS 169, 196, 207, 210–3, 218, 220–1, 228–9, 235–6, 238, 240–3, 247, 254
Antilochus 29
Antrim, HMS 23, 178–80, 185, 258, 287
Aquitania 19, 21
Arabia 19
Ardent, HMS 169, 197, 207, 209–10, 212–3, 218, 228–9, 231–2, 236–7, 241–4, 246–7, 254
Argonaut, HMS 210
Atlantic Causeway 18, 29, 147, 150, 257, 261
Atlantic Conveyor (1969) 18, 29, 87, 93, 169–70, 260, 296
Atlantic Conveyor (1984) 169
Aurania 20
Australasia 19
Bahía Paraíso 16
Baltic Ferry 66, 77, 145
Bayleaf, RFA 221, 225, 258–60
Black Rover, RFA 297
Bransfield, RRS 118
Britannia, HMY 237, 242, 259
British Wye 201, 206, 212
Broadsword, HMS 209, 211
Brockenhurst (tug) 75, 256
Bustler (tug) 86
Calshot (tug) 75, 244, 256, 259
Canberra 18, 23, 152–3, 186–8, 194, 196–9, 209, 228, 258, 287–9, 295
Cap Trafalgar 19–20
Caria 20
Carinthia (1925) 20
Carmania (1905) 19–20
Carpathia 20
Catfish, USS: see *Santa Fe*

Chale (tug) 244, 259
Clausentum (tug) 75
Clio, HMS 12
Conqueror, HMS 31
Cordella (trawler) 186–7
Coventry, HMS 169, 197, 199, 207, 211–4, 217–8, 226, 228–9, 231, 235–6, 238, 240–2, 244, 247, 254
Culver (tug) 244, 259
Cunard Adventurer 29
Cunard Countess 262, 296
Desire 11
Dumbarton Castle, HMS 146, 229, 257, 259
Endurance, HMS 12–15, 186, 258
Farnella (trawler) 186, 258
Fearless, HMS 153, 287
Feltria 20
Folia 20
Fort Austin, RFA 211
Fort Halket 29
Franconia (1922) 20–1
General Belgrano 31–2
Grey Rover, RFA 93–4, 97, 103, 220, 256
Hecla, HMS 207
Hercules 206
Hermes, HMS 18
Intermani (tug) 120, 257
Invincible, HMS 18
Ivernia 20
Junella (trawler) 186, 189
Laurentic 20
Lancastria 21
Leeds Castle, HMS 186–7, 194–5, 197, 258
Londonderry, HMS 242
Lusitania 20
Lycia 20
Mauretania (1906) 19
Mentor 29
Nelson, HMS 238

Nordic Ferry 66, 145
Norland 8, 66, 152, 186–8, 194, 196–9, 210, 228, 287
Northella (trawler) 186, 258
Persia 19
Phoenix, USS: see *General Belgrano*
Pict (trawler) 186, 258
Queen Elizabeth (1938) 7, 20–2, 29, 75, 87, 295
Queen Elizabeth 2 (QE2): see Subject Index
Queen Mary 7, 20–2, 29, 75, 87
Queen Mary 2 298
Rio de la Plata 210
Romsey (tug) 75, 256
Saga Rose 298
Saga Ruby 298
Santa Fe 16, 178–9, 200–1
Saxonia 18, 194, 198, 262
Sea Goddess 298
Sea Princess 60
Sena (tug) 120, 257
Seven Seas Voyager 298
Shackleton, RRS 13
Sheffield, HMS 32, 207
Sir Galahad, RFA 237, 296
Sir Tristram, RFA 237
Star Flyer 298
Stromness, RFA 197, 199–200, 211, 287, 295
Titanic 20, 176
Tor Caledonia 66
Typhoon (tug) 186–7, 205, 258
U-20 20
U-55 20
U-106 29
Uganda 207, 211, 217
Veinticinco de Mayo 16
Venerable, HMS: see *Veinticinco de Mayo*
Ventnor (tug) 244, 259
Welfare, HMS 11
Yarmouth, HMS 209